Stephen Skinner, co-author of **TECHNIQUES OF HIGH MAGIC**, brings us the first comprehensive guide to the ancient and secret method of prediction in over 1,000 years. Like the **I CHING**, which has been relatively unknown until recent years, the method of geomancy was a closely held secret by a handful of initiates. Thanks to the careful and extensive research of Stephen Skinner, this powerful technique is now disclosed in a clear and simple fashion, enabling any reader to fathom the mystery of his future and to unlock the universal wisdom of the Cosmos.

The romance of geomancy has thrilled the imagination of practitioners from the mysterious East through Arabia to Europe. Now it is your turn!

**THE ORACLE OF GEOMANCY,
YOUR DOORWAY INTO THE FUTURE.**

THE ORACLE OF GEOMANCY

Divination By Earth

by

Stephen Skinner

PRISM PRESS

Bridport, Dorset · San Leandro, California

First published in 1977

This edition published in the United Kingdom 1986 by
PRISM PRESS
2 South Street
Bridport, Dorset

in the USA by
PRISM PRESS
Box 778
San Leandro
California, 94577

and in Australia by
UNITY PRESS
Lindfield
N.S.W. 2070

ISBN 0 907061 82 6

© Stephen Skinner

Cover Illustration: Linda Garland

Printed in Great Britain by The Guernsey Press

ACKNOWLEDGMENTS

First and foremost to Helene who had the idea, to Cornelius Agrippa who laid bare the foundations of geomancy, and to Beverly Lawton and Claudia Macleod for undertaking the arduous task of typing the book.

CONTENTS

Chapter 1
Geomancy—What Kind of A Subject
Is That? 9

Chapter 2
How Does It Work? 17

Chapter 3
The Man With The Black Dog 27

Chapter 4
All The Mothers, Daughters, Nephews,
Witnesses And Judges You Need 39

Chapter 5
Summary of The Technique 47

Chapter 6
Sixteen Eyes On The Future 51

Chapter 7
Using The Eyes of Fa 74

Chapter 8
The Geomantic Print-Out Terminal 87

Chapter 9
As On The Earth Below, So In The
Sky Above 221

Chapter 10
Astro-Geomancy: Houses And Dots 248

Chapter 11
Answers From Sky And Earth 266

Chapter 12
Silkweavers And Bonaparte's Book
of Fate 294

Chapter 13
    Gerard of Cremona's Astro-Geomancy   309

Chapter 14
    Questions For All The Houses   315

Chapter 15
    Geomancy Today   337

Appendix I
    Alternative Zodiacal Attributions of The Geomantic Figures   339

Appendix II
    Element Attributions of The Geomantic Figures   343

Appendix III
    Allocation of The Geomantic Figures To The Houses   345

Appendix IV
    Times of Planetary Days And Hours   348

Appendix V
    Constituents of Each Line of The Geomantic Figures   350

Appendix VI
    Generation of The Geomantic Figures   353

Appendix VII
    Logical Grouping of The Geomantic Figures   355

Appendix VIII
    Names of The 16 Geomantic Figures In Latin, Arabic, Hebrew, And Malagasy (From a work published in 1665)   357

Appendix IX
    The Geomantic Figures of *The Philosophical Merlin*   362

Bibliography   398

CHAPTER 1

GEOMANCY—WHAT KIND OF A SUBJECT IS THAT?

Ptolemy and the Pope, until the time of Copernicus and Kepler, held that the earth was the center of the universe, or at least of man's universe.

They were right! Although Copernicus proved to the satisfaction of science that Ptolemy was wrong and that the earth orbited around the sun, this was merely the astronomy of the phenomena.

The *geomancy* of the subject is another matter altogether!

That which man can feel beneath his feet is the earth, the soil and rocks from which he sprang *is* the center of his universe. Although the earliest object of scientific investigation was the stars, the earliest object of man's experience was the earth, the mother from which all manifestations of nutriment and life sprang.

The ancient Greeks divided the world into four elements; fire, air, water and earth; independently the Chinese evolved a similar series, metal, wood, water, fire and earth. Although these were metaphysical as well as physical, only the most mystically inclined refer to the physical plane as illusion or Maya! And as long as this "illusion" is the plane upon which we live, love, work and die, it is very difficult not to recognize its earthiness.

Colloquial sayings, which are often a folk memory of an esoteric truth, often refer to "getting down to earth" or having "one's feet firmly on the ground," and while many systems of achievement have pointed to the heavens or the empyrean, all worthwhile effort must start with the earth.

This book is about divination by earth: it is a book on the art of geomancy.

Geomancy originally meant divination by the signs of the earth. Webster's dictionary defines geomancy as "divination by means of figures or lines (as in natural or artificial configurations of earth or by connecting dots jotted at random on paper)." The word is derived from two Greek words, *gaie* or *gé* meaning the earth and *manteia* meaning divination.

The techniques of geomancy are many and varied. They include inspecting the configurations made by scattered pebbles, the blowing of dust upon a smooth surface such as a marble tabletop, the strewing of grains of sand, the throwing of handfuls of palm kernels or seeds, (themselves born of the earth), or by making marks haphazardly in the ground with a stick. Divination by marking the earth or casting things on the ground also developed into the interpretation of lines or dots made more or less haphazardly on paper with a pencil.

The earliest traceable forms of geomancy are those of the east coast of Africa around the old voodoo and slave coast of Dahomey, home of the dark Petra and Rada Loa (the good and evil voodoo gods). One of the best known forms of divination in this part of Africa is the Ifa divination of the Yoruba tribe in Nigeria.

Ifa, the oracle god, is supposed to have been the god who directed creation. Ifa took the materials of the universe from a snail shell in a "bag" suspended between the thighs of an older god, and used them to form the universe, scattering soil to form the earth. A hen and a pigeon helped him spread the soil.

Ifa later descended to earth in human form to help with childbearing, to teach medicine, and to give information on secret and hidden matters. Like the god Mercury in the west, Ifa brings messages from the gods and is a patron of divination and medicine. Also like Mercury he is multilingual and the god of language.

Ifa taught a method of divination which is performed by casting palm nuts on the earth in combinations of four and sixteen. These form a set of abstract diagrams based on the four magical elements of air, fire, earth and water (the same elements are found in Greek, Islamic and medieval European philosophy). The diagrams are built up of odd and even numbers and are related to the twelve zodiacal signs or groups of stars in much the same way as European geomancy relates its symbols to the zodiac.

A similar system of divination is practiced in Dahomey, next door to the Yoruba lands, and dedicated to the god Fa who presented the tribes with some special palm nuts brought down from heaven. The diviner is supposed to throw the nuts from one hand to another, and depending on whether the remaining nuts were odd or even, mark down the appropriate geomantic figures from the number of nuts left on the sandy ground after the throw.

Fa told him to gather up the sand which bore the resulting pattern, inscribe it on a piece of calabash, and then to put it in a small cloth bag, and so keep the secret of his fate. Since that time divination has been performed on this pattern, both for ordinary occasions and for a life reading. It is the pattern which is either traced onto the board or marked on the calabash which provides the detailed oracle.

The divination board itself was circular with the sixteen images carved into it. They included a face with tribal marks on its cheeks, birds, a crab, figures and fish together with four lozenge shapes, totaling sixteen. Fa was also said to have sixteen eyes, made of the sixteen nuts of divination, enabling him to see everything going on in the world: a parable suggesting that the sixteen figures of geomantic divination enable the diviner to discover everything going on in the world.

It was also said that the mischievious god Legba had the duty every morning of opening Fa's eyes. Fa lived on a palm tree in the sky, from where he could see all that went on in the world, and every morning Legba, who lived on the earth, climbed the palm tree to open

Fa's eyes. As Fa did not wish to speak to Legba unless he was uttering his oracles, he put palm nuts into Legba's hands to indicate how many eyes he wanted opened. However as Legba was such a mischievious god, and delighted in doing exactly the opposite of what the other gods wanted him to do, Fa used to put one palm nut in Legba's hand if he wanted two eyes opened, but two nuts if he wanted only one eye opened. When his eyes were open he looked around to see what was happening in the world below, so that he could deliver his oracles.

To this day, one palm nut thrown by the diviner means two marks on the divining board, whilst two nuts means one mark because of the deceitfulness of Legba. If you use the palm nuts, or their equivalent, correctly, you too can open the eyes of Fa, the sixteen doors of the future which reveal the answer to any question asked of the oracle.

It is interesting to speculate if divination by geomancy was originally of African origin and passed through the refining culture of Islam to appear in Europe as geomancy, or if the art had simultaneously spread north into Europe and south into Africa from the same Islamic source.

European geomancy as a formal system of divination has its roots in Arab magic and divination, the Hellenic theory of the four elements, and the astrology of the Babylonian-Egyptian axis. This is well known—but it is less well known that the original system of divination based on the four elements, twelve signs of the zodiac and odd or even dots practiced today in Dahomey is uncommonly like modern western geomancy.

The Romans used a form of geomancy which involved the use of marks in the earth. The patterns formed then became the basis for augury, much as the patterns of the flight of birds or the entrails of sacrificed animals.

Amongst the Arabs today in North Africa, there is a method of divination called *khatt ar-raml*, which relies on casting sand or "doodling" in the sand with a stick while in a receptive frame of mind. The material to be used is carefully chosen and "magnetized" by the seer. The surface upon which it is to be cast is magically consecrated and may have an elaborate diagram or design traced on it. Colored earths are selected, especially red or white earth, and the magic design is traced with the first and second finger upon the ground where the earth is to be thrown. Generally the geomancer holds a handful of earth in his left hand and, after uttering a magical formula, casts it. Occasionally the person who is asking the question is invited to hold the earth or cast it for himself. Intuition is then brought to bear on the configurations that have appeared. When the prediction has been made, all traces of these are removed by passing the right palm over them.

Khatt originally meant a straight furrow or line drawn in the sand by a stick or with the finger. In time the word came to mean a line drawn on parchment or paper, or a line of writing. For our purpose, the earlier meaning is the most interesting because it applied especially to the lines that the diviner (*hazi*) drew in the sand to prognosticate the happy or unlucky outcome of an undertaking or event about which he was consulted. This practice dates back to well before the coming of Islam.

For this purpose the diviner, accompanied by an assistant or acolyte, drew with the utmost haste a quantity of lines in the sand, allowing himself to be carried away so that he did not know how many lines he had drawn. Then he slowly wiped out two lines at a time, whilst his assistant recited the words:

"Ye two sons of Iyan hasten with the explanation!"

If in the end two lines were left (i.e. there were an *even* number of lines drawn) then this foretold success. If however only one line remained (an *odd* number of lines drawn) then disappointment was certain.

Here you can see the germ of the later and more complex practice, where each line is reduced to odd (only one left) or even (two left). In this, the simple form of *khatt,* only *one* set of marks were made, leading straight to a lucky/unlucky prediction.

A more modern Arab version of this technique involves the making of lines in the sand. Onto these lines, corns of barley or date-stones (or even cubes resembling dice with combinations of one of two marks on each face) are thrown. The resultant patterns provide a more complex prognostication.

Discerning clear configurations in earth or sand is not

easy and a simpler method for the would-be geomancer to use is to take a number of sticks (rather like the fifty yarrow sticks of the *I Ching*), hold these for a few moments while concentrating and then throw them down.

Another form of divining uses dry silver sand poured into a tray to a depth of two to three inches and smoothed flat. The seer closes his eyes and holds an ivory stick, reed or long pencil. His hand is guided over the tray while he goes into a trance. The person who seeks information poses the question. After a while the diviner will feel an impulse to press the stick into the sand and the stick begins to move by itself. It is allowed to wander as it pleases but only when it stops of its own accord does the diviner open his eyes. He scrutinizes the marks, signs, letters, numbers, words or sentences that have been traced and uses his intuition to interpret them. The flowing Arabic script particularly lends itself to this type of divination.

A simple "yes' or "no" answers many questions, but the initials of people concerned with the questioner's request, a quantity, time, age or date, may also appear. Sometimes a message may be written out, occasionally written backwards or as a mirror-image of ordinary writing.

The Islamic passion for symmetry generated a system of translating the marks into four line figures which by simple mathematical operations transmuted one into the other. In Europe these marks in the earth became dots on paper and the science of geomancy developed into a medieval exercise in divination by binary arithmetic.

In this form, it became a more precise engine of divination, providing quite detailed information.

How can this be of use today? Well, for most types of questions about either the past, present or future requiring a fairly simple answer, geomancy can provide the instrument which will "open the eyes of Fa."

Among the questions that geomancy undertakes to answer are: how long one will live, whether one will better one's present position, whether one should enter the clergy or remain a layman, whether a journey will be dangerous, whether a rumor is true or false, whether to buy or not, whether the year will be a fertile one, and concerning gain and loss, hidden treasure, the condition of a city or castle, and which side is stronger in a war.

Whether a child will be born or not, of what sex it will be, and whether it is legitimate or a bastard. Which of two magistrates is superior in wisdom, whether a scholar can by study become an honor to the convent or not, whether the soul of some dead person is in paradise or before the doors of paradise or in purgatory or in hell.

Of course these questions rather quaintly reflect the hopes and the desires of several centuries ago and the oracle could equally well be asked for news of possible promotion, success of a business venture, trustworthiness of a partner, employees or a spouse, the development of a love affair, marriage, the whereabouts of a thief or of stolen goods and so on. The range of possible questions is limitless.

Let us try a very simple geomantic divination, using either stick and sand tray, or paper and pencil.

First formulate the question and write it at the top of the paper. Place the paper or sand tray at arm's length. Then with eyes half closed and your mind as blank as possible or thinking only of the question, make four lines of random dashes along the paper or in the sand. Make as many dashes as you feel inclined to make in each line. Put down your pencil or stick and count the number of dashes you have made in each line. Take each line in turn and use the following code to draw up the geomantic figure on your piece of paper:

* if there is an uneven number of dashes—one dot
* * if there is an even number of dashes—two dots

Start with the first line and write down either one or two dots according to the above code. Below this, mark either one or two dots for the second line. Do the same with the third and fourth lines. You have now created your first geomantic figure.

Somewhere in the following sixteen possible combinations of one or two dots will be the figure you have generated. Look it up and read off the answer to your question.

```
* *                          *   Success,
* *  Victory, great fortune, *   external aid.
 *   self-aid.               * *
 *                           * *
```

```
* *
 *     The head, entrance or        *    Departing, exit,
 *     beginning.                   *    ill-fortune.
 *                                 * *

 *                                 * *   Misfortune, sadness.
* *    Joy, health.                * *
* *                                * *
* *                                 *

* *                                 *    Loss.
 *     Gain.                       * *
* *                                 *
 *                                 * *

 *                                  *
* *    Girl, softness.              *    Boy, rashness.
 *                                 * *
 *                                  *

 *                                 * *   People, reunion,
 *     The way, street,            * *   congregation.
 *     journey.                    * *
 *                                 * *

* *                                * *
* *    White, wisdom,               *    Red, temper,
 *     spirituality.               * *   passion.
* *                                * *

* *                                 *
 *     Meeting, union.             * *   Prison, isolation.
 *                                 * *
* *                                 *
```

These in a simple form are the heart of geomancy, the sixteen figures, the equivalent of the sixteen eyes of Fa, the eyes with which you can see into the future or answer any questions.

It might seem as if these are a very simple set of meanings with which to discover the answer to any question. You are right, these are just the beginning, but useful for getting quick answers to simple questions.

CHAPTER 2
HOW DOES IT WORK?

It is important to get a clear idea of what exactly is meant by divination. It does not necessarily mean fortune-telling; in fact fortune telling is a debasement of the art of divination which used to be one of the highest functions performed by the priests of most religions. As Crowley said, with tongue in cheek, that the vast majority of people who go to fortunetellers have nothing else in mind but the wish to obtain supernatural sanction for their follies, and that apart from occultism altogether, every one knows that when people ask for advice, they only want to be told how wise they are. Crowley felt that hardly anyone acted on the most obviously commonsense counsel if it happened to clash with his previous intentions. Indeed, who would take counsel unless he were warned by some little whisper in his heart that he was about to make a fool of himself, which he is determined to do, and only wants to be able to blame his best friend, or the oracle, when he is overtaken by the disaster which his own interior mentor foresees?

Correctly used, divination is firstly a method of examining the full potential and circumstances of any given situation, that is, delineating all the possible outcomes. Secondly as an instrument for "lateral thinking," it adds another dimension to the tried and proven but uninspired processes of step-by-step reasoning. It enables someone who has "worried a problem to death" to suddenly see it from a different point of view and cut through its Gordian knot.

The legend of the Gordian knot is incidentally an excellent example of lateral thinking. The knot in question bound the yoke to the pole of the chariot of Gordius, the king of Phrygia. It was said that whoever undid the knot would become king of all of Asia (or that part of the Middle East known at the time). When Alexander the Great arrived at the city and heard of the prophecy concerning the knot, he went straight to where the chariot was housed, and instead of messing around with the knot as so many people had done before, he merely drew his sword and sliced through it with one clean stroke!

So with divination, quite often a problem which may have appeared to be a very knotted collection of factors can in fact be solved by thinking about it in a completely different manner. This then is the second function of divination, to suggest a clear path through the difficulty.

Thirdly, divination can promote not only "lateral thinking" in the practitioner, but a clearly improved intuitive faculty: a real case of practice makes perfect! Divination is as old as man, and has stood him in good and bad stead for many centuries. Records of divinations are both copious and detailed, and date back as far as any written document. The Romans were especially careful to record their divinations accurately, as often public office hung on the results of auguries. The records of the emperor Flavius Valens were as detailed as any in the history of the Roman Empire.

Flavius Valens was worried about his succession. It was the fourth century, the power of Rome was waning, the Catholics were persecuting the Aryans, there was a lot of civil strife and the Goths had crossed the Danube and were threatening the lands farther to the south. He summoned his court magicians and diviners and after listening to their claims and suggestions, settled upon the diviner who was a master of alectromancy (divination by the random pickings of a bird). A white cock was brought in and having been deprived of its claws and appropriately consecrated, it was charged with the task of discovering the emperor's successor. While the appropriate eimprecations were said over it, a circle of letters was chalked upon the floor, corn was strewn over them, and the cock unceremoniously dropped into the center of the circle.

Curious to know the outcome, the throng of court hangers-on pressed closer and watched as the cock pecked randomly at the corn. The first letter to appear was Th, then E, O, and less rapidly D. A cry went up and the cock was snatched from the circle.

The emperor being fully aware of the implications, and being brought up in a very practical manner, immediately issued orders for the execution of Theodorus, one of his favorites. It did not do to take chances, especially if it involved an early succession!

At the same time not very far away, another divination was taking place, using tripod-turning, a Roman version of the ouija board. This time, however, it was a group of conspirators who desired to see Flavius Valens deposed and wished to determine his successor. History would never have recorded the second divination if it were not for the drunken babbling of one of them at a tavern which later resulted in their arrest. At the trial they confessed: "We constructed this accursed little tripod, in the semblance of the Delphic tripod, and we fashioned it with solemn incantations, from the branches of a consecrated laurel. In accordance with ancient custom, we surrounded it with various ornaments, and consecrated it by means of imprecations and charms."

The report goes on to describe how the conspirators perfumed and incensed the room in which the divination was to occur before placing the tripod in a metal basin inscribed with all the letters of the alphabet. Each then laid a hand on the tripod, and the officiating priest, robed in white linen, skull shaven and bearing a sprig of vervain in his hand, took note of the letters that were struck by the rings suspended from the tripod as it turned.

The rings singled out Th and then E. Immediately the same conclusion was reached and the conspirators took this as confirmation of the popular belief that Theodorus would be the future emperor.

Both oracles were right, for although Theo*dorus* was executed, Valens was soon succeeded by Theo*dosius*.

Divination certainly works but *why* it works is a difficult and bewildering question; of the many answers, the two clearest are Carl Jung's theory of synchronicity and Aleister Crowley's theory of "intelligences."

Aleister Crowley's explanation of the mechanics of divination is more traditional, more medieval in fact, than Jung's so we will examine his first.

He suggests that there exist "intelligences" which are either beings with a separate existence (elementals) or parts of the subconscious mind of the diviner of which he is not normally aware (intuition if you like).

It does not matter to the theory whether the communicating spirit so called is an objective entity or a concealed portion of the diviner's mind as both are abstract concepts, each as likely to be as real as the other. We assume that these intelligences are able to reply, within limits to the questions asked. Otherwise it makes no sense to say that accurate information which was not previously known consciously by the diviner can be obtained from a purely mechanical operation. Anyway, if you take the attitude when divining that you are dealing with intelligences external to your own mind (whether it be true or not) this helps to "distance" the question and helps to prevent interference by your own hopes and desires. (It is necessary for the diviner to banish from his mind all interest in the outcome if the divination is to be accurate and unbiased.)

Now to communicate with these "intelligences" it is necessary to have a kind of shorthand, "a compendium of hieroglyphs sufficiently elastic in meaning to include every possible idea." Crowley assumes that these will be understood by the intelligences with whom we wish to communicate in the same sense as it is by ourselves; that we have therefore a sort of language.

Now the answers to questions in divination cannot be conveyed directly (except in the case of spoken oracles such as at Delphi in ancient Greece) but must be conveyed by the standard "hieroglyphs" of the form of divination being used. These in turn have to be interpreted by the diviner in terms of the problem, as it is not possible to have enough "hieroglyphs" to answer every conceivable question in specific detail.

The system of symbols can vary from the almost unlimited combination of symbols of horary astrology, through the 78 cards of the Tarot, the 64 hexagrams of the I Ching to the 16 figures of Geomancy, but each system must be flexible enough to give a complete representation of any outcome or relationship in the universe, so they can be employed to answer questions at any level of truth or complexity.

Geomancy has the advantage of being completely mathematical, but limited by the number of its symbols. To represent the universe by no more than sixteen combinations of dots throws a lot of work upon them. Conversely the very simplicity of geomancy both makes it admirably suited to the beginner and a fairly precise medium for conveying a limited message. It is best adapted for answers to material rather than spiritual questions.

Divination therefore, according to this theory, rests on the existence of intelligences (external or internal) who will hopefully give accurate answers, the system of symbols used to convey the answers, and the ability of the diviner to interpret them accurately with regard to the question. Quite often the interpretation is at fault rather than the intelligence or the method used to convey the meaning, as was the case in fourth century Rome which we talked about earlier. There are certainly many well-attested cases of accurate divination or correct omens misapplied by faulty interpretation.

A classical example of such faulty interpretation is Shakespeare's story of the Scottish lord, Macbeth. Returning home from a battle, he and his fellow general Banquo are accosted by three witches in the form of bearded women. They greet Macbeth as lord of Glamis and Cawdor who "shall be King hereafter," although *at the time* he was only the lord of Glamis. Banquo is greeted as one whose children shall be kings, although he himself will not.

Minutes later messengers arrive to confirm Macbeth's new title as lord of Cawdor. Convinced by this event that the witches tell the truth he sets about aiding its fulfillment by murdering Duncan, the current king, at the first opportunity. Unfortunately, his attempt to thwart the witches' prophecy about Banquo (by also having the latter murdered) is not successful, as Banquo's son escapes.

Having come to power through murder, Macbeth finds that peace eludes both him and his wife, even to the point of seeing Banquo's ghost. As events continue to feed his paranoia and he begins to lose the loyalty of his followers, he is tempted to return to the heath to again seek out the three witches, who have so far told him the *literal* truth.

This time however he is not being told a prophecy but is actively asking questions, and it is here that he falls down in his interpretation of the answers. The four answers are:

i) "Beware Macduff"
ii) "None of woman born shall harm Macbeth"
iii) "Macbeth shall never vanquish'd be until great Birnam wood to high Dunsinane Hill shall come against him."
iv) A vision of eight kings, all descendants of Banquo.

Macbeth interprets each of these in his own manner:

i) He decides to murder Macduff.
ii) If none "of woman born" can kill him, he concludes that he will die naturally.
iii) The wood can never move, so Macbeth feels secure in the knowledge that he will never be overthrown.
iv) The vision confirms the earlier prophecy.

Unfortunately for Macbeth each of these answers is literally true, but not as he interpreted them:

i) Macduff has already left for England to raise a rebel army.
ii) Macduff kills Macbeth in the ensuing battle, after pointing out that he, Macduff, was not "born," but delivered by caesarian section.
iii) The army which accompanies Macduff brings with it to Macbeth's castle at Dunsinane all the greenery of Birnam wood, for the purpose of camouflage.

iv) Of course Banquo's children inherit the throne.

A great play based partly on history, but also a great example of divinatory trickiness, although in this case three witches gave the answers, rather than a formal divination system.

It is therefore essential to be very careful in the construction of questions as well as in their interpretation; you must not leave the smallest loophole for being tricked, befogged, or mocked. It is common, especially in geomancy, for the intelligence to render an answer that is literally true, and yet deceives you. For example, one might ask whether some business transaction will be profitable, and find, after getting an affirmative answer, that the answer really referred to the other party to the affair!

If you find the theory of intelligences rather hard to swallow, then Jung's theory of synchronicity might be more your cup of tea. Jung felt it was possible to examine patterns or happenings in one place to discover what was happening in another part of the universe.

A simple example of this is the primitive weatherman who predicts rain with a high accuracy factor by examining the activities of ants, who invariably prepare their nests against any possibility of flood before rain.

Modern weathermen basically predict weather (with considerably less accuracy) by the unlikely process of correlating the height to which mercury rises or falls in glass tubes at various places across the surface of the earth. What connection there is between the tubes of mercury and the behavior of the clouds is not at first glance very obvious.

Jung says that similar predictions can be made by watching the fall of dice or the chance flight of a beetle, but stresses that there is not meant to be any direct logical connection between the events observed and the predictions made.

In the divinatory ritual of casting earth, sand, pebbles, sticks, arrows, small bones, marbles or jewels, as in the inspection of tea leaves, coffee grounds, ink blots and other kinds of intentional, if random, splodging or scratching, the seer looks for and attempts to interpret certain formations, numbers and patterns. It is by no means easy to put down in writing what these are likely to be and exactly what they signify as these methods entail a degree of intuitional interpretation of the divinatory equations. However, having discovered a pattern of one sort or another, this pattern can then be applied to the question in hand to provide an answer.

Jung's theory of synchronicity is difficult to set out in an easily comprehended manner for it does not rely on the old idea of cause and effect which is the basis of everyday logical thinking, but instead, suggests that some things happen at the same time as others and according to similar patterns, but are not causally connected. Thus there appears to be an underlying link that connects all methods of divination from the most primitive, naive or humble to the most advanced, complex and exalted; from the geomantic casting of pebbles, colored marbles or semi-precious stones, from tea-leaf or coffee-ground reading, to the reading of hands; from the interpretation of the bumps of the head or the moles of the body, to astrology. For if that which is above is reflected in that which is below, it follows that the patterns revealed in the heavens by planets and the patterns revealed in the apparently random fall of a handful of earth, should both reflect the changes in the tide of the life of man.

Whatever the technique, the principle is the same, that everything in the universe is linked to everything else in the universe.

Thus no matter what happens anywhere it effects many other things. One change of plan puts a whole new sequence into action. You might for example miss a bus, catch the next one, and meet someone who later takes you to a party where you meet your future marriage partner. There are innumerable instances where people can say if I had not done such-and-such-a-thing, it would never have happened. No matter how small or apparently inconsistent a change might be, it could still affect the whole course of one's life.

It is as if we were living in a garden of branching paths where each decision to do one thing and not another leads us to another part of the maze where we might otherwise never have arrived.

Not only are these choices conscious, but a million and one external influences contribute to steering a particular course, any one of which, if removed, changes the whole pattern.

So if we accept this net of relationships between man and his surroundings as something far more complex than is usually imagined, it becomes possible to see that the pattern can be mirrored in the movements or forms of the most unlikely and apparently unconnected things. If we have the key to these patterns that are produced by the general interaction of all things, then we can perhaps interpret from it the specific changes or chances that will affect us personally. Such a pattern is what is looked for when divining. The pattern can be formed in cards, tea leaves, the stars, omens, or the earth itself. It is the system derived from the patterns of earth, geomancy, and from the stars, astrology, which go to make up the technique of astro-geomancy outlined in this book.

Geomancy is one of the three or four great classical methods of divination, and like the Tarot or astrology, is a foundation stone of western occult practice. It is also the most easily apprehended of the four elemental modes of divination; pyromancy (divination by fire), hydromancy (by water), aeriomancy (by air), and geomancy (by earth).

Pyromancy is familiar to us all, for who has not stared into an open fire and perceived many figures therein? The same vision applies to candles or any other flames.

Hydromancy works rather like a crystal ball, except the diviner looks for images and visions in the depths of pools or the ebbing and flowing of some natural watercourse or fountain. Omens are also drawn from the contortions of molten wax or lead poured into water, or the washed entrails of sacrificed animals.

Aeriomancy is divination by the shape of clouds, the winds, rainbows and the other phenomena of the sky.

Unlike the other methods, geomancy is like its element, very down to earth, and needs no great natural clairvoyant ability, as does the interpretation of the oracles and omens of the other three *'mancies*.

Geomancy is the art of obtaining insight into the present or future by observing the combinations of patterns made in the earth or on paper by a diviner allowing his intuition or "the spirits of the earth" to control the movement of his wand or pencil.

Let us go back to the late Middle Ages to discover more about it.

CHAPTER 3

THE MAN WITH THE BLACK DOG

On a dark night early in 1535, Monsieur Vachon, the Receiver General of the Province of Wanphine was disturbed by a rapping on his door. The man who staggered across his threshold was prematurely aged, ill and under the penalty of death. Earlier that year he had been exiled from Bonn by Emperor Charles V, forced to divorce his wife, hounded by the Inquisition, shunned as the most pestilent heretic and feared as a sorcerer. He had with him a large black dog, his only companion in his flight from Germany.

His name was Henry Cornelius Agrippa and his reputation had spread across the whole of Europe. Monsieur Vachon had long hoped to meet him. Before the year was out Agrippa died, worn out by a life more strenuous and more persecuted than most. Ironically, he was buried in a Dominican convent, the very Order which instigated the Inquisition and helped to hound him to his death.

Why was he so infamous and why did the Inquisition take so much interest in him despite powerful patrons and allies?

For the populace, it was his large black dog who accompanied him across half of Europe. Such a dog had also been seen with Simon Magus, Pope Sylvester, Dr. Faustus, Bragandin of Venice and other magicians who were reputed to have "familiars" disguised in animal form.

For the Inquisition, the reason lay in the three volumes, and part of a fourth entitled, *De Occulta Philosophia*, one of the most important and comprehensive books on magic ever written. Despite the friendly warning of that kindly scholar, Abbot John of Trittenheim, Agrippa went ahead and in 1531 published the first volume. From then until his death he had little peace, especially from the Holy Office of the Inquisition.

For that volume contained a summary and popularization of all the basic doctrines of magic, the qabalah and divination known at that time. It is to Agrippa that we owe the first methodical and clear description of the whole qabalistic system. His book was practically the only starting point of qabalistic knowledge amongst Latin reading scholars in Europe. Consequently, it enjoyed an immense repute, and for this reason was especially feared by the church. Strangely enough, most of the information in the book came rather from the mythology and philosophy of Greece and Rome rather than the later Hebraic qabalah. In his third book which he devoted to "theology" there is much concerning angels, demons and the souls of men, linked together by an extremely competent system of correspondences based wherever possible on the numbers one to twelve, and tied in extensively with classical mythology.

Agrippa was born in 1486 in Nettesheim, a small town southwest of Cologne, of a family of scholars who insured that he acquired the fundamentals of a good education, specifically Latin, the *lingua franca* of Europe during the Middle Ages, together with the writings of the ascetics, scholastics and canonists of the period. At this period some Latin, but very few Greek texts had come to light, and even then many had arrived in Europe via Arabic translations.

As printing was still a very new invention the dissemination of rarer texts depended very much on the scholar gaining access to patronage and private manuscript collections. Because Agrippa's accomplishments included foreign languages, he was taken from his studies in 1501 to serve the Holy Roman Emperor, Maximillian II of Germany, first as a secretary and then afterwards for seven years as a soldier. Towards the close of this period he traveled to Paris University, ostensibly as a scholar, but in fact as an observer of political developments there for Maximillian (a combination of activities which later occupied one of Agrippa's admirers, Dr. John Dee, who undertook similar missions for Elizabeth I, half a century later).

During his travels Agrippa was often forced to live by his wits, and was engaged at different times in the roles of theologian, alchemist, magical writer, faith healer, astrologer, lawyer, doctor, historian and demonologist. Not the least of his wide range of skills included that of financial adviser and secret political agent working for both the Pope and his rival Maximillian. He switched sides as and when the need arose, sometimes in favor of one, sometimes of the other. His fortunes ran the gamut of experience, one minute mixing with royalty and the next in prison for debt. Because of these sudden shifts in fortune, like Paracelsus, he moved restlessly about Europe, so that very few details of his career have survived. Even before his death he had become the center of stories in which he figured as a master black magician. Goethe drew on some of these stories for his background material about Faust, although in reality Agrippa was much more of a scholar than a Faustian figure. Agrippa concluded that man "containeth in himself all things which are in God," and maintained that in a sense the magician can make himself a god and wield the natural powers of the universe to his own ends.

One of the many stories told about Agrippa tells of a day when he left his house to go into town. The key of the secret room which he used for magical purposes was left with his wife. Unfortunately she foolishly lent it to the lodger who was a student of Agrippa's, and who had been eager to see the contents of Agrippa's room ever since he had arrived at the house. In the room the student found a huge book of spells, a grimoire, which he began to read aloud.

After a while he was disturbed by a noise in the room, and looking up, found a demon standing in front of him demanding to know why he had been summoned. The student attempted to banish the demon, but not knowing the correct formula stood helpless while the demon gained in strength. Before Agrippa could return the demon strangled the student. When Agrippa discovered the murder he compelled the demon to restore the student to a semblance of life for a few hours, so that the body could walk through the streets to the market square. Here the student was seen to walk about by many of his friends, so that when the demon's power wore off and the body collapsed no one was any the wiser.

Desirée Hirst says of Agrippa that he never lacked courage and that most of the disasters that came upon him resulted from the basic honesty which he was unable to control and which drove him to dangerous outbursts of tactlessness. An example of this was the treatise that he wrote after having been appointed as court physician to Louisa of Savoy. Queen Louisa who was known for her flirtations was surprised to find that Agrippa's treatise dwelt on the benefits of matrimony. Other examples of Agrippa's tactlessness included his book, *On the Vanity of Sciences and Arts*, which set out to prove how men of learning such as himself were ill-used by princes who should have supported them financially. Two of Agrippa's recent patrons, Emperor Maximillian I and François I both took offence at this, and Agrippa had to flee to Lyons where he was thrown into prison, understandably enough, by order of the king.

His life in some ways was almost an exercise in bad timing, and he almost cuts the figure of a "knight errant of scholarship." In fact as far as his behavior on the battlefield was concerned there was no possibility for reproach; he has even been portrayed going into battle with his pockets overflowing with manuscripts, while his pupils desperately try to rescue these priceless masterpieces as they fly abroad in all directions during the fight. Fortunately many of these manuscripts survived, some being printed after his death by his disciples. Amongst these works were a wealth of traditional and sometimes verbal lore concerning geomancy. In them, he succinctly outlined the conditions under which the art may be practiced: "not on a cloudy or rainy day, or when the weather is stormy, nor while the mind is disturbed by anger or oppressed with cares."

It is easy to see why the diviner should be in a calm state of mind, for obviously the intuition is going to function better if the person is not depressed or thinking of other things, or acting in an offhand manner. For the same reasons, geomancy or any form of divination should not be attempted lightheartedly at a party, for gratifying idle curiosity or mere amusement. All of these circumstances will tend to destroy any feeling or facility you have for divination. Similarly, do not keep asking the same question, hoping that a "better answer" will be produced. If the first answer is not easy to understand then the second will not be any easier, besides repeated asking of the oracle is as rude as continually demanding the same thing from a person, who may be answering you, but whom you cannot hear.

If an answer is genuinely perplexing, try asking a different corroborative question rather than using the same form.

The first half of Agrippa's stipulations are a bit harder to understand: not only is the diviner to be in a peaceful mood, but also the weather. This specification, however, is the same as that made for evocation in many of the grimoires, the practical "grammars" of sorcery, so it seems that disturbed weather makes it difficult to attract and get answers from the earth elementals necessary for the divination.

The Equipment

Having established the right conditions for practice, it is necessary to consider the equipment of divination. In its original form, geomancy used the earth itself or a sand tray in which to make the initial marks. If you want to be this authentic you should obtain a shallow square box, several inches deep and up to a couple of feet square. Having painted your box, fill it with either dry earth or sand, which should be obtained from an inland site and not from the seashore (because of the association of the latter with water).

Henry Cornelius Agrippa, *of Geomancy.*

GEOMANCY is an Art of Divination, wherby the judgement may be rendred by lot, or destiny, to every question of every thing whatsoever, but the Art hereof consisteth especially in certain points whereof certain figures are deducted according to the reason or rule of equality or inequality, likenesse or unlikenesse; which Figures are also reduced to the Cœlestiall Figures, assuming their natures and proprieties, according to the course and forms of the Signes and Planets; notwithstanding this in the first place we are to consider, that whereas this kinde of Art can declare or shew forth nothing of verity, unless it shall be radicall in some sublime vertue, and this the Authours of this Science have demonstrated to be two-fold : the one whereof consists in Religion and Ceremonies; and therefore they will have the Projectings of the points of this Art to bee made with signes in the Earth, wherefore this Art is appropriated to this Element of Earth, even as Pyromancy to the fire, and Hydromancy to the Element of Water: Then whereas they judged the hand of the Projector or Worker to be most powerfully moved, and directed to the terrestriall spirits; and therefore they first used certaine holy incantations and

B   deprecations,

Illustration 1: The first page of Agrippa's *Of Geomancy*

You should then obtain a rounded stick, perhaps a length of dowel, or preferably, a wand which you have cut for yourself. According to the grimoires, this should be cut from a hazel bush at dawn with one blow of the knife. But as this is not an evocation, but a divination, you need not go to these lengths.

If you wish to be less traditional, a pencil and paper may be used just as effectively for making the rows of dots from which the geomantic figures are calculated, and this method will be referred to when explaining the technique of divination later in this chapter.

Two other methods for producing the initial geomantic figures have been suggested by Israel Regardie. The first consists of using a bowl full of large pebbles. From it are drawn a handful of pebbles at a time for each line. If the number of pebbles drawn is uneven, then one dot is written down, if even then two dots. Sixteen draws are needed to complete the initial geomantic figures as will be explained later in this chapter.

His second suggestion was simply to use two dice to produce odd or even number combinations, with the same result in terms of dots. Both techniques are considerably simpler than the traditional methods but the pebbles have more of the quality of earth about them than the dice. At any rate, you should choose from the four methods given above, according to which appeals most to your temperament, stick to it and don't flit from one method to another.

Having assembled your equipment, you may now like to consecrate it to the service of the earth elementals, thereby establishing a point of contact between them and the equipment. A simplified form of consecration could consist of anointing them with olive oil or sprinkling salt over them whilst reading an Invocation to the Gnomes of your own devising. Read through books like Tolkein's *Lord of the Rings* or some similar work for inspiration along these lines, or another book in this series, *Techniques of High Magic*, by Francis King and Stephen Skinner. When your equipment is charged, it should be kept wrapped or covered and out of sight unless in use.

Before we go any farther though, you should acquire a book in which to keep your astro-geomantic exercises, in which the questions, charts and interpretations should be fully and truthfully recorded. There is no good in fooling yourself about your correct predictions, if you forget your less accurate answers. Keep a fair score as to the correctness or otherwise of each of your divinations. This will give you a clear indication if you need to refine your technique, or conversely, will demonstrate beyond doubt the emergence of your intuitive faculty. As you improve this ability your score should rise to at least eighty percent accuracy, or even better. Divination, after all, should be much more reliable than guessing, or there is no point in doing it!

The Question

Let us assume that you have selected a method from the above four possibilities, and are provided with the necessary equipment, be it pencil and paper, wand and sand tray, pebbles, or dice. Now you must formulate your question. It is no good just trying out geomancy for fun. If you want a reliable device to give you serious answers to your serious questions, and serve you well, then you must treat it as such. Imagine that your tools of divination are in fact a person whose advice you respect. Immediately, it is obvious that you do not ask fatuous questions or invent questions whose answers you already know, just to try it out. If you have no faith in its abilities to reveal the unknown to you, it will treat your flippant questions to a dose of nonsense or flippant answers.

So, when selecting your question, think seriously and write down the question in your book of astro-geomantic exercises so that there is no possible ambiguity in it or room for evasive answers. Then check to see which of the following categories it falls into. In each case the appropriate planet is given with the sigil (or signature) of its ruler, who is the correct "intelligence" to answer your question.

Question	Sigil and Ruler
If the question is of the astrological nature of *Mars*—that is to say concerned with war, struggle, fighting, victory, weapons or dissension	 use the sigil of Bartzabel
If the question is of the astrological nature of *Jupiter*—that is to say concerned with good fortune, general happiness, church matters, or holding office in an organization concerned with spiritual matters	 use the sigil of Hismael
If the question is of the astrological nature of *Saturn*—that is to say concerned with gardening, farming, crops, sorrow, bereavement, death, legacies, or long-standing problems	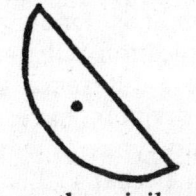 use the sigil of Zazel
If the question is of the astrological nature of *Mercury*—that is to say concerned with science, learning, trickery, theft, knowledge, or books	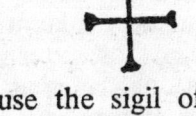 use the sigil of Taphtharttarath
If the question is of the astrological nature of *Venus*—that is to say concerned with love, music, pleasure or luxury	 use the sigil of Kedemel

If the question is of the astrological nature of the *Moon*—that is to say concerned with traveling, fishing, childbirth, reproduction, or tidal change use the sigil of Chashmodai

If the question is of the astrological nature of the *Sun*—that is to say concerned with music, feasting, success, power and rulership use the sigil of Sorath

If you wish to take great pains with your divination, then you might choose to perform it at certain times, which are more propitious for some types of question than others. The time is dependent on the planetary category into which the question falls, as in the above list. Why the time should make a difference is hard to say, except that as magicians and diviners have been using certain days or hours for certain types of question or operation for many centuries now, perhaps the constant usage has "worn into" the time the associated qualities. Details of times may be found in Appendix IV for those who care to use them.

According to the planetary category the question falls into, you can discover which intelligence is responsible for the answer. Even assuming that you prefer Jung's synchronistic explanation of divination, it is as well to think in terms of external "intelligences" and observe all the traditional rules at first until you have mastered the technique, before you try eliminating any part of the system.

The Action

The physical process of geomantic divination is similar to the trial run simple divination outlined in Chapter I, except that instead of drawing only four lines to generate one figure, we use sixteen lines to generate four figures. Greater complexity generates greater accuracy.

Having decided on the intelligence and planet relevant to your question, take a clean page in your book and write out your question as specifically as possible. Then draw a circle and inscribe inside it a pentagram of earth commencing at the point marked by the arrow as shown in the illustration.

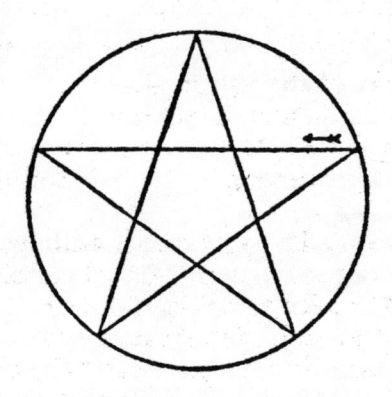

In the center of the pentagram inscribe the sigil of the planet appropriate to your question, drawn from the above table. If you are using a geomantic box, also draw the same sigil circle and pentagram in the earth or sand.

With your wand and box (or pencil and paper) make a row of a random number of dots, at the same time thinking clearly of the question. In all a total of sixteen rows of dots should be made. The pencil or wand is to be held firmly in the hand while making the dots quickly and mechanically from left to right, without counting. It is best to avoid the temptation of anticipating or counting them which can result in unconscious manipulation of the divination. If you are working with the sand tray you may have to note the number of digs every four lines or so and after transferring the numbers to your paper, rub them out and proceed to the next four lines. However if you are working solely with a pencil and paper you can go ahead until you have done at least sixteen lines of dots. A few more won't matter as you just discount any lines after the sixteenth.

Count the number of dots in each row and mark each row as either odd or even, so that you now have something like this:

Row	Dots	
1	***	odd
2	*****	odd
3	****	even
4	********	even
5	**	even
6	****	even
7	*********	odd
8	******	even
9	***	odd
10	*****	odd
11	*******	odd
12	****	even
13	******	even
14	********	even
15	*****	odd
16	*******	odd

Here ends the physical work of the divination. From here on, the figures formed from the above dots are manipulated to give an answer to the question, so you can lay aside your sand tray, pebbles or dice and work from here on solely on paper.

CHAPTER 4

ALL THE MOTHERS, DAUGHTERS, NEPHEWS, WITNESSES AND JUDGES YOU NEED

If you now examine your rows of dots you will find that there is either an odd or an even number of dots in each line. To continue with the above example, where there is an *odd* number you should put one dot at the end of the line, where there is an *even* number you should put two. Your figure now looks like this:

odd	*
odd	*
even	* *
even	* *
even	* *
even	* *
odd	*
even	* *
odd	*
odd	*
odd	*
even	* *

even   * *
even   * *
odd   *
odd   *

Now divide them into four groups of four as above.

Mothers

The four geomantic figures so formed are called the four Mothers and are the basis for the whole geomantic chart. From here on the geomantic figures and calculations are generated solely out of these four figures. Let us put them side by side from right to left and examine them carefully:

Mothers	IV	III	II	I
head	* *	*	* *	*
neck	* *	*	* *	*
body	*	*	*	* *
feet	*	* *	* *	* *

Look at each Mother: you will see that each line containing either one or two dots is labeled according to the parts of the body. From these four figures the rest of the chart is formed, and although the operations that follow look complex, in fact they only take about three minutes once you have got the hang of them. Read the instructions through first, then come back to this point and, using a pencil and paper, construct each of the figures given in this example as outlined in the instructions.

Daughters

First, the Mothers give birth to the four Daughters, which are generated by taking all the heads from Mothers I to IV and placing them on top of the other. This forms the first Daughter.

First Daughter—Figure V

```
      *           from the head of I
     * *          from the head of II
      *           from the head of III
     * *          from the head of IV
```

Then take all the necks from Mothers I to IV and place them on top of each other to produce the second Daughter, the bodies to form the third Daughter and the feet for the fourth Daughter.

Second Daughter—Figure VI

```
      *           from the neck of I
     * *          from the neck of II
      *           from the neck of III
     * *          from the neck of IV
```

Third Daughter—Figure VII

```
     * *          from the body of I
      *           from the body of II
      *           from the body of III
      *           from the body of IV
```

Fourth Daughter—Figure VIII

```
     * *          from the feet of I
     * *          from the feet of II
     * *          from the feet of III
      *           from the feet of IV
```

To recapitulate, the figures so far generated are:

	Daughters				Mothers		
VIII	VII	VI	V	IV	III	II	I
* *	* *	*	*	* *	*	* *	*
* *	*	* *	* *	* *	*	* *	*
* *	*	*	*	*	*	*	* *
*	*	* *	* *	*	* *	* *	* *

41

Nephews

Next comes the generations of the Nephews, which are produced in a different manner. Look at the eight figures laid out above, take them two at a time and "add" them together thus:

	Mother I	plus	Mother II		Nephew IX
head	*	+	* *	= odd	= *
neck	*	+	* *	= odd	= *
body	* *	+	*	= odd	= *
feet	* *	+	* *	= even	= * *

In this example, the heads together make up three dots (*odd*), so mark down one dot. Taking the necks of these Mothers, we again have an *odd* number, so again mark down one dot. Likewise the bodies make one dot (*odd*). But the feet together make up four dots (*even*), so mark down two dots. The figure of the first Nephew is now:

Nephew IX

*
*
*
* *

For the next Nephew repeat the same process but with Mothers III and IV.

Mother III	plus	Mother IV		Nephew X
*	+	* *	= odd =	*
*	+	* *	= odd =	*
*	+	*	= even =	* *
* *	+	*	= odd =	*

For the next two Nephews, repeat the same process but with the Daughters.

Daughter V	plus	Daughter VI		Nephew XI
*	+	*	= even =	* *
* *	+	* *	= even =	* *
*	+	*	= even =	* *
* *	+	* *	= even =	* *

Daughter VII	Plus	Daughter VIII		Nephew XII
* *	+	* *	= even =	* *
*	+	* *	= odd =	*
*	+	* *	= odd =	*
*	+	*	= even =	* *

So far we have got:

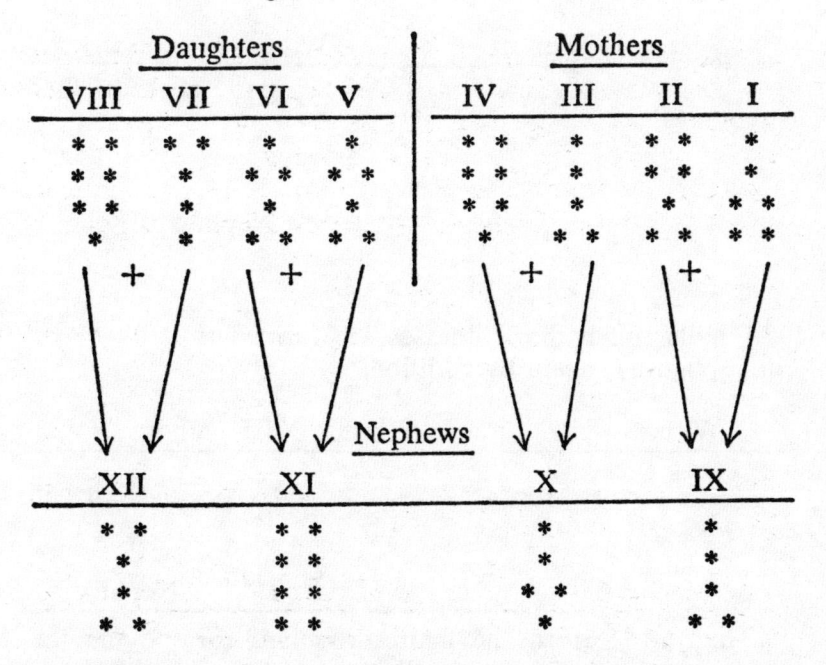

Daughters					Mothers			
VIII	VII	VI	V		IV	III	II	I
* *	* *	*	*		* *	*	* *	*
* *	*	* *	* *		* *	*	* *	*
* *	*	*	*		*	*	*	* *
*	*	* *	* *		*	* *	* *	* *

Nephews

XII	XI	X	IX
* *	* *	*	*
*	* *	*	*
*	* *	* *	*
* *	*	*	* *

Witnesses

From the four Nephews are constructed the two Witnesses (Coadjutrices or Testes) in the same manner, that is the first Witness from IX and X, and the second from XI and XII.

Nephew IX	plus	Nephew X		Witness XIII
*	+	* = even	=	* *
*	+	* = even	=	* *
*	+	* * = odd	=	*
* *	+	* = odd	=	*

Nephew XI	plus	Nephew XII		Witness XIV
* *	+	* * = even	=	* *
* *	+	* = odd	=	*
* *	+	* = odd	=	*
* *	+	* * = even	=	* *

The two Witnesses look like this:

Witness XIV		Witness XIII
* *		* *
*		* *
*	and	*
* *		*

Finally, from the Witnesses are formed the Judge (or Index figure), again by addition.

Witness XIV	plus	Witness XIII		Judge XV
* *	+	* * = even	=	* *
*	+	* * = odd	=	*
*	+	* = even	=	* *
* *	+	* = odd	=	*

Thus are formed the figures required for judging the outcome of the geomantic divination, the four Mothers, four Daughters, four Nephews, the right Witness, left Witness and the Judge.

We can now lay out the fifteen figures!

The Whole Spread

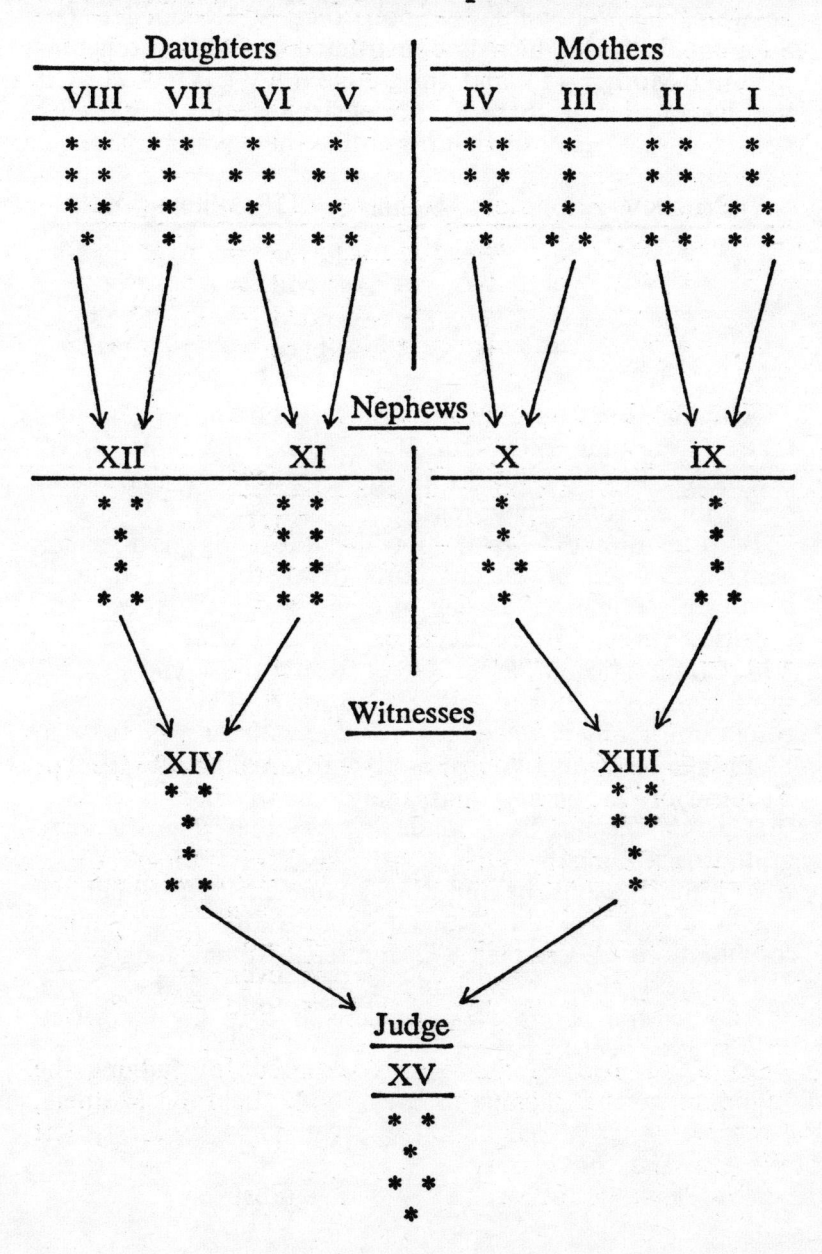

Daughters				Mothers			
VIII	VII	VI	V	IV	III	II	I
* *	* *	*	*	* *	*	* *	*
* *	*	* *	* *	* *	*	* *	*
* *	*	*	*	*	*	*	* *
*	*	* *	* *	*	* *	* * *	* * *

Nephews

XII	XI	X	IX
* *	* *	*	*
*	* *	*	*
*	* *	* *	*
* *	* *	*	* *

Witnesses

XIV	XIII
* *	* *
*	* *
*	*
* *	*

Judge

XV
* *
*
* *
*

Sometimes if the divination still provides conflicting answers, it is possible to construct a Reconciler (or Supreme Judge) which is constructed by adding together the first Mother (I) and the Judge (XV). Only consult the Reconciler if there is no clear answer. Don't ever consult it just because you do not like the answer you have.

Judge XV	plus	Mother I		Reconciler XVI
* *	+	* = odd	=	*
*	+	* = even	=	* *
* *	+	* * = even	=	* *
*	+	* * = odd	=	*

All this sounds frightfully complex but it isn't, it just takes a long time to explain. If we set out the evolution of the figures in a graphic form, the simplicity of the whole operation becomes apparent.

Because of the manner in which the Judge is formed, being composed of various parts of all the other figures, it can only come out as one of eight possible figures: Acquisitio, Amissio, Fortuna Major, Fortuna Minor, Populus, Via, Conjunctio or Carcer—in fact only those whose *total* number of dots add to either 4, 6, or 8. This provides a rough but handy check, for if a Judge with an odd number of points turns up, you should check your calculations. Because of the binary mathematics involved it is certain that a mistake has been made if any other figure is generated as a Judge.

For the reasons behind this statement, see Appendix V. As a result of this, the tables of Judge and Witness combinations in Chapter 8 is limited to eight Judges.

The next chapter contains a summary of the above operations and forms which can be used to lay them out on a single sheet of paper.

CHAPTER 5
SUMMARY OF THE TECHNIQUE

1. Choose the time, hour and day in which to carry out the divination (see Appendix IV).
2. It is is decided to go ahead immediately, lay out the sand tray, pebble bowl or dice and paper and pencil.
3. Formulate the question precisely and write it down at the top of the page. Decide which House and planet the question belongs to: write this down also.
4. Inscribe pentagram and appropriate sigil.
5. Make sixteen rows of random dots with eyes half closed and mind blank or concentrating on the question.
6. Divide the sixteen rows into four groups of four lines.
7. Count each line and mark down two dots for an even number and one dot for an odd number.
8. Write the four figures so formed on the paper from right to left, side by side. These are the four Mothers. It is useful to make copies of the diagram in this chapter and fill in the figures in the appropriate boxes, as they are worked out.
9. Form the Daughters. The first Daughter is formed

from the heads of each Mother written down one above another, the second Daughter from the necks of the Mothers, the third Daughter from their bodies, and the last Daughter from their feet.
10. Form the Nephews. The first Nephew is created by "adding together" Mothers I and II, the second from adding together Mothers III and IV. The third Nephew is formed from adding together the first and second Daughters (Figures V and VI). The fourth Nephew is formed from adding together the third and fourth Daughters (Figures VII and VIII).
11. Form the two Witnesses. The right Witness is formed by adding together the first and the second Nephews (Figures IX and X). The left Witness is formed by adding together the third and the fourth Nephews (Figures XI and XII).
12. Form the Judge by adding together the two Witnesses.
13. Lay out the figures from I to XV.
14. If the answer is not clear at this point, form a Reconciler by adding together the first Mother (Figure I) and the Judge (Figure XV).
15. Interpret the answer with reference to the Judge and the two Witnesses. If your question is one of the standard ones, use the tables of divinatory meanings of these figures (see Chapter 8).
16. If more detail is required, refer back to the Mothers (Figures I-IV) for details of the commencement (Figure I) and termination of the matter (Figure IV).
17. If even more information is required, allocate the figures to the Houses of the horoscope as outlined in the chapters on astro-geomancy.

Although the above method looks fairly complex at first glance, you will find as soon as you have done two or three divinations that the manipulation becomes almost automatic. It is simply a matter of getting the sequence right. It helps if you draw up a plan such as the following and fill the figures in the boxes as each is generated. You can choose whether to use the modern plan or the more traditional "crest-shaped" chart.

Illustration 2a: A modern geomantic chart

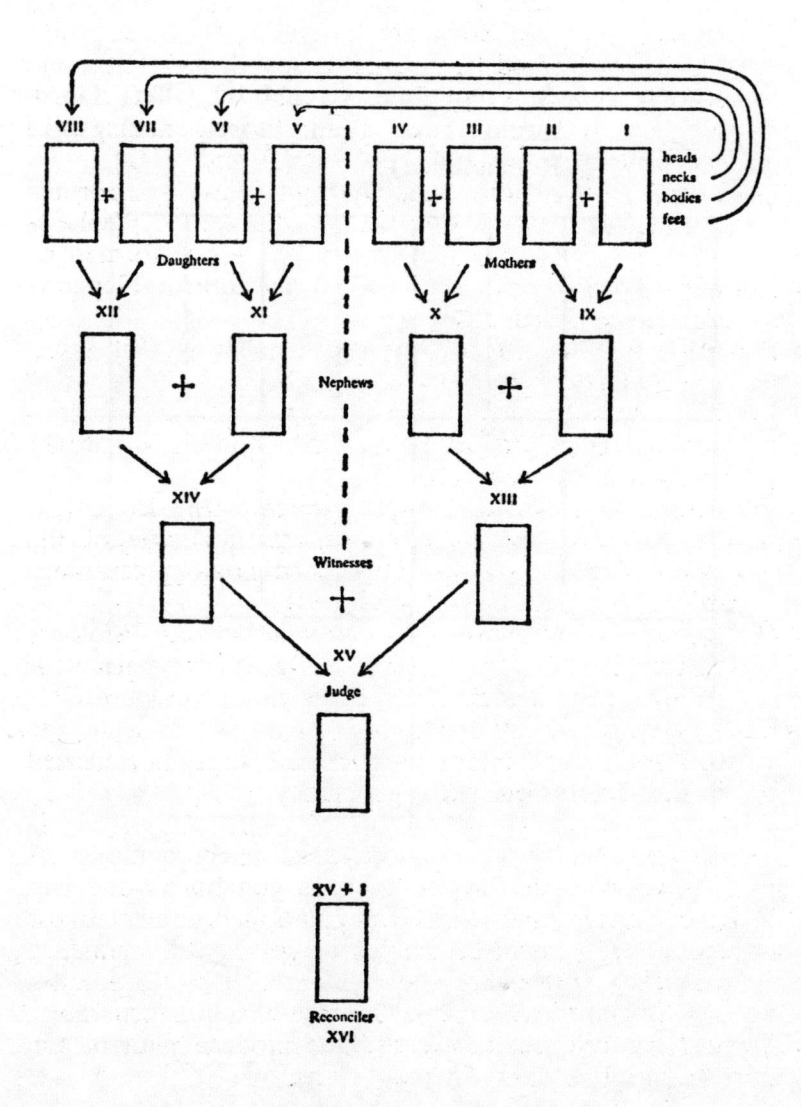

Illustration 2b: A Traditional Geomantic Chart (as it would have been drawn during the Renaissance)

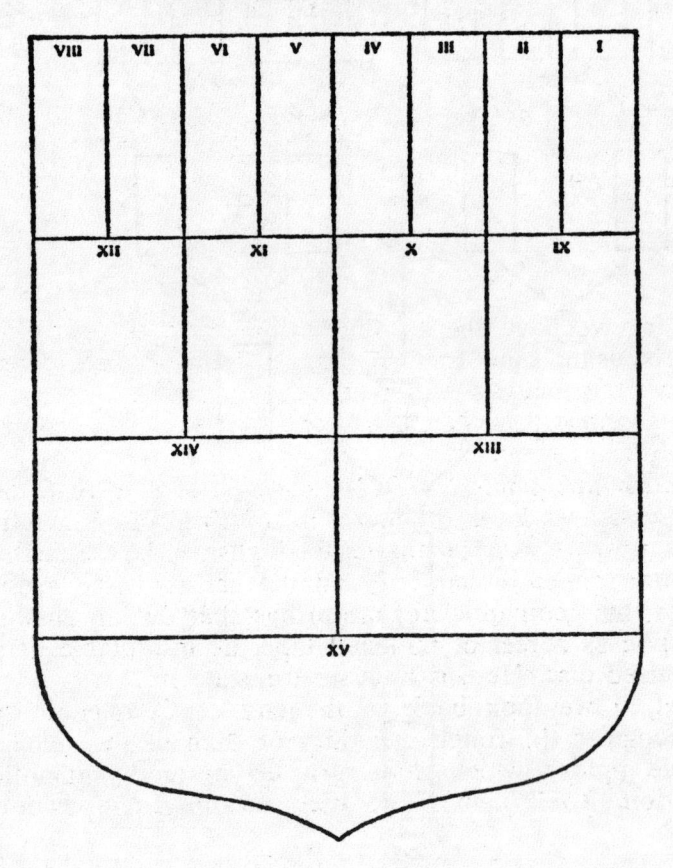

CHAPTER 6
SIXTEEN EYES ON THE FUTURE

So far we have the techniques for creating the four Mothers using sand tray, paper, pebbles or dice. Then we have the analysis and manipulation which forms the four Daughters, four Nephews, two Witnesses, Judge, and possibly the Reconciler.

What happens now? Well we must be able to read the hieroglyphs: we have an answer in the form of geomantic figures, now we want an answer in English. Like the digital computer whose circuits run on the same binary mathematics, the geomantic divination has spat out an answer as cryptic as a reel of punched tape, as inscrutable as a magnetized disc. Here is how we translate it:

First, if we look back to the end of Chapter 1 we can recognize the rough meanings of each of the sixteen possible figures which may turn up in any geomantic divination. Their names and their meanings are as follows:

Fortuna Major—major fortune	Fortuna Minor—minor fortune
* * * * * *	* * * * * *
Via—street	Populus—crowd
* * * *	* * * * * * * *
Acquisitio—acquisition	Laetitia—joy
* * * * * *	* * * * * * *
Puella—girl	Amissio—Loss
* * * * *	* * * * * *
Conjunctio—conjunction	Albus—white
* * * * * *	* * * * * * *
Puer—boy	Rubeus—red
* * * * *	* * * * * * *

Carcer—prison	Tristitia—sorrow
* * * * * *	* * * * * * *

Caput Draconis— head of the dragon	Cauda Draconis— tail of the dragon
* * * * *	* * * * *

According to Bartholomew of Parma, the geomantic figures divide evenly into two groups:

Favorable	Unfavorable
Acquisitio	Amissio
Albus	Rubeus
Puella	Puer
Laetitia	Tristitia
Caput Draconis	Cauda Draconis
Populus	Via
Conjunctio	Carcer
Fortuna Major	Fortuna Minor

Each of the seven classical planets has two geomantic figures allocated to it. Thus the Sun, a beneficent planet in astrology is associated with the two fortunes (Fortuna Major and Fortuna Minor). Jupiter is associated with the figures of acquisition (Acquisitio) and joy (Laetitia) while Mars is subsumed under Puer (boy or warrior) and Rubeus (the figure symbolizing red, the color of blood and war). Saturn, the other malefic of astrology, has imprisonment (Carcer) and sorrow (Tristitia). The moon has two opposites, Via (a solitary journey) and Populus (a crowd) attributed to it, and Venus has Puella (pretty girl) and Amissio (loss) given to it. Mercury is shown by Conjunctio (union or bringing together) and Albus (whiteness).

The remaining figures, Caput Draconis and Cauda Draconis are represented in the heavens by the nodes of the Moon, the point where the Moon crosses the Ecliptic. These last two are strange inasmuch as they are not heavenly bodies but mathematical points in the sky. They are not used much in modern astrology but their old meanings especially the evil of Cauda Draconis are still very necessary parts of a divination.

The reason for the introduction of astrological terms at this point is twofold. First, they will be of great help later when applying the geomantic figures to the Houses of heaven, (an extremely detailed and accurate extension of ordinary geomantic divination). Secondly and most importantly, they help to bring alive the rather stilted geometric shapes of the geomantic figures. For who has not got some dim idea of the characteristics of the Roman gods after whom the planets are named, if not some memory of the astrological meanings of the planets, which will be gone into greater detail in future chapters.

Look carefully now at the table (Illustration 3a) and notice the pairs of figures which are brought together by their association with a particular planet.

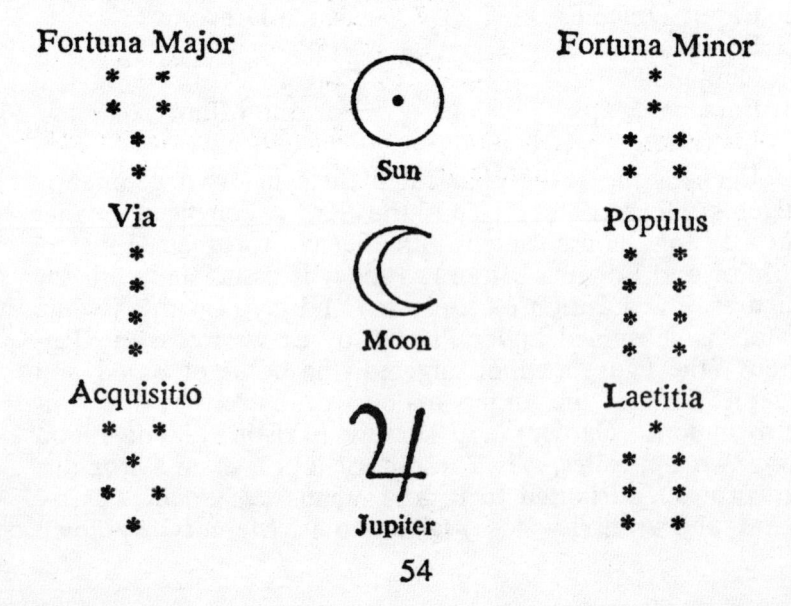

Fortuna Major	Sun	Fortuna Minor
Via	Moon	Populus
Acquisitio	Jupiter	Laetitia

Puella
*
* *
*
*

Conjunctio
* *
* *
* *
*

Puer
*
*
*
* *

Carcer
* *
* *
* *
*

Caput Draconis
* *
*
*
*

♀
Venus

☿
Mercury

♂
Mars

♄
Saturn

☊ ☋
Dragon's
Head and Tail

Amissio
*
* *
* *
* *

Albus
* *
* *
*
* *

Rubeus
*
* *
*
*

Tristitia
* *
* *
* *
*

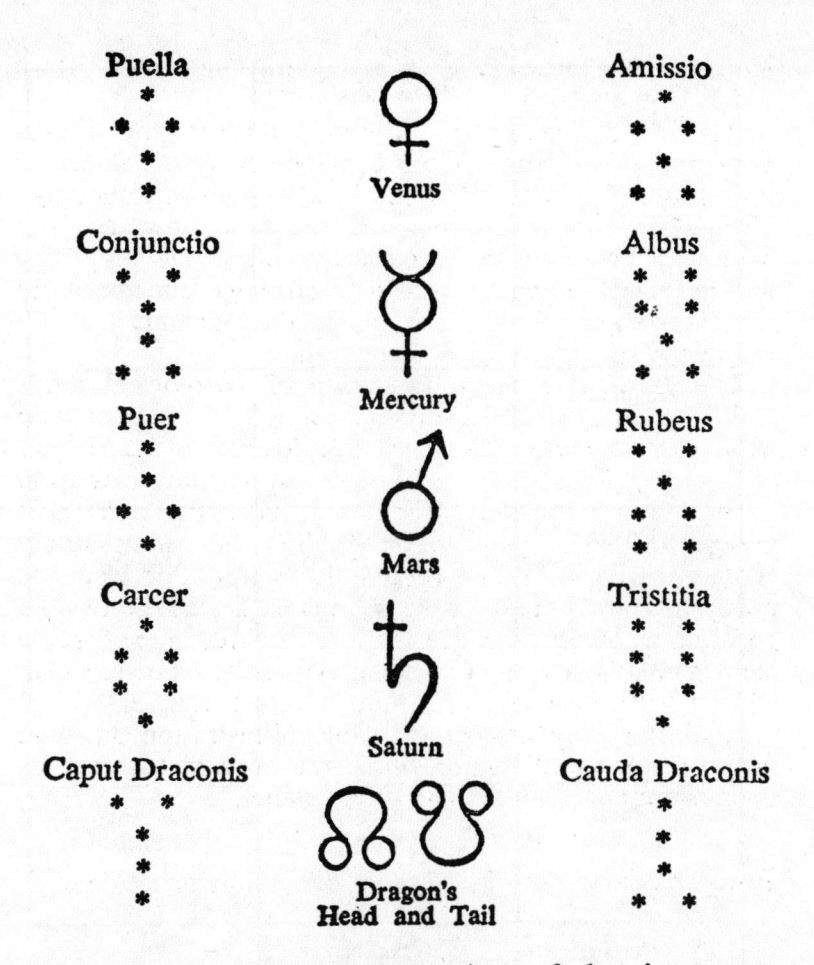

Cauda Draconis
*
*
*
* *

Illustration 3a: Planetary groupings of the sixteen geomantic figures

The greater Fortune. * * * * * *	The Lesser Fortune. * * * * * *	Solis. ☉
Via. * * * *	Populus. * * * * * * * *	Lunæ. ☽
Acquisitio. * * * * * *	Lætitia. * * * * * * *	Jovis. ♃
Puella. * * * * *	Amissio. * * * * * *	Veneris. ♀
Conjunctio. * * * * * *	Albus. * * * * * * *	Mercurii. ☿
Puer. * * * * *	Rubeus. * * * * * * *	Martis. ♂
Carcer. * * * * * *	Tristitia. * * * * * * *	Saturni. ♄
☊ Dragons head. * * * * *	☋ Dragons taile. * * * *	

Illustration 3b: Planetary Groupings of the sixteen Geomantic Figures (from Cornelius Agrippa *Of Geomancy*)

Let us now take the geomantic figures one at a time, adding in their divinatory meaning and further attributes. In the case of Zodiacal ascriptions the various authorities do not agree. Consequently the traditional ascriptions of the Golden Dawn have been used here, and a table of alternate ascriptions has been provided in Appendix I, for those who want to pursue them.

The traditional ascriptions are based on the Zodiacal Signs which are ruled by the planet ascribed to the geomantic figure. Thus, in each case, the planet, Sign and element are in perfect agreement.

In each case, the geomantic figure is given first with its Latin name, planet, element and astrological Sign. Following these are the various divinatory meanings which will "decode" the answer given by the oracle each time. The simplest form of decoding is simply to locate the Judge amongst these sixteen possible forms and read off the meaning of the figure, ignoring for the moment the associated astrological material. If more information is required, read off the meaning of each of the Witnesses which contributed to the judgment of the Judge.

If the combination of these three meanings into an answer is difficult then Chapter 8 gives an interpretation for *every possible* combination of Judge and Witness, but only for a limited number of possible questions.

You see now how flexible geomancy is; you can use it either to get a snap judgment from the Judge and Witnesses as given in Chapter 8 or you can encourage your own intuitive abilities by combining the more detailed meanings of these three figures from the following explanations of each figure, for a richer and more detailed answer. Let us take them one at a time:

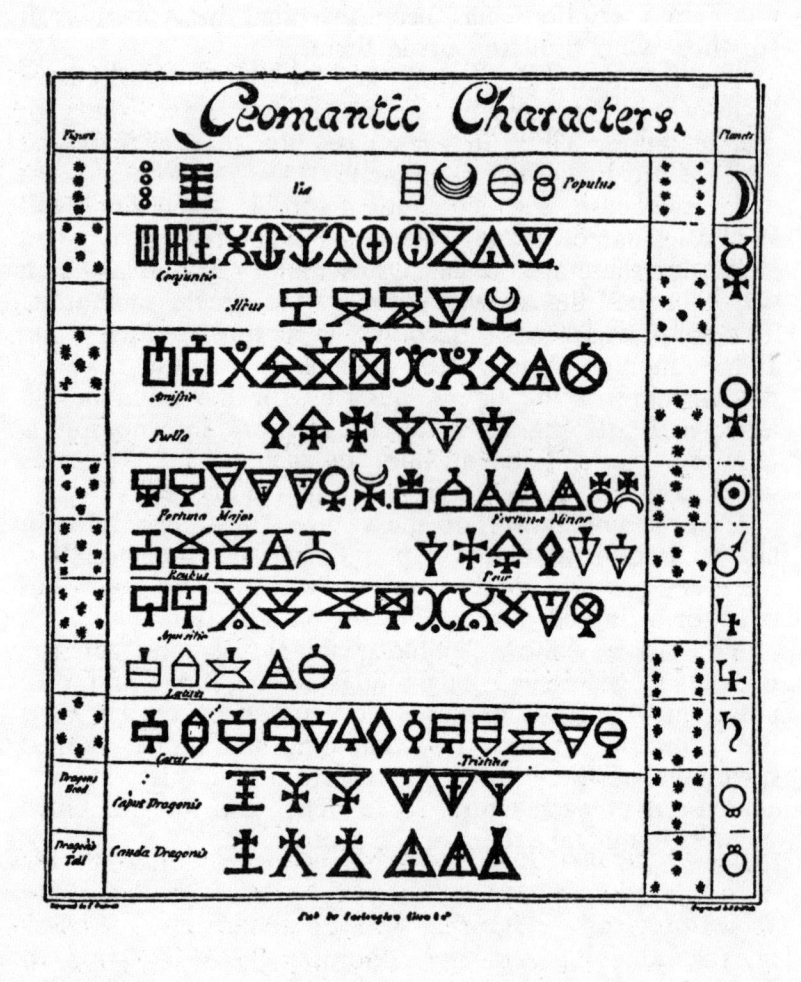

Illustration 4: Characters formed from the geomantic figures in Francis Barrett's *The Magus*

1.	Puer	Mars	Fire	Aries
∴∗∗ ∗		♂	△	♈

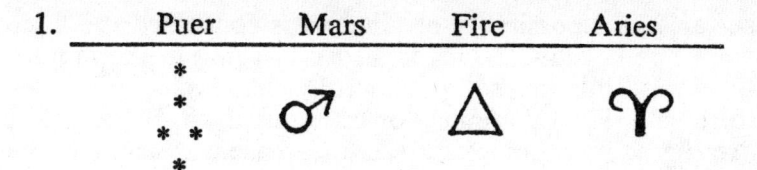

Puer means "a boy" in Latin. The figure also means yellow, beardless, rash and inconsiderate. The nature of the figure depends upon its position in the geomantic spread. The figure is basically neutral, but is rather good than bad. The traditional description of Puer is "evil in most demands, excepting those relating to war or love." Puer is the malevolent and destructive side of Mars. Associated ideas include son, servant, slave, page and bachelor. Its symbol is sometimes written in a disguised manner.

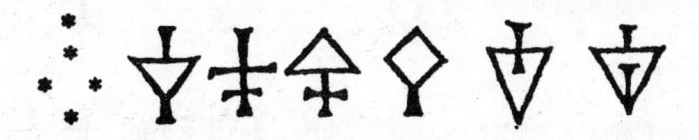

2.	Amissio	Venus	Earth	Taurus
∗ ∗∗ ∗ ∗∗		♀	▽	♉

Amissio means "lost," comprehended without, and that which is taken away: it is a bad figure. Although Venus is astrologically a benefic, the geomantic figure Amissio means quite the opposite. Traditionally it is "good for loss of substance and sometimes for love, but very bad for gain." Regardie gives a telling example of the action of Amissio: "If a woman were seeking counsel as to whether she should divorce her husband, Amissio in the appropriate house would indicate a positive answer. On the other hand, so far as the possibility of alimony is concerned the figure would be negative." This is also a warning to the inquirer to phrase his questions carefully. Amissio is the less fortunate side of Venus, or as it used to be put, it is "retrograde or combust." Associated ideas include that of loss through death. Alternate symbols include:

3.　　Albus　　Mercury　　Air　　Gemini

The Latin literally means "white, dead white." Its divinatory meanings include "white head" fair, wisdom, sagacity, clear thought, all Mercurial concepts. As the traditional explanation has it, "good for profit and for entering into a place or undertaking." Associated ideas include pale, bright (as in Lucifer's brightness), white paint, cement, egg whites and newspapers.

4.　　Populus　　Moon　　Water　　Cancer

The Latin means "the people," forming a community or state, a congregation or crowd. It is essentially a neutral figure and reflects its surroundings (or the adjoining geomatic figures), as does a crowd or gathering. The element water and the Moon which are attributed to this figure demonstrate its reflective properties. Populus is "sometimes good and sometimes bad; good with good, and evil with evil." It rules the waning part of the Moon's cycle, and is therefore less auspicious than Via who rules the Moon with it. Associated meanings include: a host, a multitude, a free state, the people as opposed to their rulers.

---

5. Fortuna Major   Sun   Fire   Leo

   * *
   * *
    *
    *

Fortuna means "chance, luck, lot, fate, or fortune." Fortuna Major means the greater fortune and is attributed to the Sun which is the source of light and life, and is a very good figure. Fortuna Major also means safeguard, entering, success, and interior aid and protection. This figure is ascribed to the Sun during its daylight hours when it is "posited in his dignities." Associated ideas include: property, possessions and a good position in life.

6. Conjunctio   Mercury   Earth   Virgo

* *
*
* .
* *
☿   🜃   ♍

Conjunctio means assembling, "uniting or joining together." It is rather good than bad, and its old definition was "good with good or evil with evil, recovery of things lost." Conjunctio is more fortunate than Albus which is the second geomantic figure of Mercury. Ideas associated with Conjunctio include marriage, allies and relationships.

7. Puella   Venus   Air   Libra

*
* *
* *
*
♀   🜁   ♎

Puella means "a girl or a maiden." Its divinatory meanings include a pretty face, a pleasant daughter, or a young wife. It is not very fortunate, and the mere possession of beauty does not promise underlying beneficence. Puella is the better side of Venus and used to be considered "good in all demands, especially in those relating to women."

8.	Rubeus	Mars	Water	Scorpio
* * * * * * *		♂	▽	♏

Rubeus means red or reddish and has the divinatory meaning of redhead, passion, vice, and fiery temper. It is a bad figure, and covers the traditionally evil associations of Scorpio. The violently sexual aspects of Scorpio are also implied.

9.	Acquisitio	Jupiter	Fire	Sagittarius

* *
  *
* *
  *
		♃	△	♐

Acquisitio in Latin means "acquisitions or additions, to existing possessions, or money." Its divinatory meanings include success, obtaining, absorbing, receiving, gain and good fortune, all attributes of Jupiter: it is a very good figure. The old meaning was "generally good for profit and gain." If it appears as the significator in a geomantic figure, or as the Judge then great success is indicated. Acquisitio is the better half of the two figures which are ruled by Jupiter. In a sense the gain or acquisition occurs as a direct result of inquiry or supplication.

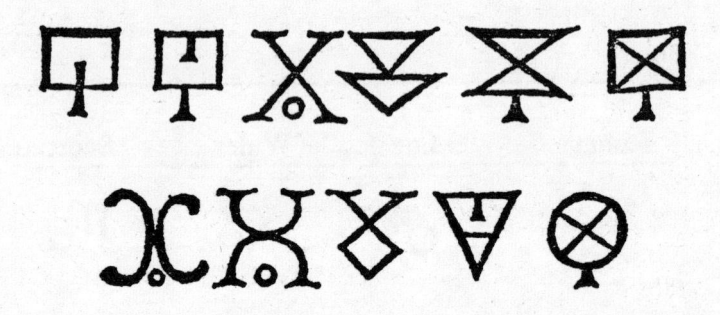

10.	Carcer	Saturn	Earth	Capricorn
	* * * * * *	♄	▽	♑

Carcer means "a prison, jail or cell." Its divinatory meanings include: being bound or confined, and it is good or bad according to the nature of the question. Traditionally, if Carcer occurs in the 1st House of the geomantic map then the divination is to be immediately discontinued and the details destroyed. No further attempt to ask the question should be made for some hours. The old meaning was "generally evil, delay, binding, bars, and restriction." Carcer has the distinction of being the more malevolent of the two Saturnian figures.

11. Tristitia	Saturn	Air	Aquarius
* * * * * * *	♄	△	≈≈

Tristitia in Latin means sadness, sorrow and melancholy. Its divinatory meanings also include: perversion and condemnation, with the old meaning "evil in all things" except useful Saturnian qualities like fortification, earthworks, retrenchment, or strangely enough, debauchery. Additionally it can apply to moroseness, ill-humor, severity and sternness.

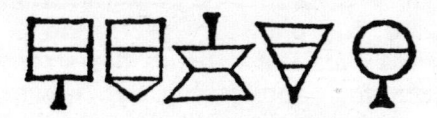

12. Laetitia	Jupiter	Water	Pisces
* * * * * * *	♃	▽	♓

Laetitia literally means joy, expressed and unrestrained gladness or delight. It implies health and laughter and is a very fortunate figure, "good for joy, present, or to come." Additional meanings include: a pleasing appearance, beauty and grace.

---

13. Cauda Draconis   Saturn & Mars   Fire   Scorpio

Cauda Draconis, the dragon's tail, has as its divinatory meanings: the exit, lower kingdom or outer or lower threshold. It is "good for evil, and for terminating affairs of any kind." It represents the harbinger of disaster, and is thoroughly evil. If this symbol ☋ occurs in the 1st House, the divination should be abandoned and the forms destroyed. Again, the planetary ascription is convenient, the two so-called "malefics" being the strongest kind of planetary attribution applicable, but nowhere near as strong as the meaning of the dragon's tail.

---

14. Caput Draconis Jupiter & Venus Earth Capricorn

66

Caput Draconis is the dragon's head, and is named after the constellation Draco. It refers to the moon's northern node, which is the point at which the moon's orbit intersects the plane of the Ecliptic. Its divinatory meanings include: the entrance, upper threshold, or upper kingdom. Its symbol is ☊. The planetary ascription is tentative and mainly for the sake of tidiness: in effect the head and tail of the dragon are points in the sky in their own right.

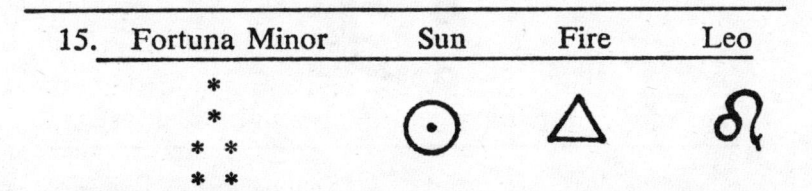

15.	Fortuna Minor	Sun	Fire	Leo
	* * * * * *	☉	△	♌

Fortuna Minor means the lesser fortune, external aid and protection, and is not nearly as good a figure as Fortuna Major. Like the latter it is also attributed to the Sun, but the Sun at night, "or placed in lesser dignities." Sometimes Fortuna Minor has the element of air attributed to it, which balances the attribution of geomantic figures to elements better by providing four figures per element, rather than a surplus of figures for fire.

16.	Via	Moon	Water	Cancer
	* * * *	☾	▽	♋

The Latin means "street or way," literally the way along which one goes, and hence its divinatory meaning also includes journey. Again it is essentially neutral, being reflective like the Moon. Via is "injurious to the goodness of other figures generally, but good for journeys and voyages." Via governs the waxing half of the moon's cycle. Associated meanings include: a highway, a way through, a wind-pipe, a march and a method.

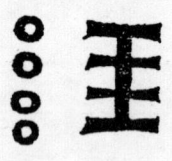

It is very useful to memorize the sixteen geomantic figures, their short divinatory meaning and planetary ascriptions. Of course these can be repeatedly looked up in the course of divination, but there is a greater fluidity and facility, a greater sureness if they are known before commencing divination.

They are easier to memorize if they are grouped together. In fact it is quite a good idea to draw the figures, one per page in an exercise book and before learning their meanings, look at them and observe their shapes. As these shapes suggest things to you, write them down without worrying if they are "correct" or not. In this manner you will develop a feel for the figures before trying to learn them.

When you have a fair selection of your own intuitions and feelings about each figure, start matching these with the traditional meanings. You will probably now find that it only takes an intelligent guess to match figures with traditional meaning.

If however your memory is "visual" rather than "verbal" it may help to match the figures in opposite pairs.

```
   *                    * *
   *     Via and        * *     Populus
   *                    * *
   *                    * *
```

The single line of Via is obviously a street, while Populus is the most crowded figure of all, having as many dots as is possible in a geomantic figure.

```
   *                     *
  * *    Puella and      *      Puer
   *                    * *
   *                     *
```

With some imagination these two figures can be seen to reflect the sexual characteristics of girl and boy respectively.

TABLE OF GEOMANTIC FIGURES

(For easy reference these details and meanings have been tabulated together with the name of the ruler of each 'figure')

No.	Geom. Fig.	Name	Meaning	Sign	Element	Ruler	Planet
1	* * * * * *	Puer	Boy, yellow, beardless, rash & inconsiderate, is rather good than bad.	♈	△	Bartzabel	♂
2	* * * * * *	Amissio	Loss, comprehended without, that which is taken away, a bad figure.	♉	▽̶	Kedemel	♀
3	* * * * * * *	Albus	White, fair, wisdom, sagacity, clear thought, is a good figure.	♊	△̶	Taphthartharath	☿
4	* * * * * * * *	Populus	People, congregation, an indifferent figure.	♋	▽	Chashmodai	☽
5	* * * * * * *	Fortuna Major	Greater fortune, greater aid, safeguard entering, success, interior aid and protection, a very good sign.	♌	△	Sorath	☉
6	* * * * * *	Conjunctio	Conjunction, assembling, union or coming together, rather good than bad.	♍	▽̶	Taphthartharath	☿
7	* * * * * * *	Puella	A girl, beautiful, pretty face, pleasant, but not very fortunate.	♎	△̶	Kedemel	♀

70

8	∴ ∴ ∴ ∶	Rubeus	Red, reddish, redhead, passion, vice, fiery temper, a bad figure.	♏	▽	Bartzabel ♂
9	∶ ∴ ∴ ∴	Acquisitio	Obtaining, comprehending within, success, acquisition, absorbing, receiving, a good figure.	♐	△	Hismael ♃
10	∴ ∶ ∶ ∴	Carcer	A prison, bound, is good or bad according to the nature of the question.	♑	⟟	Zazel ♄
11	∴ ∴ ∶ ∴	Tristitia	Sadness, damned, cross, sorrow, grief, perversion, condemnation, is a bad figure.	♒	⟟	Zazel ♄
12	∴ ∶ ∴ ∴	Laetitia	Joy, laughing, healthy, bearded, is a good figure.	♓	△	Hismael ♃
13	∶ ∴ ∴ ∶	Cauda Draconis	The threshold lower, or going out, dragon's tail, exit, lower kingdom, is a bad figure.	♌	▽	Zazel & Bartzabel ♄ ♂
14	∶ ∴ ∴ ∴	Caput Draconis	The head, the threshold entering, the upper threshold, dragon's head, entrance, upper kingdom, is a good figure.	♋	⟟	Hismael & Kedemel ♃ ♀
15	∴ ∶ ∶ ∴	Fortuna Minor	Lesser fortune, lesser aid, safeguard going out, external aid and protection, is not a very good figure.	♋	△	Sorath ☉
16	∶ ∴ ∶ ∴	Via	Way, street, journey, neither good nor bad.		▷	Chashminodai ☽

Illustration 5: Complete table of the sixteen geomantic figures

71

```
     *                              * *
     *     Cauda and                 *     Caput Draconis
     *                               *
    * *                              *
```

These are obviously the tail and head obverse of each other.

```
     *                              * *
    * *    Laetitia and             * *    Tristitia
    * *                             * *
    * *                              *
```

Joy is firm-based, sorrow looks as if it's going to topple over.

```
    * *                              *
    * *    Fortuna Major and         *     Fortuna Minor
     *                              * *
     *                              * *
```

These two are complementary, one to the other and are like a square on a stick, one being the reverse of the other. Fortuna Major is the stronger of the two.

```
    * *                              *
     *     Acquisitio and           * *    Amissio
    * *                              *
     *                              * *
```

The upward-pointing triangles or arrows indicate loss of possessions, while the down-pointing triangles bring gain.

```
    * *                              *
     *     Conjunctio and           * *    Carcer
     *                              * *
    * *                              *
```

These two are the opposite of each other, Conjunctio looking like the shape glue makes when joining two things, and Carcer looking like a pen or prison.

```
  * *                    * *
* *    Albus and          *     Rubeus
  *                      * *
* *                      * *
```

Also opposite designs, being white and red.

Anyway, your own images should by now have sprung to mind and the effort involved in distinguishing the figures one from another considerably reduced.

Let us now look at some typical applications of this system of divination.

CHAPTER 7

USING THE EYES OF FA

As an indication of the degree of accuracy obtainable in expertly done geomantic readings, it is interesting to go back three centuries and listen to Robert Fludd's account of one of his readings.

Robert Fludd was an English physician, Rosicrucian and mystical philosopher, born in Kent in 1574. He studied at St. John's College, Oxford, and then spent five years in Europe, taking his medical degree in 1605. He was a follower of Paracelsus whose advances in medicine were to revolutionize the whole medieval and classical attitude to it. Fludd was author of many obscure Latin works on theosophy, philosophy and mathematics. He approached these subjects, however, in a typical medieval manner, treating them as interrelated parts of one divine science rather than separate fields of inquiry.

His father had been "Treasurer of War" to Elizabeth I and he therefore was part of a reasonably important family and consequently had the money to travel widely and to study medicine in France, Spain, Italy and Germany. He poured out such an amazing stream of complex treatises that it was said that he employed an amanuensis regularly so that he could dictate his numerous works at odd moments throughout the day.

Apart from his interest in philosophy and medicine, he became a supporter of the Rosicrucian cause and wrote several works supporting this almost mythical brotherhood of sages which had first come to the notice of the scholars in Europe in the early seventeenth century. As he was an influential writer in his own time, much of what has later come to be considered as Rosicrucian was in fact based on Fludd's treatises rather than directly Rosicrucian material.

He was also important in other fields of endeavor and became a close correspondent of the astronomer Kepler who we mentioned on the very first page of this book. Fludd's contribution to astronomy was more in the nature of cosmological speculations, but because of the logic of the time, Kepler felt that in amongst Fludd's cosmological speculation were principles which he could possibly apply to deducing the physical nature of the universe. It was not unusual in the seventeenth century for thinkers to subscribe to the "as above so below" theory, and use the conclusions of one science to answer questions in another.

Kepler was so fascinated with Fludd's theories explained in the *Utriusque Cosmi* that when he wrote his own treatise on the solar system he included an appendix specifically addressed to Fludd. However, where Fludd saw the universe animated by a living soul and ruled by spiritual essences, angelic powers and the whole machinery of planetary intelligences, Kepler took a more modern view and described the system in terms of mathematics. In some ways Fludd and Kepler represent the division between ancient and modern approaches to cosmology; on Fludd's side is the platonic theory of the world soul integrated with the Christian ideas of his period, on the other side Kepler adheres rigorously to those things which he can prove by figures.

Fludd's speculation on Creation and natural history mixed theories of thunderbolts with addresses on anatomy, military manuvers, theological theories, religious rationalizations, and cabalistic conjectures. For Fludd, there was no difference, no dividing line between science and religion.

As Fludd saw geometry and its attendant science, mathematics, at the root of the whole cosmos, it is not unusual that he felt that the binary mathematics of geomancy were a reliable means for probing the future. Fludd describes one of his experiences with geomancy in the section on "the internal principle of terrestrial astrology or geomancy" in his *Historia Macrocosmi*. The translation of which is based on the work of C.H. Josten.

"In (1601-2) . . . I was compelled to spend the whole winter in the city of Avignon, because the winter was very severe, with so much snow covering the mountains of [St.] Bernard that the passage into Italy was entirely blocked. With many other young men of good background, and of sound education (former pupils of the Jesuits) I received board and lodging at the house of a certain captain.

"One evening, while we were drinking at table, I discussed philosophical subjects with the others and noticed their various opinions on geomantic astrology. Some of them denied its usefulness altogether; others, with whom I sided, stoutly defended the truth of that art. I set out many arguments whereby I proved myself fairly well versed in geomancy.

"The meal being over, I had no sooner returned to my bedroom, when one of my companions followed me and asked me to try my skill (in geomancy) (which, he said, he had seen was considerable) in the resolution of a problem of some importance which greatly troubled him. Having made many excuses, I was at last prevailed upon by his entreaties. So, instantly I marked out the geomantic dots for the question he had proposed. This question was: whether a girl with whom he had vehemently fallen in love returned his love with equal fervor with her entire mind and body, and whether she loved him more than anyone else.

"Having drawn up the (geomantic) chart, I assured him that I could describe the nature and appearance of his beloved and, having duly described to him the stature and shape of the girl's body, I indicated also a particular and rather noticeable mark, a kind of wart on her left eye-lid, which he agreed was there. I said also that the girl loved vineyards, and this detail, too, was confirmed by him with pleasure. He said that her mother had for that very reason built her house among the vineyards. Finally I gave the following answer to the question: that his beloved was unfaithful and by no means steady in her love of him, and that she loved somebody else more than him. Whereupon he said that he had always very much suspected that this was the case and that he was [now] seeing it with open eyes.

"He left my room in haste and then related to his companions with some admiration the truth and virtue of my art. Yet some of them, who knew the girl well, denied altogether that she had any such mark on her eye-lid as I had described, until they talked to her the following day and saw the correctness of that detail which I had foretold by the art of geomancy, and which even they had never previously noticed."

This interesting episode however could have led to serious trouble for Fludd as the papal town of Avignon contained a number of clergy who considered such practices unlawful and harmful, if not exactly demoniac. Let Fludd continue his story:

"Thus I became better known than I desired, so much so that rumours of this matter reached the ears of the Jesuits. Two of them went secretly to the Palace and, impelled by envy, reported to the Vice-Legate that there was a certain foreigner, an Englishman, who had made predictions of future events by the science of geomancy, which science was not approved of by the Catholic Church. The following morning this was related to me by a captain of the Palace, named John."

John put Fludd's fears to rest for he had heard the Vice-Legate's reply that:

"Truly this is not so serious an offence as you are trying to make out. Is there indeed a single Cardinal in Italy who does not possess an interpretation of his nativity after the astrological or the geomantic method?"

A few days later the Vice-Legate invited Fludd to have a meal with him and discuss geomancy. Just to be on the safe side, and to have a witness, in case his words later be twisted by a court, Fludd took his old friend,

Monsieur Malceau, the well-known papal apothecary. After the usual formalities the Vice-Legate broached the reason for his invitation and asked Fludd for his real opinion of geomancy. The Vice-Legate also wanted to know how a scientific method of divination could be based on an apparently random and accidental jotting. By this time Fludd saw that there was no trap concealed in the conversation, and that his questioner really wanted to know the inner mechanics and rationale of geomancy. Accordingly, Fludd replied that

". . . the principle and origin of those dots made by the human hand was inward and very essential, since the movement [of the hand by which the dots are produced] emanated from the soul. I added that the errors of geomancy are not caused by the soul but by the unrefined nature of the body distorting the intention of the soul. For that reason it is a general rule in this art that the soul (of the geomancer) must be in a peaceful condition, and a condition in which the body is obedient to the soul; also that there must be no disturbance of body or soul, nor any bias concerning the question; that the (geomancer's) soul must be like a just and impartial judge . . . Likewise it is necessary for the practitioner to think intensely of the question that had been proposed so that he might not be seduced by any extraneous thoughts."

Let us try and make this clearer, by taking a divination suggested by Aleister Crowley:

"We will suppose that one wishes to divine by geomancy whether or not one should marry, it being assumed that one's emotional impulses suggest so rash a course. The man takes his wand and his sand; he traces the question, makes the appropriate pentagram, and the sigil of the spirit. [In this case the sigil Kedemel, Ruler of Venus]. Before tracing the dashes which are to determine the four 'Mothers,' he must strictly examine himself. He must banish from his mind every thought which can possibly act as an attachment to his proposed partner. He must banish all thoughts which concern himself, those of apprehension no less than those of ardour . . . So long as his mind is stirred, however slightly, by one single aspect of the subject, he is not fit to begin to form the figure . . . he must await the impulse to trace the marks on the sand;

and, as soon as it comes let it race to the finish. Here arises another technical difficulty. One has to make 16 rows of dots; and, especially for the beginner, the mind has to grapple with the apprehension lest the hand fail to execute the required number. It is also troubled by fearing to exceed; but excess does not matter. Extra lines are simply null and void, so that the best plan is to banish that thought and make sure only of not stopping too soon.

"The lines being traced, the operation is over as far as spiritual qualities are required, for a time. The process of setting up the figure for judgment is purely mechanical."

Suppose that the lines of dots were traced as follows:

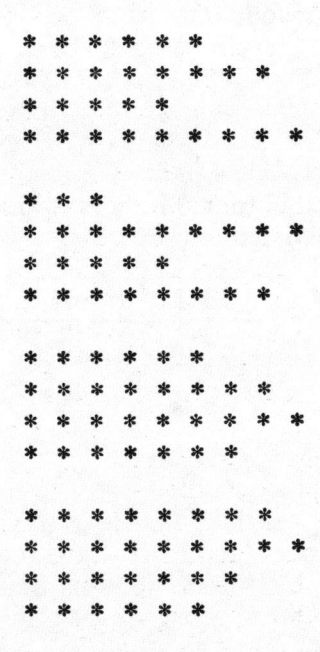

```
      * * * * * *
      * * * * * * * *
      * * * * *
      * * * * * * * * *

      * * *
      * * * * * * * * *
      * * * * *
      * * * * * * * *

      * * * * * *
      * * * * * * * *
      * * * * * * * * *
      * * * * * * *

      * * * * * * * *
      * * * * * * * * *
      * * * * * * *
      * * * * * *
```

Now translate this into odd (one dot) and even (two-dot figures) and separate the sixteen lines into four groups of four (steps 6 and 7 in the summary in Chapter 5).

```
         even        * *
         even        * *
         odd          *
         odd          *
```

79

odd	*
odd	*
odd	*
even	* *
even	* *
even	* *
odd	*
odd	*
even	* *
odd	*
odd	*
even	* *

Step 8

This gives us the four Mothers which we must now write from right to left.

	IV	III	II	I
M	* *	* *	*	* *
O				
T	*	* *	*	* *
H				
E	*	*	*	*
R				
S	* *	*	* *	*

Step 9

Now you will remember that the Daughters are formed from the Mothers by taking:
 all the heads of the Mothers for the first Daughter V
 all the necks of the Mothers for the second Daughter VI
 all the bodies of the Mothers for the third Daughter VII
 all the feet of the Mothers for the fourth Daughter VIII

Write them also from right to left:

	VIII	VII	VI	V
D	*	*	* *	* *
A				
U	* *	*	*	*
G				
H	*	*	* *	* *
T				
E	* *	*	*	* *
R				
S				

Step 10

Now for the Nephews, which are formed using the "addition formula":
Mother I + Mother II = Nephew IX
Mother III + Mother IV = Nephew X
Daughter V + Daughter VI = Nephew XI
Daughter VII + Daughter VIII = Nephew XII

These are also written right to left:

	XII	XI	X	IX
N	* *	* *	* *	*
E				
P	*	* *	*	*
H				
E	* *	* *	* *	* *
W				
S	*	*	*	*

Step 11

Likewise Witnesses are formed by addition.
Nephew IX + Nephew X = Witness XIII
Nephew XI + Nephew XII = Witness XIV

	XIV	XIII
W	* *	*
I		
T	*	* *
N		
E	* *	* *
S		
S	* *	* *
E		
S		

WITNESSES

Step 12

These two are then added to form the Judge.
Witness XIII + Witness XIV = Judge XV

```
              XV
      J       *
      U       *
      D       *
      G      * *
      E      * *
```

Step 13

Before proceeding to interpretation, let's lay out the full fifteen figures on the form designed for this purpose. (See Geomantic Chart, page 83.)

Interpretation

Now, having gone through the mechanical generation of the fifteen figures of the geomantic spread, comes the work of interpretation (*steps 14-15* in the summary given in Chapter 5). Before we can determine the meaning of the chart we have to identify the name of each of the fifteen figures. In the chart, each figure has been given its

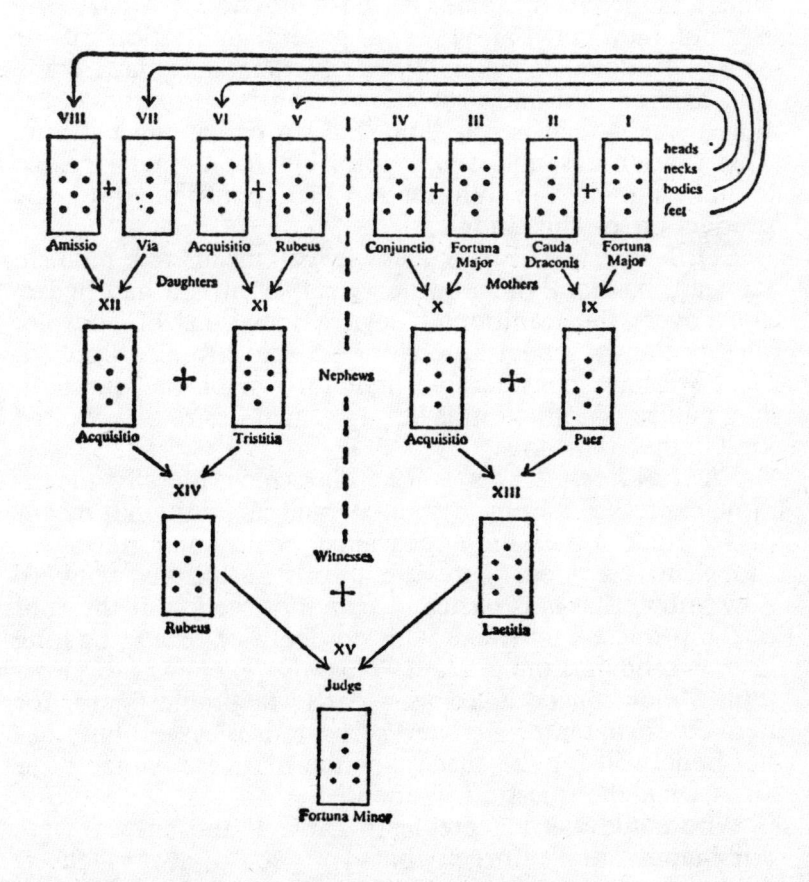

VIII	VII	VI	V	IV	III	II	I	
• • • • • • •	• • • • • •	• • • • • • •	• • • • • • •	• • • • • •	• • • • • •	• • • • •	• • • • • •	heads necks bodies feet
Amissio	Via	Acquisitio	Rubeus	Conjunctio	Fortuna Major	Cauda Draconis	Fortuna Major	

Daughters   Mothers

XII   XI   X   IX

Acquisitio   Tristitia   Nephews   Acquisitio   Puer

XIV   XIII

Witnesses

+

Rubeus   XV   Laetitia

Judge

Fortuna Minor

name. Observe particularly the figures that are in the Witness and Judge boxes. If you have not memorized these figures and their names, write them down from Illustration 5, on page 70–7.

As the question is not one of the set specified in Chapter 8, you can't take the easy way out and merely look up the Judge and Witness tables in that chapter, so let's take the figures in turn. The Judge is Fortuna Minor which is grouped amongst the unfavorable figures by Bartholomew of Parma as a general indication of its nature. In detail it means "lesser fortune, safeguard going out, external aid and protection," and is attributed to the Sun at night, that is, the cold, hidden or vanquished Sun. This does not sound very promising for a marriage, so let us examine the Witnesses which contributed to the production of this Judge.

Left Witness: This is Rubeus, which means red, reddish, redhead, passion, vice and fiery temper; it is a bad figure, and covers the traditionally evil associations of Scorpio. The violently sexual aspects of Scorpio are also implied. Here we have considerable light thrown on the question. The nature of attraction is strong sexual desire of a violent kind rather than love.

Right Witness: This is Laetitia which literally means "joy, expressed and unrestrained" and its additional meanings include a pleasing appearance, beauty and grace. Although it is a good figure it confirms beautifully what we now know, that is is basically sexual attraction at the root of the proposed marriage with no depth of feeling or long lasting good fortune implied. This also explains how Fortuna Minor can be listed as a partly favorable figure, for here the sexual attraction and pleasure is pleasant, but does not bode well for the success of the marriage, which after all is what the question is about.

Who could ask for greater clarity? If the answer were ambiguous, don't forget that you could always resort to that back-stop, the Reconciler (Figure XVI), which is formed by adding together Figures I and XV, that is, the first Mother and the Judge. However don't form a Reconciler if you have already got a satisfactory answer, as this is rude persistence in the face of a perfectly adequate reply by the oracle!

Step 16

If more detail is required, refer back to the first Mother (Figure I) for the beginning of the matter. This figure is Fortuna Major, indicating that the relationship commenced with a good figure which means "the greater fortune" and is attributed also to Leo and the Sun, but the Sun during the day. Thus both this figure and the Judge are attributed to the Sun and Leo but the relationship moves from the Sun during the day to the Sun at night, in short the relationship cools off and dies. Fortuna Major also includes among its divinatory meanings "safeguard, entering success, and interior aid and protection" indicating the beginning of the relationship, which perhaps commenced with some elements of a desire on the part of one partner to protect or look after the other.

The termination or end of the relationship is indicated by Figure IV which is Conjunctio or "uniting or joining together," more good than bad but "good with good or evil with evil." Associated ideas include marriage.

This is interesting because it indicates clearly that although the Judge warns against the marriage as being the lesser fortune, the likely upshot of the matter is that the marriage will take place nevertheless. As Conjunctio is "good with good or evil with evil" the mixture of Rubeus and Laetitia (violent sexual attraction and good looks) will draw the two into a marriage which will nevertheless wane in quality as the Sun at day (Figure I, Fortuna Major) reverts to the Sun at night (Figure XV, Fortuna Minor).

Crowley neatly sums up the operation of judgment, emphasizing the need of a meditative frame of mind untouched by bias in assessing the correct interpretation of the information supplied by the geomantic chart:

"In the judgment, the diviner stands once more in need of his inmost and utmost attainments. He should exhaust the intellectual sources of information at his disposal, and form from them his judgment. But having done this, he should detach his mind from what it has just formulated, and proceed to concentrate it on the figure as a whole, almost as if it were the object of his meditation. One need hardly repeat that in both these operations, detachment from one's personal partialities is as necessary as it was in the first part of the work."

For the moment this is the limit of information obtainable from the chart till we progress to astro-geomancy (Chapter 10), but for now let us take a break and look at a shortcut method of getting easy answers from a geomantic chart without having to exercise any judgment or intuition at all. Like a computer the next chapter will take in the data in the form of Judge and Witnesses and "print out" an instant answer to your question, although the answer should not be taken quite as seriously as a "real" divination.

CHAPTER 8

THE GEOMANTIC PRINT-OUT TERMINAL

This chapter is by way of a diversion. It could be likened to the print-out terminal of a computer, from which you can derive an almost automatic answer from the material fed in. In this chapter we do the same for geomancy. The feed-in material is of course your question and the result of your sand tray or dot-making, which has to be arranged in the usual manner, Mothers, Daughters, Nephews, Witnesses and Judge.

Feed in your information (the question), draw your lines of dots, produce the two Witnesses and Judge, look them up in this chapter, and presto you have the answer! Here you can match any combination of Witnesses and Judge against a short answer for certain basic questions. The only proviso is that you must choose your question from among the following possible questions. In each case, the question can refer either to yourself or to another person. The questions are numbered 1-16 so you can find your particular answer, which will have the same number, in the answer pages.

Questions

1. Will he have a long life?
2. Will he become rich?
3. Should I undertake this project?
4. How will the undertaking end?
5. Is the expected child a boy or a girl?
6. Are the servants/employees honest?
7. Will the patient soon recover from his illness?
8. Will the lover succeed in getting his girl, or vice versa?
9. Will the inheritance be obtained?
10. Will the lawsuit be won by me?
11. Will he get the job?
12. How will he die?
13. Will the expected letter arrive?
14. Will the voyage be successful?
15. Will good news arrive soon?
16. Will the adversary be conquered?

For example, let us suppose that you wanted a quick and easy answer to the question "Is the expected child a boy or a girl." This is question no. 5 in the above list.

Use your paper or sand tray in the normal manner. You put down the four Mothers, and from them work out the Daughters, Nephews, two Witnesses and Judge, following the usual method. Suppose that the two Witnesses were Populus (left Witness) and Acquisitio (right Witness) then the Judge formed is therefore also Acquisitio.

You now turn to page 91, where the index of Witnesses and Judges tells you to look at page 93. On this page question no. 5 (your question) is answered by "Son." The answers, which are almost always very short, have been taken from part of a sixteenth-century German work on geomancy, and are a medieval try at establishing a compendium of answers to take the hard work out of divination!

Of course your possible questions are limited to the sixteen given earlier in this chapter, and there are many possible questions that could have been asked, but this "shortcut" is essentially just that, and no substitute for careful analysis and interpretation of the figures, using your own intuition and the information provided so far. Despite this, there are over two thousand answers packed tightly into this chapter!

For those who are interested in the mathematics, there are 8 possible Judges that can be formed in any geomantic operation. These Judges are made in 2 ways (left taken with right Witness, or right taken with left Witness) from 8 combinations of Witnesses, for a total of 16 questions. Multiply these together and we get $8 \times 2 \times 8 \times 16 = 2048$ possible answers, that is, 2 raised to the power of 11.

Remember that in each case, the Judge is the central figure with the Witnesses flanking it on the right and the left. Take good care when looking up the tables that you identify which is the right and which the left Witness. Because of the nature of the binary calculations which finally generate the Judge, there are only *eight possible* Judge figures (out of the total of sixteen geomantic figures) which can turn up as Judges. There is one for each planet with the exception of the Sun and the Moon, which have two representative figures each. The Judges follow in the order that they appear in these tables:

♃	Acquisitio
♀	Amissio
☉	Fortuna Major / Fortuna Minor
☾	Populus / Via
☿	Conjunctio
♄	Carcer

89

In each case, find the pages appropriate to the Judge, then locate the correct flanking Witnesses. The number indicating the question asked is repeated in the answer pages, so you can select the appropriate answer.

The general rules which govern the generation of these answers are:

1. A good Judge made of two good Witnesses is good.
2. A bad Judge made of two bad Witnesses is bad.
3. A good Judge made of one good Witness and one bad Witness means success, but delay and vexation.
4. If the two Witnesses are good and the Judge bad, the result will be obtained; but it will turn out unfortunately in the end.
5. If the first Witness is good and the second bad, the success will be very doubtful.
6. If the first Witness is bad and the second one good, the unfortunate beginning will take a good turn.

WHERE TO FIND YOUR JUDGE AND WITNESS:

Judge	Witnesses		Page
Acquisitio	Populus	+ Acquisitio	93
	Via	+ Amissio	95
♃	Puer	+ Laetitia	97
	Rubeus	+ Tristitia	99
	Albus	+ Caput Draconis	101
	Puella	+ Cauda Draconis	103
	Conjunctio	+ Fortuna Major	105
	Carcer	+ Fortuna Minor	107
Amissio	Populus	+ Amissio	109
	Via	+ Acquisitio	111
♀	Albus	+ Laetitia	113
	Puella	+ Tristitia	115
	Puer	+ Caput Draconis	117
	Rubeus	+ Cauda Draconis	119
	Carcer	+ Fortuna Major	121
	Conjunctio	+ Fortuna Minor	123
Fortuna Major	Populus	+ Fortuna Major	125
	Via	+ Fortuna Minor	127
	Conjunctio	+ Acquisitio	129
☉	Puella	+ Laetitia	131
	Caput Draconis	+ Rubeus	133
	Cauda Draconis	+ Puer	135
	Amissio	+ Carcer	137
	Albus	+ Tristitia	139
Fortuna Minor	Populus	+ Fortuna Minor	141
	Carcer	+ Acquisitio	143
	Rubeus	+ Laetitia	145
☉	Puer	+ Tristitia	147
	Puella	+ Caput Draconis	149
	Albus	+ Cauda Draconis	151
	Conjunctio	+ Amissio	153
	Via	+ Fortuna Major	155
Populus	both	Acquisitio	157
	both	Populus	158
☾	both	Laetitia	159

Judge	Witnesses		Page
Populus	both	Amissio	160
	both	Caput Draconis	161
☾	both	Tristitia	162
	both	Puella	163
	both	Cauda Draconis	164
	both	Albus	165
	both	Puer	166
	both	Fortuna Major	167
	both	Rubeus	168
	both	Fortuna Minor	169
	both	Via	170
	both	Conjunctio	171
	both	Carcer	172
Via	Via	Populus	173
	Acquisitio	Amissio	175
☾	Laetitia	Caput Draconis	177
	Tristitia	Cauda Draconis	179
	Puella	Rubeus	181
	Puer	Albus	183
	Conjunctio	Carcer	185
	Fortuna Major	Fortuna Minor	187
Con-junctio.	Conjunctio	Populus	189
	Acquisitio	Fortuna Major	191
	Amissio	Fortuna Minor	193
☿	Laetitia	Cauda Draconis	195
	Caput Draconis	Tristitia	197
	Fortuna Major	Acquisitio	199
	Rubeus	Albus	201
	Via	Carcer	203
Carcer	Carcer	Populus	205
	Acquisitio	Fortuna Minor	207
♄	Amissio	Fortuna Major	209
	Laetitia	Tristitia	211
	Puella	Albus	213
	Rubeus	Puer	215
	Caput Draconis	Cauda Draconis	217
	Conjunctio	Via	219

ACQUISITIO AS JUDGE

Left Witness	Judge	Right Witness
☾	* *	♃
Populus.	*	Acquisitio.
* *	* *	* *
* *	*	*
* *		* *
* *		*

Acquisitio.

♃

1. Feeble in youth, afterwards strong.
2. Wealthy in youth, afterwards poor.
3. Do not doubt.
4. The end is good.
5. Son.
6. Reliable, but greedy.
7. He will die soon.
8. After waiting a long time.
9. At last something will be had.
10. The judge is favorably inclined.
11. The aspect is favorable if it refers to lawyers.
12. Death by water or watery diseases.
13. Slowly.
14. Fortunate.
15. Tolerable.
16. Yes.

Left Witness	Judge	Right Witness
♃	* *	☾
Acquisitio.	*	Populus.
* *	* *	* *
*	*	* *
* *		* *
*		* *

Acquisitio.

♃

1. A long and happy life.
2. Will be rich in old age.
3. It will be successful.
4. The object will be slowly attained.
5. A boy.
6. Do not trust them too much.
7. He dies after a long sickness.
8. Success.
9. Yes, but it will take a time.
10. Money will gain the day.
11. No success.
12. Dropsy.
13. Yes.
14. Fortunate, but slow.
15. Good news will arrive.
16. Yes.

Left Witness	Judge	Right Witness
☾	* *	♀
Via.	*	Amissio.
*	* *	*
*	*	* *
*		*
*		* *

Acquisitio.

♃

1. Average.
2. A little in the beginning, but nothing in the end.
3. Doubtful.
4. Tolerable.
5. Daughter.
6. They are thieves.
7. Dies.
8. She is inconstant.
9. The inheritance is not good.
10. Success through women.
11. Fortunate with ladies of high position.
12. The fever will kill him.
13. No.
14. A good voyage on land in female company.
15. Only tolerable news.
16. Victory.

Left Witness	Judge	Right Witness
♀	* *	☾
Amissio.	*	Via.
*	* *	*
* *	*	*
*		*
* *		*

Acquisitio.

♃

1. He will die early.
2. Inconstant fortune.
3. Many disappointments.
4. Difficult beginning but a good end.
5. Daughter.
6. Worthless.
7. Dies.
8. He may obtain her by strategy.
9. The legacy is bad.
10. Loses.
11. Inconstant fortune.
12. Fever.
13. Yes.
14. In no way favorable.
15. Trifles.
16. The adversary is stronger than you.

Left Witness	Judge	Right Witness
♂	* *	♃
Puer.	*	Laetitia.
*	* *	*
*	*	* *
* *		* *
*		* *

Acquisitio.

♃

1. Strong in youth, feeble in old age.
2. That which is inherited will nearly all be lost.
3. Fails.
4. A good beginning and a bad end.
5. Son.
6. Reliable.
7. Recovers.
8. He will obtain his wish.
9. A good inheritance.
10. Gains.
11. Success with clergymen.
12. Congestion or apoplexy.
13. They will arrive.
14. No obstacles.
15. News about advancement in office.
16. The adversary loses.

Left Witness	Judge	Right Witness
♃	* *	♂
Laetitia.	*	Puer.
*	* *	*
* *	*	*
* *		* *
* *		*

Acquisitio.

♃

1. Feeble in youth, strong in old age.
2. Final success.
3. Success.
4. The beginning bad, the end good.
5. Son.
6. They are faithful.
7. Recovers.
8. Embrace.
9. Good inheritance gained by law.
10. Loses
11. Fortunate with clergymen.
12. Febrile diseases.
13. No.
14. Beware of robbers.
15. Bad news.
16. The adversary gains.

Left Witness	Judge	Right Witness
♂		♄
Rubeus.		Tristitia.
* *	* *	* *
*	*	* *
* *	* *	* *
* *	*	*

Acquisitio.

♃

1. Painful and feeble.
2. What you gain will be taken away.
3. The undertaking will be abandoned.
4. Bad ending.
5. Son.
6. Thieving and unreliable.
7. Dies.
8. Loss on account of neglectfulness.
9. The legacy is worthless.
10. Gains, but receives no advantage from it.
11. No luck except in war.
12. Beware of fire and lead.
13. The messenger does not arrive.
14. The voyage will cost his life.
15. Worthless.
16. Victory by strategy.

Left Witness	Judge	Right Witness
♄	* *	♂
Tristitia.	*	Rubeus.
* *	* *	* *
* *	*	*
* *		* *
*		* *

Acquisitio.

♃

1. Short and painful life.
2. Be not deluded.
3. Cease to think of it.
4. Bad end.
5. Son.
6. They steal secretly and openly.
7. He will have to go.
8. Vain hope.
9. Obtains.
10. Loses.
11. Unlucky.
12. Cold steel.
13. Waits in vain.
14. Wounded during the voyage.
15. Bad news.
16. The adversary gains by cheating.

Left Witness	Judge	Right Witness
☿	* *	☊
Albus.	*	Caput Draconis.
* *	* *	* *
* *	*	*
*		*
* *		*

Acquisitio.

♃

1. Happy old age.
2. A fortune by marriage and employees.
3. Keep your undertaking secret.
4. The end is as it is desired.
5. Daughter.
6. Faithful and discreet.
7. Danger.
8. He will obtain her.
9. Slow success.
10. The adversary has the advantage.
11. Fortunate with clergymen and ladies.
12. Natural death.
13. Soon.
14. Fortunate.
15. Good.
16. You will wish to settle.

Left Witness	Judge	Right Witness
☊	* *	☿
Caput Draconis.	*	Albus.
* *	* *	* *
*	*	* *
*		*
*		* *

Acquisitio.

♃

1. Long life.
2. Fortune acquired by writing.
3. Fortunate.
4. Good end.
5. Daughter.
6. Honest and industrious.
7. Recovers after a long illness.
8. Will ultimately succeed.
9. A fat legacy.
10. Settlement.
11. Fortunate with mercurial people.
12. Dies quietly in bed.
13. Soon.
14. Good but slow.
15. Agreeable.
16. Adversary is feeble and desires to settle.

Left Witness	Judge	Right Witness
♀ Puella.	* * * * * *	☋ Cauda Draconis.
* * * * *		* * * * *

Acquisitio.

♃

1. Feeble youth, happy old age.
2. Your wife will cause your ruin.
3. If the object is robbery, it will succeed.
4. The end is better than the beginning.
5. Son.
6. Thievish and unchaste.
7. Dies.
8. There are enemies in the way.
9. The legacy will go into the hands of strangers.
10. You will lose because ♀ is against you.
11. No luck.
12. Beware of being wounded.
13. No letters.
14. The voyage is very dangerous.
15. News about war.
16. Your enemy is stronger than you.

Left Witness	Judge	Right Witness
☋	* *	♀
Cauda Draconis.	*	Puella.
*	* *	*
*	*	* *
*		*
* *		*

Acquisitio.

♃

1. Not very long. Feeble old age.
2. Means by marriage.
3. Fortunate in love affairs.
4. The end very doubtful.
5. Son.
6. Unchaste and thieving.
7. Dies.
8. Obtains her.
9. Obtains the inheritance.
10. Gains through the influence of women.
11. Fortunate with ladies.
12. Dies of venereal disease.
13. The letters will arrive.
14. Happy voyage, but great expenses.
15. News about love affairs.
16. You will be victorious over your malicious enemy.

Left Witness	Judge	Right Witness
☿		☉
Conjunctio.		Fortuna Major.

Acquisitio.

♃

1. Happy and very old age.
2. Great riches.
3. Good success.
4. Good.
5. Daughter.
6. Useful.
7. Regains his health.
8. Success by negotiation.
9. Obtains an excellent inheritance.
10. Gains.
11. Fortunate in high places.
12. Natural death.
13. Not as soon as expected.
14. Fortunate but slow.
15. Happy news.
16. Meet him without fear.

Left Witness	Judge	Right Witness
☉	* *	☿
Fortuna Major.	*	Conjunctio.
* *	* *	* *
* *	*	*
*		*
*		* *

Acquisitio.

♃

1. Long life.
2. Rich by trade.
3. Doubtful.
4. Tolerable.
5. Daughter.
6. Faithful.
7. Dies.
8. Certain success.
9. Obtains the legacy.
10. Settlement.
11. Fortunate by means of the pen.
12. Dies in his bed.
13. Soon.
14. Quick and fortunate.
15. Advantageous.
16. You will conquer.

Left Witness	Judge	Right Witness
♄	* *	☉
Carcer.	*	Fortuna Minor.
*	* *	*
* *	*	*
* *		* *
*		* *

Acquisitio.

♃

1. Average.
2. Fortune through ladies.
3. Final success.
4. Tolerable.
5. Son.
6. Vain and idle.
7. Recovery.
8. Success.
9. The adversary obtains the legacy.
10. Gain.
11. Some success.
12. Dies of a fever.
13. No letters.
14. Tolerable.
15. Letters from high personages.
16. You will not gain.

Left Witness	Judge	Right Witness
☉	* *	♄
Fortuna Minor.	*	Carcer.
*	* *	*
*	*	* *
* *		* *
* *		*

Acquisitio.

♃

1. Average.
2. Little gained by a great deal of trouble.
3. You will cease to think of it.
4. Success slow.
5. Daughter.
6. Lazy and vain.
7. Dies.
8. Yes, if she is a widow.
9. The legacy is poor.
10. The adversary gains.
11. Fortunate in the country.
12. Dies of a cold.
13. No letters.
14. Slow and a great deal of annoyance.
15. The news is worthless.
16. The enemy will be victorious.

AMISSIO AS JUDGE

Left Witness	Judge	Right Witness
☾		♀
Populus.	*	Amissio.
* *	* *	*
* *	*	* *
* *	* *	*
* *		* *

Amissio.

♀

1. Feeble and short life.
2. Fortune easily lost.
3. Untimely love is injurious.
4. A bad end.
5. Son.
6. Careless and unfaithful.
7. Recovery.
8. He will obtain his wish.
9. The legacy will be very meagre.
10. The opponent has the advantage.
11. Success by being genteel.
12. Danger of death by venereal disease.
13. Delay.
14. Interference from water.
15. Contents are love affairs.
16. You will conquer all enemies.

Left Witness	Judge	Right Witness
♀		☾
Amissio.		Populus.

Amissio.

♀

1. Short and feeble life.
2. Small fortune.
3. Disappointment.
4. Unsuccessful.
5. Boy.
6. Quick, but unchaste.
7. Dies.
8. Loses her on account of a long voyage.
9. Another person obtains the legacy.
10. Neither one of the opposing parties will have an advantage.
11. Unfortunate.
12. Danger of drowning.
13. Soon.
14. He will go to see his sweetheart.
15. News about voyages.
16. The enemy will do no harm.

Left Witness	Judge	Right Witness
☽ Via.	* * * * * *	♃ Acquisitio. * * * * * *

Amissio.

♀

1. Healthy youth, feeble old age.
2. The older he becomes, the poorer will he be.
3. The prospect is good.
4. Good.
5. Boy.
6. Yes.
7. A long disease.
8. You will get her.
9. Legacy obtained through females.
10. Victory.
11. You will be welcome.
12. Peaceful and natural.
13. Long delay.
14. Delayed.
15. Joyful contents.
16. You are superior to him.

Left Witness	Judge	Right Witness
♃ Acquisitio. * * * * * *	* * * * * *	☾ Via. * * * *

Amissio.

♀

1. Average.
2. Poor in youth and old age. Rich in middle years.
3. The chances are against it.
4. Tolerable.
5. Daughter.
6. Good but inconstant.
7. He regains his health.
8. Your inconstancy will cause you to lose her.
9. Not by you.
10. You will lose.
11. Fortunate on a voyage.
12. Dies in a foreign country.
13. Receives letters.
14. Rapid voyage on land and water.
15. Unimportant.
16. Powerful enemies.

Left Witness	Judge	Right Witness
☿		☿
Albus.		Laetitia.

Amissio.

♀

1. Long life and health.
2. Rich by service.
3. The wish will be fulfilled.
4. The beginning is better than the end.
5. Son.
6. Reliable and good.
7. Health.
8. Will get her.
9. You will get the best part.
10. Gains.
11. Honorable positions in the church.
12. Peaceful and easy death.
13. Certainly.
14. Very good.
15. Agreeable.
16. The enemy will do no harm.

Left Witness	Judge	Right Witness
♃	*	☿
Laetitia.	* *	Albus.
*	*	* *
* *	* *	* *
* *		*
* *		* *

Amissio.

♀

1. Long, joyful life.
2. The older he becomes the richer he will be.
3. Very good prospect.
4. The end will show your ability.
5. Girl.
6. Honest and useful.
7. Dies.
8. Will get her through writing.
9. Another one will get the best part.
10. Amicable settlement.
11. Your pen will be your recommendation.
12. Natural death.
13. They have already arrived.
14. Fortunate.
15. Good.
16. You should try to obtain a settlement.

Left Witness	Judge	Right Witness
♀ Puella. * * * * *	* * * * * *	♄ Tristitia. * * * * * * *

Amissio.

♀

1. Long but troubled life.
2. A little by agriculture and hard labor.
3. Useless.
4. Worthless.
5. Girl.
6. Idle and dishonest.
7. Recovery.
8. Lost on account of carelessness.
9. A little, but not much.
10. The adversary gains.
11. Unlucky in the country.
12. Gloom and discouragement.
13. No letters.
14. Slow.
15. Bad news.
16. The enemy gains the day.

Left Witness	Judge	Right Witness
♄	*	♀
Tristitia.	* *	Puella.
* *	*	*
* *	* *	* *
* *		*
*		*

Amissio.

♀

1. Average duration. Troublesome.
2. Means by way of marriage.
3. Yes, if it is a love affair.
4. Tolerable.
5. Son.
6. Not very faithful.
7. Will gain strength.
8. Most certainly.
9. You may hope for a little.
10. Gains through ladies of rank.
11. All favors by female influence.
12. Melancholy.
13. Letters from ladies.
14. Tolerable.
15. The contents are love matters.
16. Look out for treachery.

Left Witness	Judge	Right Witness
♂		☊
Puer.		Caput Draconis.

Amissio.

♀

1. Strong in youth, feeble afterwards.
2. A little by marriage.
3. This time you will have success.
4. Fortunate end.
5. Girl.
6. Good.
7. Recovers his strength slowly.
8. The marriage will not take place.
9. A small legacy.
10. Fortunate ending.
11. Fortunate at the court.
12. Natural death.
13. Slowly.
14. Fortunate.
15. Very agreeable.
16. You have the advantage.

Left Witness	Judge	Right Witness
☊	*	♂
Caput Draconis.	* *	Puer.
* *	*	*
*	* *	*
*		* *
*		*

Amissio.

♀

1. Sickly in youth, afterwards stronger.
2. Nothing to be expected except by force.
3. Unsuccessful.
4. Bloody.
5. Son.
6. Average.
7. Will gain strength.
8. The marriage will take place.
9. There is nothing to be inherited.
10. The adversary gains.
11. Fortune in war.
12. Beware of fire.
13. Soon.
14. Dangerous.
15. News about war.
16. Your enemy is too sly for you.

Left Witness	Judge	Right Witness
♂	*	☋
Rubeus.	* *	Cauda Draconis.
* *	*	*
*	* *	*
* *		*
* *		* *

Amissio.

♀

1. Feeble youth; healthy old age.
2. Obtains some means in old age.
3. It will be abandoned.
4. Unfortunate.
5. Son.
6. Worthless.
7. Dies.
8. The marriage will take place.
9. Another person will get it.
10. The adversary has the advantage.
11. Go to the country or to the war.
12. A fever will make an end to his life.
13. Very slowly.
14. There is danger from robbers and lewd women.
15. Disagreeable news.
16. Your enemy is too powerful for you.

Left Witness	Judge	Right Witness
☊	*	♂
Cauda Draconis.	* *	Rubeus.
*	*	* *
*	* *	*
*		* *
* *		* *

Amissio.

♀

1. Long life. Feeble old age.
2. Considerable means.
3. Success.
4. Fortunate end.
5. Daughter.
6. Average.
7. Dies.
8. It will come to nothing.
9. A small amount.
10. It will not be to your advantage.
11. A good position at the court.
12. Taking cold.
13. Soon.
14. Fortunate.
15. Good.
16. You are superior to the other.

Left Witness	Judge	Right Witness
♄	*	☉
Carcer.	* *	Fortuna Major.
*	*	* *
* *	* *	* *
* *		*
*		*

Amissio.

♀

1. Long life.
2. Abundance.
3. There will be some success.
4. The end will be as desired.
5. Girl.
6. Good and useful.
7. This time he will escape.
8. He will not get his darling.
9. Persons of high positions will divide it with you.
10. The judgment will be in your favor.
11. Success in view.
12. Quietly.
13. No.
14. Fortunate but slow.
15. News speaking of persons of high rank.
16. Take courage.

Left Witness	Judge	Right Witness
☉		♄
Fortuna Major.		Carcer.
* *	*	*
* *	* *	* *
*	*	* *
*	* *	*

Amissio.

♀

1. A long life.
2. Means by agriculture and mines.
3. That which seems difficult now will become clearer.
4. Average and slow success.
5. Girl.
6. Good and useful.
7. Dies.
8. You ought to dismiss all thoughts of marrying.
9. The legacy is destined for you.
10. The adversary will receive the judgment.
11. Your fortune is to be found in the country.
12. A natural death.
13. No letters.
14. Fortunate but slow.
15. Letters on agricultural matters.
16. You had better remain away.

Left Witness	Judge	Right Witness
☿	*	☉
Conjunctio.	* *	Fortuna Minor.
* *	*	*
*	* *	∗
*		* *
* *		* *

Amissio.

♀

1. Considerably long but eventful life.
2. Riches by obtaining honorable positions.
3. It will turn out well.
4. Good.
5. Son.
6. They are excessively vain.
7. Recovers.
8. Certain success.
9. After a dispute.
10. The adversary offers a settlement.
11. Advantage.
12. Hot fever.
13. Slow messages.
14. Average.
15. Agreeable.
16. Take courage and go ahead.

Left Witness	Judge	Right Witness
☉	*	☿
Fortuna Minor.	* *	Conjunctio.
*	*	* *
*	* *	*
* *		*
* *		* *

Amissio.

♀

1. Average and changeful.
2. Fortune by trade.
3. Will be abandoned.
4. Tolerable.
5. Twins.
6. They are of the average kind.
7. Dies.
8. He must have her.
9. The legacy will be lost.
10. You will want a settlement.
11. Your fortune is in trading.
12. In bed.
13. The messenger is entering the house.
14. Fortunate.
15. Good.
16. Your adversary is very fortunate.

FORTUNA MAJOR AS JUDGE

Left Witness	Judge	Right Witness
☾	* *	☉
Populus.	* *	Fortuna Major.
* *	*	* *
* *	*	* *
* *		*
* *		*

Fortuna Major.

☉

1. Long life and contented.
2. The possessions are excellent.
3. Go ahead with it.
4. The end will be very good.
5. Girl.
6. You may hire them.
7. Recovers.
8. The other admirers will have to take a back seat.
9. The inheritance is sure.
10. You will gain.
11. You will find what you are seeking.
12. Dies peacefully.
13. Slowly.
14. The voyage on land will be fortunate.
15. Jolly.
16. Attack him.

Left Witness	Judge	Right Witness
☉	* *	☾
Fortuna Major.	* *	Populus.
* *	*	* *
* *	*	* *
*		* *
*		* *

Fortuna Major.

☉

1. Long happy life.
2. Abundance by things connected with water.
3. Fulfillment of wish.
4. As desired.
5. Girl.
6. Many and good servants.
7. Dies.
8. There is nothing to prevent him.
9. Another person has the advantage.
10. Loses.
11. Fortunate on the water or with things connected with it.
12. Beware of danger by water.
13. The messenger will arrive soon.
14. Fortunate voyage by water.
15. Average.
16. Go out of the way.

Left Witness	Judge	Right Witness
☾	* *	☉
Via.	* *	Fortuna Minor.
*	*	*
*	*	*
*		* *
*		* *

Fortuna Major.

☉

1. Average life.
2. Poverty.
3. Partly.
4. The end is better than the beginning.
5. Daughter.
6. Very vain.
7. Recovers.
8. She will be his.
9. Inheritance.
10. Favorable.
11. Some danger is connected with it.
12. Fever.
13. They are coming.
14. Fortunate.
15. Good news.
16. You will be victorious.

Left Witness	Judge	Right Witness
☉	* *	☾
Fortuna Minor.	* *	Via.
*	*	*
*	*	*
* *		*
* *		*

Fortuna Major.

☉

1. Short life, full of disappointments.
2. Very little fortune.
3. Disappointment.
4. Only tolerable.
5. Girl.
6. Faithful.
7. Recovers.
8. It is very doubtful.
9. No.
10. The adversary succeeds.
11. Disfavor.
12. Dropsy.
13. Soon.
14. Tolerable.
15. Tolerably good news.
16. The enemy is stronger than you.

Left Witness	Judge	Right Witness
☿	* *	♃
Conjunctio.	* *	Acquisitio.
* *	*	* *
*	*	*
*		* *
* *		*

Fortuna Major.

☉

1. Long life.
2. Sufficient money.
3. Success.
4. The end is good.
5. Son.
6. You may hire the servant.
7. He will die at last in spite of all hope.
8. The marriage will take place.
9. Unexpected inheritance.
10. You will gain by settling the matter.
11. Fortunate with lawyers.
12. Painless and peaceful.
13. The messenger is on the way.
14. Very good ending.
15. As desired.
16. Your enemy offers a settlement.

Left Witness	Judge	Right Witness
♃	* *	☿
Acquisitio.	* *	Conjunctio.
* *	*	* *
*	*	*
* *		*
*		* *

Fortuna Major.

☉

1. Long life.
2. Average fortune.
3. Yes.
4. Average success.
5. Son.
6. Honest and useful.
7. Dies.
8. He will get what he wants.
9. The profit will not be very great.
10. Settlement with loss.
11. Some success in mercantile positions.
12. Natural.
13. Soon.
14. Tolerable.
15. Tolerably good.
16. Seek a settlement.

Left Witness	Judge	Right Witness
♀	* *	♃
Puella.	* *	Latitia.
*	*	*
* *	*	* *
*		* *
*		* *

Fortuna Major.

☉

1. Long and healthy.
2. Abundance.
3. Success.
4. As desired.
5. Son.
6. Good.
7. He will leave his couch.
8. She loves him very affectionately.
9. Inheritance and fortune.
10. A good end.
11. Fortunate with the clergy.
12. Dies in his bed.
13. The letters are detained.
14. Quick and successful.
15. Only good news.
16. The enemy is timorous and unjust.

Left Witness	Judge	Right Witness
♃ Latitia. * * * * * * *	* * * * * *	♀ Puella. * * * * *

Fortuna Major.

☉

1. Fortunate and healthy.
2. Riches acquired by marriage.
3. It is a love affair, it will succeed.
4. Pleasant.
5. Son.
6. Gay, but honest.
7. Will regain his health.
8. He will get his wish.
9. Fortunate.
10. The adversary gains.
11. Fortune through ladies.
12. Peacefully.
13. The messenger will arrive soon.
14. A gay and pleasant voyage.
15. They concern love matters.
16. The enemy is wise, just, and powerful.

Left Witness	Judge	Right Witness
☊	* *	♂
Caput Draconis.	* *	Rubeus.
* *	*	* *
*	*	*
*		* *
*		* *

Fortuna Major.

☉

1. Short life, full of trouble.
2. Poverty in his youth, rich in old age.
3. The calculation was made without consulting the host.
4. The end will be the ruin of the whole thing.
5. Daughter.
6. Thievish.
7. Death will release him.
8. You are in danger of death on account of your sweetheart.
9. You may inherit a lawsuit.
10. The judge favors your adversary.
11. ♂ is against you.
12. Danger of forcible death.
13. Soon.
14. Dangerous.
15. The news is useless.
16. Your enemy seeks to destroy you.

Left Witness	Judge	Right Witness
♂ Rubeus.		☋ Caput Draconis.
* * * * * * *	* * * * * *	* * * * *

Fortuna Major.

☉

1. Short and sickly life.
2. What has been gained in youth will be lost in old age.
3. Some success.
4. Good.
5. Daughter.
6. Intelligent but dishonest.
7. Recovery.
8. Enjoyment.
9. Several legacies.
10. Favorable judgment.
11. Fortunate among ladies.
12. Natural death.
13. Slowly.
14. Fortunate.
15. Good.
16. You will get the best of your enemy.

Left Witness	Judge	Right Witness
☋	* *	♂
Cauda Draconis.	* *	Puer.
*	*	*
*	*	*
*		* *
* *		*

Fortuna Major.

☉

1. Nothing but misfortune. A short life.
2. What he has will be taken from him by force.
3. Castles in the air.
4. The beginning bad; the end somewhat better.
5. Son.
6. Dishonest, useless.
7. He is on his dying bed.
8. There is many a slip between the cup and the lip.
9. It will not be worth the while to possess it.
10. The adversary loses.
11. There is nothing to be found.
12. Force, executioner, murder, or suicide.
13. You are waiting in vain.
14. You will do well to remain at home.
15. Severe disappointment.
16. You are superior to your enemy.

Left Witness	Judge	Right Witness
♂	* *	☋
Puer.	* *	Cauda Draconis.
*	*	*
*	*	*
* *		*
*		* *

Fortuna Major.

☉

1. Short and painful life.
2. Poverty and misery.
3. It will be a miscarriage.
4. Useless.
5. Son.
6. Lazy, idle, dishonest, thievish.
7. Let him make his preparations for death.
8. It will be useless to think of marriage.
9. The lawyers will divide it among themselves.
10. The lawsuit will be lost.
11. Unfortunate everywhere except in the war.
12. Death by water, drowning, or dropsy, etc.
13. No letters will come.
14. A great deal of misfortune.
15. Nothing agreeable.
16. The enemy is too powerful for you.

Left Witness	Judge	Right Witness
☿	* *	♄
Amissio.	* *	Carcer.
*	*	*
* *	*	* *
*		* *
* *		*

Fortuna Major.

☉

1. Short life, but a strong constitution.
2. Riches by agriculture or mining.
3. It will slowly succeed.
4. Tolerable.
5. Girl.
6. Average.
7. Dies.
8. There will be a wedding.
9. It amounts to very little.
10. The prospect is bad.
11. Go to the country.
12. Natural death.
13. The mail will not arrive.
14. Tolerable.
15. Neither good nor bad.
16. The advantage is on your side.

Left Witness	Judge	Right Witness
♄	* *	☿
Carcer.	* *	Amissio.
*	*	*
* *	*	* *
* *		*
*		* *

Fortuna Major.

☉

1. Long but sickly life.
2. Inconstant fortune.
3. Useless thoughts about love.
4. Good ending.
5. Daughter.
6. Idle and dishonest.
7. Recovery.
8. The engagement will be broken up.
9. Vain hopes.
10. Neither one of the opponents will gain.
11. Cease to think of it.
12. In bed.
13. They will arrive at last.
14. It will be slow.
15. Trifles.
16. Doubtful ending.

Left Witness	Judge	Right Witness
☿	* *	♄
Albus.	* *	Tristitia.
* *	*	* *
* *	*	* *
*		* *
* *		*

Fortuna Major.

☉

1. Long, melancholy life.
2. Great fortune by agriculture or mining.
3. Success, but slow.
4. Tolerably well.
5. Daughter.
6. Idle, but honest.
7. Dies.
8. Successful in the end.
9. Tolerably lucky.
10. He loses on account of his own neglect.
11. The country is more suitable for you than the city.
12. A natural death.
13. Slowly.
14. Good on the average.
15. Not worth much.
16. The enemy keeps the upper hand.

Left Witness	Judge	Right Witness
♄	* *	☿
Tristitia.	* *	Albus.
* *	*	* *
* *	*	* *
* *		*
*		* *

Fortuna Major.

☉

1. Long and healthy life.
2. Riches through writing.
3. Success.
4. The desired end.
5. Daughter.
6. Honest.
7. Will get well.
8. The marriage bells will ring.
9. Good luck.
10. Gains.
11. Fortunate in the legislation.
12. Natural death.
13. Good letters that will come quickly.
14. Fortunate and rapid.
15. Contents are good.
16. Victory.

FORTUNA MINOR AS JUDGE

Left Witness	Judge	Right Witness
☾	*	☉
Populus.	*	Fortuna Minor.
* *	* *	*
* *	* *	*
* *		* *
* *		* *

Fortuna Minor.

☉

1. Average duration. Changeable.
2. Considerable riches.
3. It will succeed.
4. The end is good.
5. Son.
6. Not the very best.
7. Dies.
8. The wedding will take place.
9. A good legacy will be obtained.
10. Gains.
11. Changeable.
12. Natural death.
13. No.
14. Fortunate and rapid.
15. Good news.
16. Beware of too many enemies.

Left Witness	Judge	Right Witness
☉	✳	☾
Fortuna Minor.		Populus.

Fortuna Minor.

☉

1. Long life, considerably fortunate.
2. Some means by trading on the ocean.
3. It has no power to live.
4. Average.
5. Daughter.
6. They will do well enough.
7. Dies.
8. He will be disappointed.
9. Doubtful.
10. Loses.
11. Your fortune is on the water.
12. Painless.
13. The letters will come.
14. Quick and fortunate.
15. Tolerable.
16. The enemy will do no damage.

Left Witness	Judge	Right Witness
♄	*	♃
Carcer.	*	Acquisitio.
*	* *	* *
* *	* *	*
* *		* *
*		*

Fortuna Minor.

☉

1. Long life and health.
2. Rich by practising law.
3. It will take place.
4. A good ending.
5. Daughter.
6. They are good.
7. The tomb is waiting for him.
8. Marriage.
9. There is cause for hope.
10. Gains.
11. Fortunate with lawyers.
12. A natural death.
13. They will not arrive.
14. Fortunate.
15. Doubtful.
16. The enemy is harmless.

Left Witness	Judge	Right Witness
♃		♄
Acquisitio.		Carcer.
*　*	*	*
*	*	*　*
*　*	*　*	*　*
*	*　*	*

Fortuna Minor.

☉

1. Long and healthy life.
2. Rich by works belonging to ♄.
3. No.
4. Average.
5. Son.
6. Honest and industrious.
7. Dies.
8. It is useless to attempt it.
9. Vain hopes.
10. Loses by not coming to time.
11. Ill luck.
12. In bed.
13. No letters.
14. It will be slow.
15. Good on the average.
16. Stay away.

Left Witness	Judge	Right Witness
♂	*	♃
Rubeus.	*	Laetitia.
* *	* *	*
*	* *	* *
* *		* *
* *		* *

Fortuna Minor.

☉

1. Long and healthy.
2. Rich from rents.
3. It will take place.
4. The end is good.
5. Son.
6. Good.
7. Recovery.
8. You will be left in the cold.
9. A good legacy.
10. Gains.
11. Fortunate among the clergy.
12. Dies a natural death.
13. Soon.
14. Fortunate.
15. Good news.
16. Your enemy will give way.

Left Witness	Judge	Right Witness
♃	*	♂
Laetitia.	*	Rubeus.
*	* *	* *
* *	* *	*
* *		* *
* *		* *

Fortuna Minor.

☉

1. Short, unhealthy life.
2. Loss of property.
3. It will go the wrong way.
4. Unfortunate.
5. Son.
6. Thievish.
7. Dies.
8. Marriage.
9. Worthless.
10. Loss.
11. Fortunate in the army.
12. Forcible death.
13. The letters will be stolen.
14. Unfortunate.
15. Disagreeable.
16. The enemy will come out first best.

Left Witness	Judge	Right Witness
♂ Puer.		♄ Tristitia.

Fortuna Minor.

☉

1. Long and very fortunate life.
2. A little, obtained with great labor.
3. Extremely doubtful.
4. Doubtful.
5. Daughter.
6. They are lazy.
7. He must die.
8. There will be no marriage, because he will be too careless.
9. A good legacy.
10. Will win at last.
11. Expect nothing.
12. Natural death.
13. No.
14. Delay.
15. Mournful news.
16. The enemy must succumb.

Left Witness	Judge	Right Witness
♄	*	♂
Tristitia.	*	Puer.
* *	* *	*
* *	* *	*
* *		* *
*		*

Fortuna Minor.

☉

1. Short and painful.
2. He will have nothing whatever.
3. His attempts are useless.
4. The end is of no use.
5. Son.
6. Dishonest.
7. Dies.
8. He will marry the woman.
9. Not worth the while to take it.
10. Loses.
11. The stars are against it.
12. He will be killed in battle.
13. Soon.
14. Dangerous voyage.
15. Bad news.
16. The enemy has the advantage.

Left Witness	Judge	Right Witness
♀	*	☊
Puella.	*	Caput Draconis.
*	* *	* *
* *	* *	*
*		*
*		*

Fortuna Minor.

☉

1. Pleasant life but not very long.
2. Good circumstances.
3. Some is true and some of it false.
4. Slow.
5. Daughter.
6. They are good.
7. He will die.
8. He will have no success.
9. Obtains the legacy.
10. It will be settled.
11. Fortune smiles upon you.
12. Natural death.
13. Slowly.
14. Slow but fortunate voyage.
15. Good news.
16. The whole animosity is merely pastime.

Left Witness	Judge	Right Witness
☊	*	♀
Caput Draconis.	*	Puella.
* *	* *	*
*	* *	* *
*		*
*		*

Fortuna Minor.

☉

1. Average duration of life. Good circumstances.
2. A fortune through marriage.
3. Fulfilment of wish.
4. A good end.
5. Son.
6. Faithful.
7. Will recover his health.
8. The beloved one will be obtained.
9. Inheritance from ladies.
10. Gains.
11. There is some hope.
12. A natural death.
13. The letters will arrive.
14. Gay and happy voyage.
15. Agreeable news.
16. A settlement is advisable.

Left Witness	Judge	Right Witness
☿	*	☋
Albus.	*	Cauda Draconis.
* *	* *	*
* *	* *	*
*		*
* *		* *

Fortuna Minor.

☉

1. Short but healthy life.
2. Poverty and misery.
3. Wrongly calculated.
4. Worthless.
5. Boy.
6. They are useless.
7. Dies.
8. All his efforts are in vain.
9. He will get nothing.
10. Is already lost.
11. Ill-luck.
12. Will be killed.
13. Nothing comes.
14. Unfortunate voyage.
15. Without any value whatever.
16. The enemy is too smart for you.

Left Witness	Judge	Right Witness
☋	*	☿
Cauda Draconis.	*	Albus.
*	* *	* *
*	* *	* *
*		*
* *		* *

Fortuna Minor.

☉

1. Long but unhealthy life.
2. Rich by trade.
3. Success.
4. Good ending.
5. Daughter.
6. Dies.
7. Good.
8. Never in this case.
9. A good legacy.
10. Gains.
11. Some advantage is waiting for you.
12. A natural death.
13. Very soon.
14. Fortunate.
15. Good news.
16. You will be the master.

Left Witness	Judge	Right Witness
☿		♀
Conjunctio.		Amissio.
* *	*	*
*	*	* *
*	* *	*
* *	* *	* *

Fortuna Minor.

☉

1. Short and feeble life.
2. Poverty.
3. All in vain.
4. Worthless.
5. Son.
6. They are worthless.
7. Recovery.
8. The marriage will be celebrated.
9. It is of no value.
10. Loss.
11. Bad luck.
12. A natural death.
13. The messenger does not arrive.
14. Unfortunate.
15. Worthless news.
16. A strong enemy.

Left Witness	Judge	Right Witness
♀	*	☿
Amissio.	*	Conjunctio.
*	* *	* *
* *	* *	*
*		*
* *		* *

Fortuna Minor.

☉

1. Average life. Unhealthy.
2. Average means.
3. Some success.
4. Average.
5. Twins.
6. They are of the average blood.
7. Dies.
8. The wedding will take place.
9. It is not very considerable.
10. It will be settled.
11. Fortunate in trading.
12. A natural death.
13. Soon.
14. Good on the average.
15. Neither good nor bad.
16. No harm will be done.

Left Witness	Judge	Right Witness
☾	*	☉
Via.	*	Fortuna Major.
*	* *	* *
*	* *	* *
*		*
*		*

Fortuna Minor.

☉

1. Long and healthy life.
2. Riches.
3. Fulfilment.
4. A good end.
5. Daughter.
6. Faithful.
7. Recovery.
8. Success.
9. Fortunate.
10. Gains.
11. Very fortunate this time.
12. Natural.
13. Slow.
14. Fortunate.
15. Good news.
16. You will conquer.

Left Witness	Judge	Right Witness
☉	*	☾
Fortuna Major.	*	Via.
* *	* *	*
* *	* *	*
*		*
*		*

Fortuna Minor.

☉

1. Short life, but very fortunate.
2. Some fortune.
3. Will be abandoned.
4. Doubtful.
5. Daughter.
6. Average.
7. Must die.
8. He will not get her.
9. It is worthless.
10. Lost.
11. Unfortunate.
12. A natural death.
13. Soon.
14. Quick and happy.
15. Of the average kind.
16. Avoid him.

POPULUS AS JUDGE

Left Witness	Judge	Right Witness
♃	* *	♃
Acquisitio.	* *	Acquisitio.
* *	* *	* *
*	* *	*
* *		* *
*		*

Populus.

☾

1. Long and happy.
2. Abundance.
3. You will give up the idea.
4. Average success.
5. Girl.
6. Faithful.
7. Dies.
8. His wish will be granted.
9. A good inheritance.
10. Doubtful.
11. Fortunate.
12. Natural.
13. Delay.
14. Slow but fortunate.
15. Good.
16. You will do him no harm.

Left Witness	Judge	Right Witness
☾	* *	☾
Populus.	* *	Populus.
* *	* *	* *
* *	* *	* *
* *		* *
* *		* *

Populus.

☾

1. Long life.
2. Abundant means.
3. Your dreams will come to nought.
4. The end is doubtful.
5. Daughter.
6. Honest.
7. Dies.
8. A wedding.
9. You will be disappointed.
10. Things look very bad for you.
11. You will be fooled.
12. Natural.
13. Soon.
14. Fortunate and healthy.
15. They are of the average kind.
16. Both adversaries have equal chances.

Left Witness	Judge	Right Witness
♃	* *	♃
Laetitia.	* *	Laetitia.
*	* *	*
* *	* *	* *
* *		* *
* *		* *

Populus.

☾

1. Long and healthy life.
2. Riches.
3. The idea is very good.
4. A good end.
5. Son.
6. They are good.
7. Recovery.
8. She will be his.
9. A fortune by inheritance.
10. Settlement.
11. Luck.
12. Painless and peaceful.
13. Soon.
14. Fortunate.
15. Good.
16. Settlement.

Left Witness	Judge	Right Witness
♀	* *	♀
Amissio.	* *	Amissio.
*	* *	*
* *	* *	* *
*		*
* *		* *

Populus.

☾

1. Very feeble health.
2. Poverty and misery.
3. The plans will be destroyed.
4. Worthless.
5. Girl.
6. They are useless.
7. Dies.
8. No prospect whatever.
9. Vain hope.
10. Lost.
11. He will obtain nothing.
12. Will be killed.
13. Soon.
14. Unfortunate.
15. Bad news.
16. Loss on both sides.

Left Witness	Judge	Right Witness
☋	* *	☋
Caput Draconis.	* *	Caput Draconis.
* *	* *	* *
*	* *	*
*		*
*		*

Populus.

☾

1. Average healthy life.
2. Rich by service.
3. It will work, but slowly.
4. Good.
5. Girl.
6. Good.
7. Recovers.
8. He will get her in spite of everything.
9. A good inheritance.
10. Settlement.
11. Lucky.
12. Natural.
13. They are coming.
14. Unfortunate.
15. Good news.
16. Neither one harms the other.

Left Witness	Judge	Right Witness
♄	* *	♄
Tristitia.	* *	Tristitia.
* *	* *	* *
* *	* *	* *
* *		* *
*		*

Populus.

☾

1. Long and troubled.
2. A little by hard work.
3. Missed.
4. Painful.
5. Girl.
6. Useless.
7. Dies.
8. He will not get her.
9. Worthless.
10. Lost.
11. Nothing to be expected.
12. Natural.
13. No.
14. Slow voyager.
15. Useless.
16. A tricky enemy.

Left Witness	Judge	Right Witness
♀	* *	♀
Puella.	* *	Puella.
*	* *	*
* *	* *	* *
*		*
*		*

Populus.

☾

1. Long and happy.
2. Rich.
3. Fulfilment.
4. Good.
5. Son.
6. Good.
7. Recovery.
8. He will get her.
9. Yes.
10. Settlement.
11. Unlucky.
12. Natural.
13. They will arrive.
14. Gay voyage.
15. Joyful news.
16. He will do you no harm.

Left Witness	Judge	Right Witness
☋	* *	☋
Cauda Draconis.	* *	Cauda Draconis.
*	* *	*
*	* *	*
*		*
* *		* *

Populus.

☾

1. Weak and feeble.
2. Poverty, misfortune.
3. Useless.
4. Unfortunate.
5. Son.
6. Dishonest.
7. Dies.
8. Great disappointment.
9. He will get nothing.
10. Lost.
11. Ill-luck.
12. Will be killed.
13. No.
14. Unfortunate.
15. Worthless.
16. The enemies are a worthless set.

Left Witness	Judge	Right Witness
☿	* *	☿
Albus.	* *	Albus.
* *	* *	* *
* *	* *	* *
*		*
* *		* *

Populus.

☽

1. Long and happy.
2. Riches by service.
3. It will take place.
4. Good.
5. Daughter.
6. Good.
7. Dies.
8. He will succeed.
9. A good inheritance.
10. Settlement.
11. His pen will recommend him.
12. Natural.
13. Soon.
14. Happy.
15. Good.
16. Harmless.

Left Witness	Judge	Right Witness
♂	* *	♂
Puer.	* *	Puer.
*	* * *	*
*	* *	*
* *		* *
*		*

Populus.

☾

1. Wealth and feeble.
2. Poverty in consequence of theft.
3. Non-success.
4. Useless.
5. Son.
6. Worthless.
7. Dies.
8. He will be refused.
9. Gets nothing.
10. The judge is partial.
11. Fortune in war.
12. Forcible.
13. No letters.
14. Quick.
15. Useless
16. The enemy is dangerous.

Left Witness	Judge	Right Witness
☉	* *	☉
Fortuna Major.	* *	Fortuna Major.
* *	* *	* *
* *	* *	* *
*		*
*		*

Populus.

☾

1. Fortunate and long.
2. Abundance.
3. It will go on.
4. Fortunate.
5. Girl.
6. Good.
7. Recovery.
8. He will surely get her.
9. A rich legacy.
10. It is already gained.
11. Fortunate among potentates.
12. Natural.
13. Slowly.
14. Unfortunate.
15. Good.
16. The enemy will give way.

Left Witness	Judge	Right Witness
♂ Rubeus.	* *	♂ Rubeus.
* *	* *	* *
*	* *	*
* *		* *
* *		* *

Populus.

☾

1. Short and unhealthy.
2. Loss by theft.
3. A wrong beginning.
4. A bad end.
5. Son.
6. Dishonest.
7. Dies.
8. He will be dismissed.
9. Nothing but lawsuits.
10. The judge is against you.
11. No.
12. Dies in war.
13. No letters.
14. Unfortunate.
15. Worthless.
16. A bloodthirsty enemy.

Left Witness	Judge	Right Witness
☉	* *	☉
Fortuna Minor.	* *	Fortuna Minor.
*	* *	*
*	* *	*
* *		* *
* *		* *

Populus.

☾

1. Average. Changeable.
2. Satisfactorily.
3. Incorrect.
4. Good.
5. Son.
6. Good.
7. He will gain strength.
8. He will be very fortunate.
9. Gained by a great deal of dispute.
10. A bad prospect.
11. Instability.
12. Natural.
13. Soon.
14. Quick and fortunate.
15. Not very good.
16. You will do him no harm.

Left Witness	Judge	Right Witness
☾	* *	☾
Via.	* *	Via.
*	* *	*
*	* *	*
*		*
*		*

Populus.

☾

1. Long and happy.
2. Fortunate in the silver trade.
3. Worthless plans.
4. Tolerable.
5. Daughter.
6. Tolerable.
7. Dies.
8. He is going to marry her.
9. An average legacy.
10. Tolerable success.
11. No.
12. Dies in the water.
13. Soon.
14. Quick and happy.
15. Average.
16. You will get the best of him.

Left Witness	Judge	Right Witness
☿	* *	☿
Conjunctio.	* *	Conjunctio.
* *	* *	* *
*	* *	*
*		*
* *		* *

Populus.

☾

1. Average length.
2. Tolerable.
3. Will turn out truly.
4. Good.
5. Son.
6. Good.
7. Dies.
8. He will obtain her.
9. Settlement with the opponent.
10. Settlement.
11. Fortunate in the mercantile business.
12. Natural.
13. The letters will arrive.
14. Tolerable.
15. Tolerably good.
16. Settlement.

Left Witness	Judge	Right Witness
♄	* *	♄
Carcer.	* *	Carcer.
*	* *	*
* *	* *	* *
* *		* *
*		*

Populus.

☾

1. Long and full of trouble.
2. Riches by agriculture.
3. You will give up the idea.
4. Tolerable.
5. Daughter.
6. They work hard but stupidly.
7. Dies.
8. No prospects.
9. An average inheritance.
10. Unfortunate look-out.
11. No luck.
12. Natural.
13. Slowly.
14. Fortunate.
15. Tolerably good.
16. The enemy will not harm you.

VIA AS JUDGE

Left Witness	Judge	Right Witness
☾	*	☾
Via.	*	Populus.
*	*	* *
*	*	* *
*		* *
*		* *

Via.

☾

1. Long life.
2. Sufficient means.
3. In vain.
4. Tolerable.
5. Daughter.
6. Average.
7. Dies.
8. He is going to obtain her.
9. Without any value.
10. Gained.
11. Changeable luck.
12. In bed.
13. Soon.
14. Quick and fortunate.
15. Tolerably good.
16. You are master.

Left Witness	Judge	Right Witness
☾	*	☾
Populus.	*	Via.
* *	*	*
* *	*	*
* *		*
* *		*

Via.

☾

1. Short life.
2. Mediocrity.
3. Vain hope.
4. Unfortunate.
5. Girl.
6. Useless.
7. Dies.
8. Yes.
9. Amounts to nothing.
10. Missed the time.
11. Everything is against you.
12. Natural.
13. Soon.
14. Fortunate on land.
15. Trifles.
16. The enemy appears to be master.

Left Witness	Judge	Right Witness
♃	*	♀
Acquisitio.	*	Amissio.
* *	*	*
*	*	* *
* *		*
*		* *

Via.

☾

1. Short but healthy.
2. Inconstant.
3. Useless to try it.
4. Deplorable end.
5. Son.
6. Faithful.
7. Recovery.
8. All attempts are in vain.
9. Will do more harm than good.
10. Lost.
11. It is worthless.
12. Natural death.
13. Soon.
14. Quick and fortunate.
15. Disagreeable.
16. The enemy remains on the top.

Left Witness	Judge	Right Witness
♀	*	♃
Amissio.	*	Acquisitio.
*	*	* *
* *	*	*
*		* *
* *		*

Via.

☾

1. Long but not strong.
2. Tolerably good.
3. Good success.
4. Average.
5. Son.
6. Good.
7. He will regain his health.
8. Of course.
9. A good legacy.
10. Gained.
11. Success among lawyers.
12. Peaceful.
13. Slowly.
14. Delay, but fortunate.
15. As desired.
16. The enemy will run away.

Left Witness	Judge	Right Witness
♃	*	☊
Laetitia.	*	Caput Draconis.
*	*	* *
* *	*	*
* *		*
* *		*

Via.

☾

1. Average and healthy.
2. Sufficient.
3. A mistake.
4. Good.
5. Daughter.
6. Faithful.
7. Recovery.
8. He will.
9. It will come to him.
10. Settlement.
11. It is not a very good one.
12. In bed.
13. Slowly.
14. He will not regret it.
15. Pleasant.
16. The enemy becomes a friend.

Left Witness	Judge	Right Witness
☊	*	♃
Caput Draconis.	*	Laetitia.
* *	*	*
*	*	* *
*		* *
*		* *

Via.

☾

1. Long and joyful.
2. Abundance.
3. Success.
4. Excellent.
5. Son.
6. Good.
7. Recovery.
8. He will obtain his heart's desire.
9. A good legacy.
10. He will be fortunate.
11. Fortunate with the clergy.
12. Natural.
13. They are coming.
14. Fortunate.
15. Pleasant.
16. You will gain the upper hand.

Left Witness	Judge	Right Witness
♄	*	☋
Tristitia.	*	Cauda Draconis.
* *	*	*
* *	*	*
* *		*
*		* *

Via.

☾

1. Short and painful.
2. Very little.
3. Non-success.
4. Misfortune.
5. Girl.
6. Treacherous and lazy.
7. Dies.
8. His sweetheart cheats him.
9. The inheritance is dangerous.
10. Loses the lawsuit.
11. No luck.
12. Forcible.
13. Soon.
14. Not very good.
15. Bad news.
16. A strong enemy.

Left Witness	Judge	Right Witness
☋	*	♄
Cauda Draconis.	*	Tristitia.
*	*	* *
*	*	* *
*		* *
* *		*

Via.

☾

1. Miserable, but long.
2. A little by hard work.
3. Carrying water in a sieve.
4. A bad end.
5. Girl.
6. Idle.
7. Dies.
8. She will refuse his offer.
9. There is little to be inherited.
10. Gains.
11. More luck on the land than on water.
12. Natural.
13. No.
14. Delay.
15. Mournful news.
16. The enemy loses.

Left Witness	Judge	Right Witness
♀	*	♂
Puella.	*	Rubeus.
*	*	* *
* *	*	*
*		* *
*		* *

Via.

☾

1. Short.
2. Bad.
3. Disappointment.
4. Entirely worthless.
5. Son.
6. Dishonest.
7. He will give up the ghost.
8. You may go ahead.
9. The inheritance escapes.
10. Loses.
11. High places are unhealthy for you.
12. Fever.
13. No letters.
14. Dangerous.
15. Bad.
16. The enemy has the advantage.

Left Witness	Judge	Right Witness
♂	*	♀
Rubeus.	*	Puella.
* *	*	*
*	*	* *
* *		*
* *		*

Via.

☾

1. Average.
2. Tolerable.
3. Good.
4. Very well.
5. Son.
6. Good.
7. Recovers.
8. You will soon rejoice.
9. Yes.
10. Gains.
11. Luck.
12. Natural.
13. Soon.
14. Happy.
15. Good.
16. You are superior to him.

Left Witness	Judge	Right Witness
♂	*	☿
Puer.	*	Albus.
*	*	* *
*	*	* *
* *		*
*		* *

Via.

☾

1. Long but feeble.
2. Tolerable.
3. Failure.
4. Pleasant.
5. Girl.
6. Good.
7. Dies.
8. The marriage will take place.
9. Yes.
10. Gains.
11. A good prospect.
12. Natural.
13. Certainly.
14. Fortunate.
15. Good.
16. You will make him squirm.

Left Witness	Judge	Right Witness
☿	*	♂
Albus.	*	Puer.
* *	*	*
* *	* *	* *
*	*	* *
* *		*

Via.

☾

1. Short.
2. Bad.
3. Failure.
4. Indifferent.
5. Boy.
6. Dishonest.
7. Dies.
8. Marriage.

9. Bad.
10. Lost.
11. Difficult.
12. Forcible.
13. None.
14. Worthless.
15. Bad.
16. He will conquer you.

Left Witness	Judge	Right Witness
☿	*	♄
Conjunctio.	*	Carcer.
* *	*	*
*	*	* *
*		* *
* *		*

Via.

☾

1. Long.
2. Bad.
3. Failure.
4. Useless.
5. Girl.
6. Idle.
7. Dies.
8. A wedding.
9. Yes.
10. Settlement.
11. No.
12. Natural.
13. Yes.
14. Tolerable.
15. Bad.
16. The enemy succeeds.

Left Witness	Judge	Right Witness
♄	*	☿
Carcer.	*	Conjunctio.
*	*	* *
* *	*	*
* *		*
*		* *

Via.

☽

1. Average.
2. Tolerable.
3. It will be accomplished.
4. Indifferent.
5. Girl.
6. Average.
7. He is going to travel.
8. He will be very lucky.
9. It comes in good time.
10. It will be decided in your favor.
11. A tolerably good prospect.
12. Natural.
13. Yes.
14. Tolerably good.
15. Indifferent.
16. The enemy is a loser.

Left Witness	Judge	Right Witness
☉	*	☉
Fortuna Major.	*	Fortuna Minor.
* *	*	*
* *	*	*
*		* *
*		* *

Via.

☾

1. Good and long.
2. More than enough.
3. Will disappear.
4. Good.
5. Son.
6. Tolerable.
7. Recovery.
8. She cannot escape him.
9. Good.
10. Lost.
11. Inconstant luck.
12. Natural.
13. They will come.
14. Fortunate.
15. Tolerably good.
16. Victory for the enemy.

Left Witness	Judge	Right Witness
☉	*	☉
Fortuna Minor.	*	Fortuna Major.
*	*	* *
*	*	* *
* *		*
* *		*

Via.

☾

1. Long but unfortunate.
2. Sufficient.
3. Good.
4. Good.
5. Daughter.
6. Honest.
7. Recovers.
8. Success.
9. A good legacy.
10. Gains.
11. Luck.
12. Natural.
13. Slowly.
14. Delay.
15. Gladness.
16. Victory.

CONJUNCTIO AS JUDGE

Left Witness	Judge	Right Witness
☿	* *	☾
Conjunctio.	*	Populus.
* *	*	* *
*	* *	* *
*		* *
* *		* *

Conjunctio.

☿

1. Long life, indifferent health.
2. Tolerable.
3. False.
4. Indifferent.
5. Daughter.
6. Average.
7. Dies.
8. He will get her.
9. Not much to be had.
10. Loses.
11. No luck.
12. Natural.
13. Soon.
14. Quick.
15. False reports.
16. The adversary desires the peace.

Left Witness	Judge	Right Witness
☽	* *	☿
Populus.	*	Conjunctio.
* *	*	* *
* *	* *	*
* *		*
* *		* *

Conjunctio.

☿

1. Average health, short life.
2. A little by trade.
3. A mixed-up affair.
4. Indifferent.
5. Twins.
6. Average.
7. Dies.
8. Marriage.
9. A good legacy.
10. Settlement.
11. A bad position.
12. Natural.
13. Soon.
14. Good.
15. Indifferent.
16. You will want a settlement.

Left Witness	Judge	Right Witness
♃	* *	☉
Acquisitio.	*	Fortuna Major.
* *	*	* *
*	* *	* *
* *		*
*		*

Conjunctio.

☿

1. Long and healthy.
2. Abundance.
3. Success.
4. Glad.
5. Girl.
6. Good.
7. Dies.
8. There is no one to take her from him.
9. Rich.
10. Gains.
11. Luck.
12. Natural.
13. Soon.
14. Fortunate but long.
15. As desired.
16. The adversary will be conquered.

Left Witness	Judge	Right Witness
☉	* *	♃
Fortuna Major.	*	Acquisitio.
* *	*	* *
* *	* *	*
*		* *
*		*

Conjunctio.

☿

1. Healthy and fortunate.
2. Tolerable.
3. Success.
4. Indifferent.
5. Son.
6. Good enough.
7. Dies.
8. Marriage.
9. Certainly.
10. Gains.
11. Luck among lawyers.
12. Natural.
13. Slowly.
14. Slow.
15. Good news.
16. Enemy remains victorious.

Left Witness	Judge	Right Witness
♀	* *	☉
Amissio.	*	Fortuna Minor.
*	*	*
* *	* *	*
*		* *
* *		* *

Conjunctio.

☿

1. Feeble and short.
2. Little.
3. Deluded hope.
4. Tolerably good.
5. Son.
6. Not the best.
7. Recovers.
8. Obtains his wish.
9. A bad legacy.
10. Inconstant luck.
11. Success.
12. Natural.
13. Soon.
14. In vain.
15. Useless.
16. You will succeed.

Left Witness	Judge	Right Witness
☉	* *	♀
Fortuna Minor.	*	Amissio.
*	*	*
*	* *	* *
* *		*
* *		* *

Conjunctio.

☿

1. Feeble and weak.
2. Little constancy.
3. Disappointment.
4. Doubtful.
5. Son.
6. Useless.
7. Dies.
8. Marriage.
9. Cease to think of it.
10. Loses.
11. Nothing.
12. Fever.
13. Soon.
14. Bad.
15. Worthless.
16. No.

Left Witness	Judge	Right Witness
♃ Laetitia. * * * * * * *	* * * * * *	☋ Cauda Draconis. * * * * *

Conjunctio.

☿

1. Short but healthy.
2. Bad.
3. All in vain.
4. Useless.
5. Girl.
6. Treacherous.
7. Dies.
8. The engagement will be broken up.
9. The adversary gets it.
10. Lost.
11. Misfortune.
12. Forcible.
13. Soon.
14. Quick.
15. Good.
16. The enemy will be victorious.

Left Witness	Judge	Right Witness
☋		♃
Cauda Draconis.		Laetitia.

Conjunctio.

☿

1. Long and happy.
2. Enough.
3. Success.
4. Good.
5. Son.
6. Honest.
7. Recovery.
8. Success.
9. Success.
10. Gains.
11. A good prospect.
12. Natural.
13. They will come.
14. Fortunate.
15. Glad.
16. Enemy will have to leave the field.

Left Witness	Judge	Right Witness
☋	* *	♄
Caput Draconis.	*	Tristitia.
* *	*	* *
*	* *	* *
*		* *
*		*

Conjunctio.

☿

1. Long life.
2. Tolerable.
3. Failure.
4. Indifferent.
5. Daughter.
6. Unfaithful.
7. Dies.
8. Vain hope.
9. Bad prospect.
10. Loses.
11. The stars are against you.
12. Natural.
13. They are coming.
14. Disagreeable.
15. Worthless.
16. Your enemy will be your judge.

Left Witness	Judge	Right Witness
♄	* *	☊
Tristitia.	*	Caput Draconis.
* *	*	* *
* *	* *	*
* *		*
*		*

Conjunctio.

☿

1. Long life.
2. Good circumstances.
3. Fulfilment.
4. Good.
5. Daughter.
6. Faithful.
7. Dies.
8. Success.
9. Success.
10. Success.
11. The fate is in his favor.
12. Natural.
13. They will come.
14. Fortunate.
15. Good.
16. The enemy loses.

Left Witness	Judge	Right Witness
☉	* *	♃
Fortuna Major.	*	Acquisitio.
* *	*	* *
* *	* *	*
*		* *
*		*

Conjunctio.

☿

1. Long and happy.
2. Abundance.
3. It will be done.
4. Good.
5. Son.
6. Good.
7. Recovery.
8. Success.
9. Another will get the best.
10. The adversary gains.
11. The lawyers are in your favor.
12. Natural.
13. Slowly.
14. Delay.
15. Good news.
16. Your enemy will be master of the situation.

Left Witness	Judge	Right Witness
♃	* *	☉
Acquisitio.	*	Fortuna Major.
* *	*	* *
*	* *	* *
* *		*
*		*

Conjunctio.

☿

1. Fortunate.
2. Sufficient.
3. Success.
4. Fortunate.
5. Daughter.
6. Honest.
7. Dies.
8. They will become a pair.
9. A good legacy.
10. A good prospect.
11. Favorable.
12. In bed.
13. They will come at last.
14. Postponement.
15. Glad.
16. The adversary gets the worst.

Left Witness	Judge	Right Witness
♂	* *	☿
Rubeus.	*	Albus.
* *	*	* *
*	* *	* *
* *		*
* *		* *

Conjunctio.

☿

1. Long life.
2. Average riches.
3. Success.
4. Good.
5. Daughter.
6. Faithful.
7. Dies.
8. Marriage.
9. A good legacy.
10. Gains.
11. Favorable.
12. Natural.
13. Soon.
14. Dangerous.
15. Good.
16. The adversary loses.

Left Witness	Judge	Right Witness
☿	* *	♂
Albus.	*	Rubeus.
* *	*	* *
* *	* *	*
*		* *
* *		* *

Conjunctio.

☿

1. Short.
2. Bad.
3. Wrongly calculated.
4. Bad.
5. Son.
6. Useless.
7. Dies.
8. Disappointment.
9. The inheritance will injure you.
10. Loss.
11. It will be a hell for him.
12. Forcible.
13. None.
14. Slowly.
15. Vexatious.
16. The adversary loses.

Left Witness	Judge	Right Witness
☾	* *	♄
Via.	*	Carcer.
*	*	*
*	* *	* *
*		* *
*		*

Conjunctio.

☿

1. Short life.
2. A little by hard work.
3. From bad to worse.
4. Indifferent.
5. Daughter.
6. Idle.
7. Dies.
8. A wedding.
9. Tolerably good.
10. Gained at last.
11. Secret enemies.
12. Natural.
13. None whatever.
14. Delay.
15. Good.
16. Yes.

Left Witness	Judge	Right Witness
♄	* *	☾
Carcer.	*	Via.
*	*	*
* *	* *	*
* *		* *
*		*

Conjunctio.

☿

1. Short.
2. Bad.
3. Disappointment.
4. Indifferent.
5. Daughter.
6. Average.
7. Dies.
8. Marriage.
9. Nothing.
10. Lost.
11. Nothing to be expected.
12. Natural.
13. Certainly.
14. Quick.
15. Indifferent.
16. The enemy will gain nothing.

CARCER AS JUDGE

Left Witness	Judge	Right Witness
♄	*	☾
Carcer.	* *	Populus.
*	* *	* *
* *	*	* *
* *		* *
*		* *

Carcer.

♄

1. Long life.
2. Good.
3. It will be interfered with.
4. Average.
5. Daughter.
6. Average.
7. Dies.
8. Undoubtedly.
9. The adversary inherits.
10. Lost.
11. Indifferent luck.
12. Natural.
13. A message.
14. Quick.
15. Indifferent.
16. The enemy must leave the field.

Left Witness	Judge	Right Witness
☾	*	♄
Populus.	* *	Carcer.
* *	* *	*
* *	*	* *
* *		* *
* *		*

Carcer.

♄

1. Long.
2. Tolerably good fortune in the country.
3. Backward.
4. Tolerable.
5. Daughter.
6. Average.
7. Must go.
8. Cease to think of her.
9. Things look bad.
10. Too late.
11. Nothing to be obtained.
12. Natural.
13. Letters.
14. Delay.
15. Bad.
16. The enemy conquers.

Left Witness	Judge	Right Witness
♃ Acquisitio.		☉ Fortuna Minor.

Carcer.

♄

1. Short and happy.
2. Tolerable.
3. In vain.
4. Good.
5. Son.
6. Good.
7. Recovery.
8. Marriage.
9. The legacy is against you.
10. Lost.
11. Lucky, but inconstant fortune.
12. Natural.
13. Yes.
14. Soon.
15. Tolerable.
16. You lose.

Left Witness	Judge	Right Witness
☉	*	♃
Fortuna Minor.	* *	Acquisitio.
*	* *	* *
*	*	*
* *		* *
* *		*

Carcer.

♄

1. Long life.
2. Tolerable.
3. It will go ahead.
4. Good.
5. Son.
6. Faithful.
7. Dies.
8. Wedding.
9. A good legacy.
10. Gains.
11. Nothing.
12. Natural.
13. Soon.
14. Fortunate.
15. Good.
16. The enemy returns.

Left Witness	Judge	Right Witness
♀ Amissio. * * * * * *	* * * * * *	☉ Fortuna Major. * * * * * *

Carcer.

♄

1. Long life.
2. Great fortune and durable.
3. It will slowly go on.
4. Happy.
5. Daughter.
6. As good as can be desired.
7. Recovery.
8. He will take the bride.
9. A fat legacy.
10. Gains.
11. A good start.
12. Natural.
13. Letters.
14. Fortunate.
15. Good.
16. Enemy succumbs.

Left Witness	Judge	Right Witness
☉		♀
Fortuna Major.		Amissio.

Carcer.

♄

1. Short life.
2. Poverty and misery.
3. The idea is correct.
4. Bad.
4. Bad.
5. Son.
6. Useless.
7. Must go.
8. ♀ is against you.
9. Another one will rejoice over it.
10. Gains.
11. An unlucky star.
12. In bed.
13. They have been captured.
14. It will cause you a loss.
15. Contents are vile.
16. Your enemy will step upon you.

Left Witness	Judge	Right Witness
♃	*	♄
Laetitia.	* *	Tristitia.
*	* *	* *
* *	*	* *
* *		* *
* *		*

Carcer.

♄

1. Long life.
2. Bad.
3. Disappointment.
4. Bad.
5. Daughter.
6. Lazy.
7. Good-bye.
8. At a very late hour.
9. Success.
10. Decision against you.
11. Everything works against you.
12. Natural.
13. No.
14. Delay.
15. Bad.
16. Enemy comes out first best.

Left Witness	Judge	Right Witness
♄	*	♃
Tristitia.	* *	Laetitia.
* *	* *	*
* *	*	* *
* *		* *
*		* *

Carcer.

♄

1. Long and painful life.
2. Abundant means.
3. Success.
4. Good.
5. Son.
6. Faithful.
7. Recovery.
8. No prospect.
9. Prospect very favorable.
10. Gains.
11. Good luck.
12. Natural.
13. Soon.
14. Fortunate.
15. Glad.
16. Enemy must give way.

Left Witness	Judge	Right Witness
♀	*	☿
Puella.	* *	Albus.
*	* *	* *
* *	*	* *
*		*
*		* *

Carcer.

♄

1. Long life.
2. Good.
3. It is well thought out.
4. Good.
5. Daughter.
6. Good.
7. Dies.
8. The stars are against him.
9. It is not very big.
10. Gains.
11. We congratulate.
12. Natural.
13. Soon.
14. Fortunate.
15. Good.
16. The enemy will come out second best.

Left Witness	Judge	Right Witness
☿		♀
Albus.		Puella.
* *	* *	*
* *	* *	* *
*	*	*
* *		*

Carcer.

♄

1. Short but happy.
2. Tolerable.
3. Good.
4. Indifferent.
5. Son.
6. Faithful.
7. Health.
8. He will get what he loves.
9. There is a little of it.
10. Gains.
11. Good luck.
12. Natural.
13. Soon.
14. Fortunate.
15. Good.
16. The victory is doubtful.

Left Witness	Judge	Right Witness
♂	*	♂
Rubeus.	* *	Puer.
* *	* *	*
*	*	*
* *		* *
* *		*

Carcer.

♄

1. Short but unfortunate.
2. Poor but miserable.
3. Incorrect.
4. An arrest and imprisonment.
5. Son.
6. Dishonest.
7. Dies.
8. No success.
9. It is harmful.
10. Loses.
11. Obstacles.
12. Forcible.
13. No letters.
14. Unfortunate.
15. Useless.
16. The enemy will be victorious.

Left Witness	Judge	Right Witness
♂	*	♂
Puer.	* *	Rubeus.
*	* *	* *
*	*	*
* *		* *
*		* *

Carcer.

♄

1. Long life.
2. Loss of property.
3. Let it alone.
4. Misery.
5. Son.
6. Thievish.
7. Dies.
8. The marriage will be postponed forever.
9. Nothing but quarrels.
10. Gains, but will receive no advantage from it.
11. Avoid it.
12. Forcible.
13. None.
14. Dangerous.
15. Throw them into the fire.
16. Victory.

Left Witness	Judge	Right Witness
☊		☋
Caput Draconis.		Cauda Draconis.
* *	*	*
*	* *	*
*	* *	*
*	*	* *

Carcer.

♄

1. Short.
2. Poverty.
3. A false calculation.
4. Bad.
5. Son.
6. Greedy.
7. Dies.
8. No success.
9. Nothing to inherit for you.
10. Loses.
11. The position is dangerous.
12. In prison.
13. None.
14. Unfortunate.
15. Useless.
16. The enemy is too cunning.

Left Witness	Judge	Right Witness
☋	*	☊
Cauda Draconis.	* *	Caput Draconis.
*	* *	* *
*	*	*
*		*
* *		*

Carcer.

♄

1. Short and unhappy.
2. Average means.
3. Succeeds.
4. Good.
5. Daughter.
6. Good.
7. Dies.
8. No marriage.
9. He will get it.
10. Gains.
11. Luck.
12. Natural.
13. Slowly.
14. Slow.
15. Agreeable.
16. The adversary loses the game.

Left Witness	Judge	Right Witness
☿		☾
Conjunctio.		Via.

Carcer.

♄

1. Short and painful.
2. Poor.
3. Disappointment.
4. Indifferent.
5. Daughter.
6. Average.
7. Dies.
8. The engagement will be discontinued.
9. Bad prospects.
10. Loses.
11. No luck.
12. Natural.
13. A message.
14. Quick.
15. Tolerable.
16. The enemy desires peace.

Left Witness	Judge	Right Witness
☾	*	☿
Via.	* *	Conjunctio.
*	* *	* *
*	*	*
*		*
*		* *

Carcer.

♄

1. Average.
2. Tolerable.
3. Bad prospects.
4. Bad.
5. Twins.
6. Average.
7. Dies.
8. He will get her.
9. Pays for the mourning.
10. Decided to your advantage.
11. Everything looks bad.
12. Natural.
13. The messenger is near.
14. Profitable.
15. Good.
16. Victory.

CHAPTER 9
AS ON THE EARTH BELOW, SO IN THE SKY ABOVE

When skill has been achieved in the manipulation of ordinary geomantic divination, it will become increasingly obvious that the Judge and Witness figures are really not much more than artificially derived summaries of the twelve primary figures—the Mothers, Daughters and Nephews. Consequently, the use of the Judge/Witness tables are a shade too mechanical and sometimes misleading because of their oversimplified answers.

At this stage, you might have guessed that a more flexible approach requiring a little more interpretive skill as well as involving a number of other factors is derived by integrating the two systems of astrology and geomancy.

Before this begins to sound too alarming, it is worth pointing out that no knowledge of astrology outside of what is contained in this chapter is needed, although some background reading wouldn't hurt. Also, there is no need for complex calculations, for that part of astrology is not needed for geomantic interpretation; in fact tables of planetary and Zodiacal data (an ephemeris) need never be opened.

Before proceeding with the application of astrology to geomantic interpretation, it is useful to go roughly over basic astrological ideas. As far as geomancy is concerned, astrology is merely an interpretive tool and there is therefore no need to go into it in depth.

If we ignore the relative positions of the solar system in which the planets revolve around the Sun, and think instead of the universe from the point of view of a man standing on the earth and gazing up at the dome of the sky, we will get a clearer picture of astrology. It does not matter what the complex orbital systems are, which result in planets and stars being in certain parts of the sky at certain times; what does matter is the angles they make with each other and their relationship with the spot on the earth where we are standing.

If we had to devise a system of astrology for people born on the surface of the Sun, then the present scientific model of the (heliocentric) solar system would be a perfect start. However we are dealing with the relationship of the planets and stars *with the earth*, so it is irrelevant to talk about their orbital relationship with the Sun.

Having disposed of this unnecessary complication, let us imagine that we are standing at night with feet firmly planted on the earth, some time before Copernicus, looking up into the great blue-black dome of the night. The night is lit by a film of stars, a band of which, the Milky Way, is denser than the rest.

Look carefully for a group of stars which have an unmistakable form, it may be that you notice the three very bright evenly spaced stars of Orion's belt, or in the Southern Hemisphere it might be the unmistakable Southern Cross. Watch them attentively; in an hour or two they will appear to have moved across the sky. Look for another group of stars and watch them; they too will move. Imagine the astonishment of early man when he realized that the whole sky appears to turn like a great sphere around the earth, some stars rising up from the horizon, some traversing the heights of heaven, and others sinking beyond the opposite horizon. Each star keeps the same position relative to the other stars. Those who watched this phenomenon did not think in terms of the rotation of the earth, but taking the earth as their reference point, chose to examine particular groups of stars fixed into the crystal sphere of the stars which ceaselessly turned around the earth, and they called these groups of stars, constellations.

Signs of the Zodiac

Obviously, as the dome of the sky moved it was necessary to find a fixed point of reference for measuring the movement of the Sun, Moon and planets. Twelve particularly outstanding constellations in a rough band about 16° wide round the earth were chosen as "markers" in the sky by which to plot the movement of the planets, Sun and Moon. These twelve constellations were called the twelve Signs of the Zodiac. Between the earth and this band (which stretched around the earth) moved all the then visible planets and the Moon, each following its own erratic course.

These "markers" were named after the animals and other images they were supposed to look like:

Aries	♈
Taurus	♉
Gemini	♊
Cancer	♋
Leo	♌
Virgo	♍
Libra	♎
Scorpio	♏
Sagittarius	♐
Aquarius	♒
Capricorn	♑
Pisces	♓

Since the date they were named, the constellations have moved somewhat from the positions in which they were first seen by a process called the precession of the Equinoxes. However this need not concern us as the Zodiacal Signs listed above still act as markers for the same twelve sections of the sky even if they are slightly out of line with the original constellations. The qualities of these signs are briefly summed up in this chapter.

So far we have the sphere of the stars which appears to revolve as a whole with the stars on it rising along the eastern horizon and setting along the western horizon. So in twenty-four hours each of the twelve Signs will have risen in the east, passed across the sky and set in the west, just like the sun. Of course it is not possible to observe this during daylight hours, but it continues to happen nevertheless.

Now, traveling with this belt through the sky is that closest of stars, the Sun. Watching the Sun over a period of some days it would appear that the Sun travels with one of the Signs of the Zodiac across the sky and under the earth before again rising with the same Sign. However the Sun is not fixed in the same part of the Zodiacal belt for the whole of the year. It seems in fact to travel with each Sign for approximately one month, moving slowly from one Sign of the Zodiac to another throughout the year, until in the course of the whole year the Sun will have "travelled" with each of the twelve Signs across the sky.

It is for this reason that it can be said that the Sun is in the Sign of Aries approximately from March 21st to April 20th, in Taurus from April 21st to May 20th and so on. For each of these times the Sun "travels" through the sky with this Sign.

At the same time all of the classical planets, Venus, Mercury, Mars, Saturn and Jupiter can be seen in one Sign or the other at different times of the year. The Moon, which was considered a planet by the ancients also moves through the Zodiacal Signs. These planets however move through the Signs much faster or slower than the Sun, each changing Sign at a different speed.

Houses

We now need one more system of measurement, for although we have the Signs of the Zodiac, they are moving as part of the sphere of stars and are therefore not a fixed system of measurement. For this purpose astrologers have devised the "House" system. These Houses form an imaginary but fixed grid centered on the earth and orientated according to the spot of ground on which you are standing while looking up at the sky. The twelve fixed House divisions are projected out into the sky, forming the ribs of the system (see Illustration 6).

Look back at the illustration: there is something strange

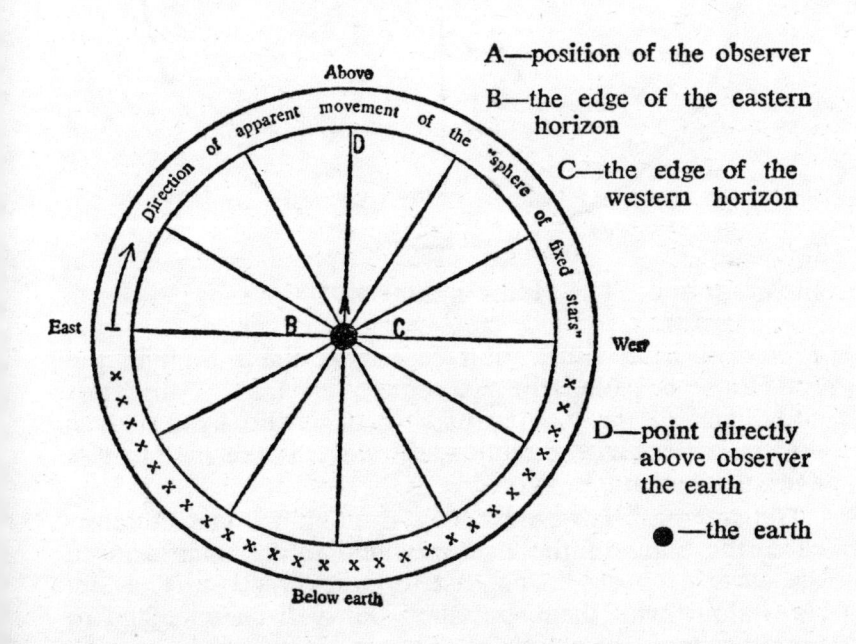

A—position of the observer
B—the edge of the eastern horizon
C—the edge of the western horizon
D—point directly above observer the earth
●—the earth

Ilustration 6: The Houses of heaven

about it. The eastern horizon is on the left side. This is the traditional manner of drawing astrological charts despite the fact that it is the reverse of the conventional manner of drawing geographical maps. The numbering of the Houses is also strange looking until you get used to it.

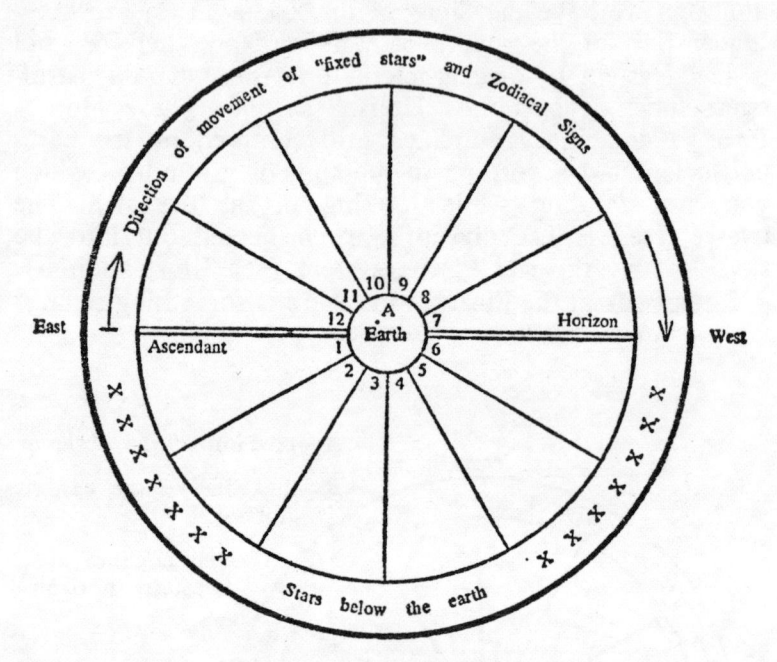

Illustration 7: The House numbers

Now look at Illustration 7. The Zodiacal Sign in the 1st House is called the Ascendant, because as the stars and Signs of the Zodiac pass through the fixed House grid in a clockwise direction, this Sign is the first to rise over the eastern horizon.

To summarize, we now have a moving frame of reference, the Signs of the Zodiac which rotate once around the earth each day in an east to west direction. The Sun rides along with them, but slips slowly from one Sign to the other over the course of the year, spending one month approximately in each Sign. The second framework of twelve Houses is fixed, the 1st House is always located just under the eastern horizon from wherever you happen to be standing. The Houses are then numbered in order around the earth until House 12 is just above the eastern horizon. This is fixed and is always so, for the Houses are a man-made fixed grid while the Zodiac is based on the natural phenomena of the moving Zodiacal Signs. These then provide two systems of reference for plotting the position of the seven classical planets (including the Sun and Moon), as a planet's position in the

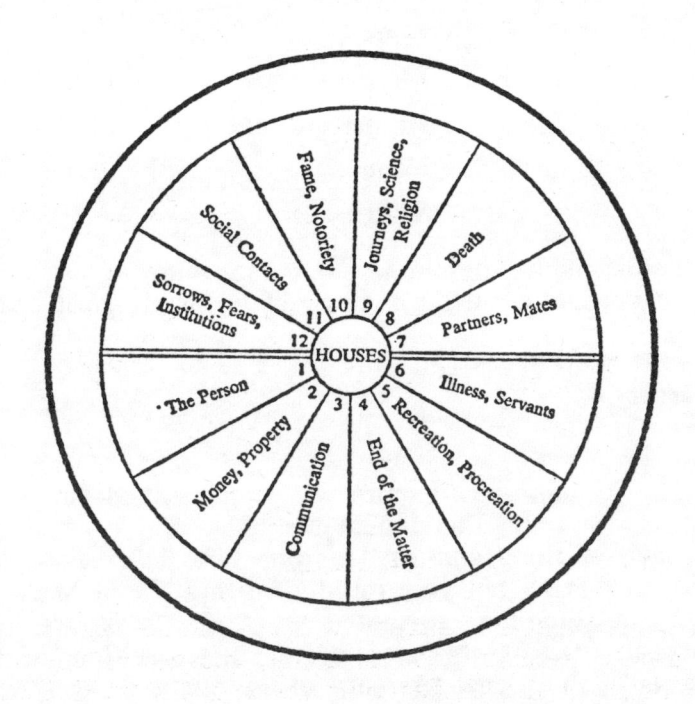

Illustration 8: Key departments of the twelve Houses

sky may be indicated by both its House and its Zodiacal Sign location.

Each of the Houses is given a meaning, so that each sector of the sky both above the earth and under the earth is associated with a particular type of question or function (see Illustration 8).

Planets

Having considered the frameworks of astrology, let us now consider the seven traditional planets which move through them. These are:

Sun	☉
Moon	☽
Mars	♂
Mercury	☿
Jupiter	♃
Venus	♀
Saturn	♄

Traditionally they are given the following qualities when considered in the context of an astrological chart:

Mercury

☿

The Roman god Mercury was equivalent to the Greek Hermes and the Babylonian Nabu.

Each of these gods had at one time been associated with that small but very rapidly moving planet Mercury, and the qualities attributed to these gods are also characteristic of the astrological interpretation of the effects of the planet Mercury in the chart.

As Nabu was the god of intellect and the scribe who was supposed to have invented writing, Mercury rules the intellect, communications of all types from writing to radio, calligraphy to computers, and the by-product of writing and literature.

Hermes, god of travelers, business chicanery and thieves, messenger to the gods, has added his attributes including that of a persuasive tongue, reason, wit and argument.

Mercury being hermaphrodite rules change, be it change of sex, in ideas, or in travel direction. Changeability is a quality Mercury shares with the Moon, with the exception that her changes are those of the tide—natural and well regulated. His changes are perverse and fickle, in fact, mercurial.

Summing up: Mercury subsumes a versatile intellect, giving literary and lecturing ability, a clever tongue, and ability with any subject or science relying heavily on logic, such as arithmetic, geometry or astrology. An interest in magic is sometimes implied. Commerce is also under the auspices of this planet and the presence of Mercury in a favorable position will help this activity flourish, especially if the trade involves travelling or communication, for example journalism or publishing.

Conversely, if Mercury is badly positioned in the horoscope or associated with one of the malefic geomantic figures, qualities such as boasting, prattling, slandering or lying may come to the surface.

Venus

♀

The Roman goddess Venus was paralleled in Babylon by Ishtar, in Egypt by Hathor or Isis, and in Greece by Aphrodite.

All these goddesses were associated with love, sensuality, lust, and to a lesser extent, with fertility. The original forms of these goddesses represented fertility and lust, the cruelty of Nature admixed with love.

Ishtar's worship involved the ancient practice of temple prostitution which was not looked upon as anything reprehensible, but in the light of a religious sacrifice to the greater glory of the goddess. The symbol of Venus represents the female sex, and its traditional qualities of emotion, warmth, eroticism and love are clearly those of this planet.

Venus, which is most clearly seen at dawn and dusk, was sometimes called the morning or evening star and has been associated with Lucifer, the light-bringer.

Ptolemy said of Venus that when she rules, she renders

the mind benignant, good, voluptuous, copious in wit, pure, gay, fond of dancing, abhorring wickedness . . . but if contrarily posited, she renders the mind dull, amorous, effeminate, timorous, indiscriminating, sordid, faulty, obscure and ignominious.

Thus Venus is a benefic planet but prey to the weaknesses of excessive emotion.

Mars

♂

The war god of Rome, Mars was red like the color of his planet, and with the fire and blood inevitably associated with war. Ares, his Greek equivalent clearly indicates the link between the planet and the sign Aries of which more soon.

Mars is the lesser of the two so-called malefics, sharing this title with the somber planet, Saturn. His qualities are, however, far from being uniformly negative. He can boast the courage of a warrior, the ability of an athlete, the drive of a leader, the sword-edged quality of a surgeon's life-saving skills, as well as the cruelty of a Caligula or the fury of a berserk warrior. There are even two sides to the fury of battle, the triumphant, exaltation of one warrior or the calculated cruelty of others.

The complementary natures of Venus and Mars, the word "martial" and the use of Mars's symbol to designate the male sex sum up the qualities of the planet admirably.

Jupiter

♃

Zeus, Jupiter's Greek equivalent, although king of the gods, was not always so. Having overthrown his father, Cronos, and taken over the command of Olympus, he was considered the beneficent overthrower of the malefic old god.

The qualities of beneficial revolution and kingly virtue, are characteristic of the effects of the planet

Jupiter. Marduk, his Babylonian opposite number, also replaced his father and initiated a golden age on earth. All favors and patronage from those higher placed are associated with Jupiter who symbolized justice, charity, liberality, good faith, honor, honesty and philanthropy. The rotund joviality of the traditional medieval churchman is also associated with Jupiter, and the word "jovial" derived from Jupiter sums up his qualities. He is obviously a benefic planet.

Jupiter is also connected with the intellect but of a more searching kind than the cleverness of Mercury. However, when the planet is ill-aspected or associated with one of the evil geomantic figures, it tends towards over-joviality and spendthrift behavior and allows himself to be easily swindled, he is in short, a sucker. Hypocrisy, religious fanaticism, carelessness and a poor choice of friends also tends to be the mark of an afflicted Jupiter.

Saturn

♄

Saturn was a dark god, the Roman equivalent of the Greek Cronos, although their shared qualities are not as marked as most Greco-Roman pairs of gods, because the Romans mistakenly identified the harmless agricultural god, Saturn, with Cronos, possibly because both gods had the sickle as their emblem.

(Cronos was in turn identified with *Ch*ronos the Greek god who created time, and with it that old timekeeper, death. Obviously, the planet associated with these gods has always been considered a malefic. Although death may be merciful sometimes, he has never been looked on with favor by those whom he harvests! Because time is so important, a feature of *Ch*ronos, inertia is also a prime quality of the god and its planet.)

Cronos also had unpleasant qualities. Having castrated his father and devoured his own children, he is associated with impotence, infertility and the process of aging.

Saturn was a more pleasant god and governed agriculture and latent fertility, the resurrection of seeds, souls and sciences. The death of seeds in the soil in winter before their later springtime resurrection connects Saturn with agriculture and the earth (in which the dead are buried).

As Cronos and Saturn were deposed by their children, the qualities of loss, regret and melancholy go with this planet. On the positive side, if the planet is well-aspected, then a certain endurance, inhibition, reserve, patience, dignity and practicality may manifest as well as success in agriculture, building and steady relationships.

The Sun

☉

The sun, although not technically a planet, nevertheless appears to rotate around the earth against the backdrop of the Zodiac, and thus appears to act like a planet. However, the Sun is special, being the most powerful of the "planets."

In a horoscope, it is considered very important because the Zodiacal Sign it happens to be in at the time of birth is the Sun Sign of the person, about which so much is written in popular astrological works.

In all cultures, the sun is the brilliant eye of heaven, the charioteer who lights the earth by day. Ra, Shemesh, Helios or Sol all banished night and conquered evil. His qualities are therefore a mixture of the best aspects of Mars and Jupiter.

His qualities include justice, prudence, stateliness, honor, confidence, bonhomie and trust. If the planet is ill-aspected, then a certain pride, restlessness, wastefulness and overbearing arrogance sometimes gain the upper hand, but on the whole the qualities of the Sun are benefic.

The Moon

☽

The Moon is the eye of the night and one of the seven

"planets" complementing the Sun. The Moon, however, by associating mainly with the night, influences dreams, sleep, mysticism, and sensitivity. It is the feminine passive opposite of the masculine Sun.

If the Moon is ill-aspected, then a certain luxuriousness and laziness, drunkness, carelessness and a general looseness of living can take the upper hand.

However, if the Moon is well placed or disciplined by its position in the horoscope, then intuition, curiosity especially in strange subjects or novelties, and mediumistic ability go hand in hand with a mercurial compulsion to travel or change residence.

Signs of the Zodiac

As the planets move against the background of that also moving division of the sky, the twelve Zodiacal Signs, it is worthwhile considering some of the traditional qualities of the twelve Signs.

To appreciate the relationships between the seven planets and their background of twelve Signs better, it is useful to consider the traditional rulership of each of the twelve Signs by the planets. This rulership gives some indication of the nature of the Signs in terms of the qualities of the planets.

Planet	Sign Ruled
Sun	Leo
Moon	Cancer
Mars	Aries, Scorpio
Mercury	Gemini, Virgo
Jupiter	Pisces, Sagittarius
Venus	Taurus, Libra
Saturn	Aquarius, Capricorn

Interestingly, the five "real planets" govern two Signs apiece, while the Sun and Moon rule only one Sign each.

We will take the Signs in the order in which the Sun passes through them commencing at the Spring Equinox.

Figure.	Name.	Element	Planet.	Sign.
* * * . * * *	Way Journey	Water	☾	♌
* * * * * * * *	People Congregation.	Water	☾	♑
* * * * * *	Conjunction An assembling	Aire	☿	♍
* * * * * *	A prifon Bound	The Earth	♄	♓
* * * * *	Great fortune Greater aid Safe-guard entering	The Earth	☉	♒
* * * * *	Lesser fortune Lesser aid Safe-guard going out	Fire	☉	♉
* * * * *	Obtaining Comprehended within	Aire	♃	♈
* * * * *	Acquisition Comprehended without	Fire	♀	♎
* * * * * * *	Joy Laughing Healthy Bearded	Aire	♃	♉
* * * * * * *	Sadnefs Damned Crofs	Earth.	♄	♏
* * * *	A Girle Beautifull	Watter	♀	♎
* * * *	A Boy Yellow Beardless	Fire	♂	♈
* * * * * *	White Fair	Water.	☿	♋
* * * * *	Reddish Red	Fire	♂	□
* * * *	The head The threshold entring The upper threshold	Earth		♍
* * * *	The Taile The threshold going out The lower threshold	Fire.		♐

Illustration 9: The geomantic figures and their astrological correspondences (from Cornelius Agrippa's *Three Books of Occult Philosophy*, Book II)

ARIES ♈

Symbol: Ram
Element: Fire
Ruler: Mars
Exaltation: Sun

Positive Characteristics: Extreme activity, especially physical, unlimited energy, daring, love of enterprise and adventure, a quick temper that is not easily restrained. The mind is often quick and able in dealing with concrete things, but Aries is essentially a Sign of action, and likes to rely on the inspiration of the moment.

Negative Characteristics: If badly aspected, it is quarrelsome, will not compromise, and is one-sided. Daring becomes foolhardiness, and there is a lack of prudence and foresight shown by ill-aspected Aries, which is also prone to outbreaks of temper and empty bravado.

Health: Aries governs the head and brain, and may indicate headaches, toothache, brain fever or neuralgia if ill-aspected.

Occupation: Actors, designers, herbalists, nature-cure doctors, guides and travelers, surveyors, architects, electricians, agents of all kinds, company promoters, free-lance journalists, novelists.

TAURUS ♉

Symbol: Bull
Element: Earth
Ruler: Venus
Exaltation: Moon

Positive Characteristics: This is in most respects the opposite of Aries. It is slow, careful, steady, practical and reserved. It is easily contented, and enjoys the simple things of life, especially those of a rural nature. It is motherly, homely, protective, patient, persevering and firm, but sometimes these qualities reflect a certain laziness. Careful with money, gentle, affectionate and sensitive.

Negative Characteristics: The temper is peaceable and not easily roused, but when provoked Taurus can be violent and unrelenting.

Health: Taurus governs the neck and the throat, hence indications of illness are likely to be sore throats, diphtheria, mumps, heart and kidney troubles, and diabetes. Laziness is fatal to their health.

Occupation: Cashiers, financial agents, municipal accountants, collectors, stockbrokers, masseurs, doctors, nurses, foremen, manufacturers of paper, sweet-stuffs or chemicals, agricultural pursuits, chefs and cooks.

GEMINI ♊

Symbol: Twins
Element: Air
Ruler: Mercury
Exaltation: (Caput Draconis)

Positive Characteristics: It is pre-eminently the Sign connected with the concrete mind, reason and logic. Hazy or sentimental thinking, leading to loose or inaccurate conclusions, are particularly distasteful to this Sign. Repartee, good conversation, debate and argument are integral features. Gemini people are very active, restless and changeful, seldom settling down, and in many respects retaining their youth for long. They make excellent clerks, teachers and students.

Negative Characteristics: The faults of the Sign are lack of concentration and the tendency to take on too many projects and enterprises, so that they have "too many irons in the fire," and leave things unfinished. There is lack of decision and a good deal of wavering and a difficulty in making up the mind. The Gemini person often excels in detail, but may fail to "see the wood for the trees." Emotionally there is a tendency to egoism, hardness and selfishness, introspection, self-centeredness and discontent. When severely afflicted, there may be deceit, untruthfulness or dishonesty.

Health: Gemini governs the lungs, arms, hands, and nerves. The constitutiion is not very strong and the health quickly breaks up when affected by worry, overwork or shock. Catarrhal trouble, pneumonia and diseases of the lungs generally, stammering and very quick speech are also associated with this Sign.

Occupation: Brokers, dealers, and auctioneers, public speakers, reporters, journalists, barristers, bookkeepers, clerks.

CANCER ♋

Symbol: Crab
Element: Water
Ruler: Moon
Exaltation: Jupiter

Positive Characteristics: Extreme sensitiveness, both physical and emotional, and rapidly varying moods usually reflecting each outside influence with which they come into contact, characterize Cancer. The emotions range from the sentimental, extremely timid and even helpless to morbidity and sensitivity. The imagination is vivid and Cancer natives easily enter into other people's feelings and thoughts, and sense "atmospheres" readily. Cancerians may show much tenacity and passive bravery and sticking power. Once they have taken up a position or idea they maintain it with a persistence that is not found in the more objective Signs. They are usually good business people, being shrewd, prudent and careful. They are home-loving and devoted to their families, clannish, prejudiced against strangers, and tend to make the family their main end.

Negative Characteristics: Cancer, as in all the water Signs, has a tendency towards moral laxity. They absorb impressions of all sorts, and are easily influenced.

Health: Cancer rules the breast and stomach. Gastric and stomach troubles, pleurisy, dropsy, and all watery and inflammatory diseases are associated with this Sign. Vitality is sometimes quite low.

Occupation: Their strong domesticity makes women under this Sign the best of housekeepers, hotel-keepers, midwives, barmaids or laundresses. Dealers in all manner of second-hand articles and curios. Real estate agents and builders' merchants are also found under Cancer, as well as seamen.

LEO ♌

Symbol: Lion
Element: Fire
Ruler: Sun
Exaltation: ――

Positive Characteristics: This Sign of the Zodiac possesses the greatest amount of power, using the word in its widest sense. There is usually strong ambition and a firm will associated with this Sign, and seldom do the natives of Leo occupy an obscure position: the inherent ability of the Sign brings it forward to a position of prominence and authority, in whatever field chosen. Most "born leaders" have a strong solar influence, and the Sun shines strongly through Leo. Leo's destiny is to deal with large issues, and leave drudgery and detail to others. It possesses all the gifts of the born commander, and produces people whom others readily respect and obey. Often apparently genial and democratic in theory, its methods are nearly always autocratic. The

Leo is temperamentally good natured, obliging and often even devotedly affectionate.

Negative Characteristics: The fault of this Sign is vanity, and it is easily flattered. Leos may surround themselves with favorites, and aim at show rather than merit, and become assuming, snobbish and worldly.

Health: Leo governs the heart and the back. Afflictions of the ribs, side and back, pleurisy, eye trouble; fevers and convulsions are illnesses to which Leo is subject.

Occupation: Organizers, leaders, managers, foremen, social welfare workers, organists and musicians showing preference for the really grand and inspiring in their art; artists, actors. They do not like manual labor and usually do better in a professional rather than a business career.

VIRGO ♍

Symbol: Virgin
Element: Earth
Ruler: Mercury
Exaltation: Mercury

Positive Characteristics: Usually artistic and literary, and gifted with considerable taste, Virgo people are generally careful with money and possess a sound commercial instinct. They are neat, methodical and very precise. They take a pride in their work, and as a rule like to be left alone to carry out their tasks in peace and quiet. They are conscientious and attend to detail, making excellent secretaries or subordinates of any kind. They do not often assume control, dislike responsibility and shrink from the limelight and self-advertisement; in fact, they are often shy and retiring and make few friends. They usually possess skill in manual craftsmanship. They have a marked interest in health, food, diet and hygiene, and may be doctors or nurses.

Negative Characteristics: Virgo is pre-eminently a sign of criticism and discrimination, especially as regards details, and therefore the commonest failings of the Sign are the outcome of this tendency. They may be chronic fault-finders, cantankerous, prejudiced and narrow in their views, with the result that they are unpopular with those who misunderstand their natures. The love of method also leads to fussiness and immersion in detail, and their refinement may develop into prudery and lack of charity towards the lapses of warmer-blooded Signs.

Health: Virgo rules the bowels, and worry and overwork causes afflictions of this part of the body. Virgo people worry a lot which reacts on their nerves, and drugs and alcohol are very harmful to them.

Occupation: Virgo people do well in all business connected with food and drugs. They make splendid analytical chemists. Editors and literary critics are found among them. They are fitted by their tact, mental ability and business aptitude for practically any professional or business vocation, bearing in mind that they may have trouble relating to others working in the same field.

LIBRA ♎

Symbol: The Scales
Element: Air
Ruler: Venus
Exaltation: Saturn

Positive Characteristics: Libra has a highly developed sense of beauty, is very sociable and companionable, and seldom leads a separate life. They are always found doing their best work and achieving more when associated with others, either in marriage or in some other form of partnership. They are affable, courteous and obliging. Their temper is even and equable, and if ruffled, subsides readily. They never bear malice; in fact there is a readiness on all occasions to forgive and forget. They find a disturbed or quarrelsome atmosphere difficult to put up with, and compromise rather than face prolonged discord. There is sometimes a longing for escape from wordly conditions, and secret unhappiness in the face of the roughness and hardship of life. They are rarely extreme in their views and tend to be impartial.

Negative Characteristics: The faults are those of weakness and complacency. They find it hard to take a firm attitude in the face of hostility, and tend to avoid unpleasantness at all costs. They consequently compromise too much, and waver from one view to another, without committing themselves to one course or another. They are often lazy and may be slovenly and careless. They cannot act on their own responsibility but instinctively seek a partner.

Health: Libra rules the kidneys. The constitution is usually strong but excess, especially drinking, affects the kidneys and the bladder. Pains in the loins and weakness of the lower part of the back are common. Libra people often allow themselves to get into a very melancholy state.

Occupation: Barristers, lawyers, musical and theatrical people generally and those having the direction and management of the artistic side of public amusements are found amongst Librans. They are clever as artists and decorators. In trade they are antique and art dealers, and often have much to do with perfumery and fabrics.

SCORPIO ♏

Symbol: Scorpion
Element: Water
Ruler: Mars
Exaltation: ——

Positive Characteristics: Scorpio has an intense emotional nature. No sign has more profound and enduring feelings, but owing to the fixity of Scorpio these become set in an unwavering devotion to principles or people. Extreme sensitiveness to imagined slights or injustice, resentment, suspicion and furious anger are also sometimes manifest. Scorpios of this kind are very prone to think themselves undervalued. The Sign is extremely thoroughgoing and courageous. Many heroes have been born under this Sign, as well as notable villains. They do nothing by halves, and having once selected their course in life, pursue it relentlessly. There is frequently an inclination towards some sort of mysticism or occultism, and a natural tendency towards what is secret and hidden, with a love of probing mysteries and getting at the bottom of things.

Negative Characteristics: There may be treachery, cruelty and revengeful traits which appear in childhood, but die out with good training. Reckless self-indulgence and powerful feelings constantly tempt the native, and few Scorpios pass through life without having run the full gamut of temptation on the physical plane.

Health: Scorpio governs the genitals. The constitution is usually strong. Scorpios suffer from diseases and infections of the generative organs, afflictions of the bladder and poisoning of the blood, pains in the groin and kidney troubles.

Occupation: Scorpios succeed in all martial employments, such as doctor, surgeon, butcher, mechanical engineers, ironmongers, smiths, etc. They are also hypnotists and magnetic healers, occultists, chemists, inventors of all kinds, detectives, etc. They are in their element at sea and make good naval officers and sailors. They excel as detectives, inspectors and investigators of all kinds.

SAGITTARIUS ↗

Symbol: Archer
Element: Fire
Ruler: Jupiter
Exaltation: Cauda Draconis

Positive Characteristics: Typical Sagittarians are high-spirited, kind, generous and honest, with a great love of outdoor life, sports and athletics. They enjoy life to the full, and their mental ability is also as a rule above the average. Interest in philosophy, metaphysics and religion is common. There is a love of travelling, exploring and wandering, the attachment to home usually being small. Freedom and personal liberty make a strong appeal. It is however, on the whole, one of the most fortunate and likeable of the Signs.

Negative Characteristics: The faults of the Sign are the result of its exuberance of life and spirits, and its restlessness and love of covering large stretches of country, both physically and mentally. There may be extravagance, carelessness over detail, waste, exaggeration, too great a faith in luck, superficiality, a tendency to know a little of everything but all of nothing, with sudden crazes for people, intellectual interests and hobbies, which blaze up and die away.

Health: Sagittarius governs the thighs and hips. Tumors and all diseases affecting the hips and thighs are associated with this Sign; sciatica, rheumatism, varicose veins and blood fevers are possible afflictions.

Occupation: Military officers, civil engineers, politicians, clergymen, college professors, and barristers are found among Sagittarians; also commercial travellers, advertising agents, inspectors, horse-dealers and book-makers.

CAPRICORN ♑

Symbol: The Goat
Element: Earth
Ruler: Saturn
Exaltation: Mars

Positive Characteristics: A careful, prudent, conscientious and ambitious type. Capricorn rising seems to give a much more emotional and introspective type, a love of music or other forms of art being a common characteristic. The conscientiousness and practical abilities are less marked, so that this Sign will often produce clever but ineffective people, who seem unable to find their right place in the world, and in consequence fret and flit capriciously from one thing to another, achieving little and often becoming hard to please, sour and disappointed. It is a restless and sometimes rather self-important Sign, many Capricornians being loquacious and pushy, and disliking to be overlooked.

Negative Characteristics: The failings which occur in weak examples are worldliness, snobbishness, a tendency to manage and even to make use of others for private ends, narrowness of outlook, too great a respect for the past and a refusal to change with the times. Selfishness and craftiness in pursuit of personal advantage, are their negative characteristics.

Health: Capricorn rules the knees. All diseases of the knees, skin complaints and rheumatism are associated with this Sign.

Occupation: Managers and organizers of all huge enterprises requiring persistent and long-sustained effort, contractors, real-estate agents and brokers, lawyers, farmers and agricultural workers and dealers, researchers and great land owners are found among Capricornians.

AQUARIUS ♒

Symbol: Water Carrier
Element: Air
Ruler: Saturn
Exaltation: ——

Positive Characteristics: A serious and grave outlook on life, but less practical than the previous Sign. The mind is more idealistic and may spend much time on speculations in the field of philosophy, religion and sociology: the result may be lack of practical common sense. There is nearly always kindness, sympathy and refinement, together with an intense love for wild nature. The native tends to be attracted to societies, clubs, associations, groups of people, and "movements" of all sorts, easily merging his own personality in "causes." There are many associates, but the temperament is often too detached to make warm friendships. Aquarius has a great love of personal freedom and resents enforced obedience, but apart from this is usually faithful, constant and affectionate. It is the Sign of truth and sincerity. At the same time Aquarians may hold extreme opinions. It is pre-eminently a human Sign.

Negative Characteristics: It is sometimes led in an opposite direction to unconventional morality, and may get a reputation for looseness. Sometimes Aquarians tend to harbor deepseated resentments.

Health: Aquarius rules the ankles and legs. Swollen legs and ankles and all diseases and weaknesses of these parts, poor circulation and cramps are peculiar to this Sign. The Moon in Aquarius, especially when badly aspected, gives trouble with the eyes.

Occupation: Railway, post-office and telegraph employees, managers, engineers, and surveyors, are largely recruited from Aquarians. Reformers and revolutionists in many spheres are among them, and they will be found much in evidence in many public companies and associations. Musicians, poets, astronomers, astrologers, literary workers, artists and secretaries are other occupations of this Sign.

PISCES ♓

Symbol: The Fishes
Element: Water
Ruler: Jupiter
Exaltation: Venus

Positive Characteristics: Pisces is the most plastic of the Signs, and it seldom possesses a very strong individual character, for it lives largely on the thoughts and feelings of those with whom it comes in contact. Hence it is, above all, the actor's Sign, giving great ability to absorb and express the emotions of others. The imagination is extremely active, as in all watery Signs, and the life is often passed in the imaginative rather than the actual world. It is often the Sign of writers, poets and artists. Religious feeling is often prominent. The sympathies are abundant and the Sign is attracted to the needy and sick, which may cause the native to connect himself with hospitals, asylums or institutions of a similar description, as well as prisons and monasteries. Pisceans however are commonly jovial and convivial and make entertaining companions.

Negative Characteristics: In some types the desire to help others seems to find expression in the giving of advice and the preaching of "sermons" in and out of season. They are often thriftless, unmethodical, and devoid of worldly wisdom, and without much sense of responsibility. Indeed a large proportion of life's wastrels are born under this Sign. Pisceans are as a rule their own worst enemy and, though not violent or cruel, they are capable of deceiving both themselves and others, and produce bad examples of hypocrisy, especially of the religious kind. Drugs have a great fascination for many

Pisceans, who seem to crave emotional and physical stimulation.

Health: Pisces governs the feet. Trouble with the feet through lameness and pains, swellings, and rheumatism proceeding from impure blood. Other marked features of the Sign are blotches, boils, ulcers, tumors, mucous diseases and discharges of the bowels, and colds and chills.

Occupation: Chiefs of department, agents of all descriptions, literary workers, bookkeepers, librarians, nurses, sailors and naval officers, caterers and hotel-keepers are found amongst Pisces people.

CHAPTER 10

ASTRO-GEOMANCY: HOUSES AND DOTS

Having considered the framework of astrology, the time has come to apply the figures derived in ordinary geomantic divination to this framework to derive a more detailed interpretation.

In almost every case a greater clarification is necessary than can be obtained merely by reading off the meaning of the Judge and Witnesses. One such method of clarification is to allocate the first twelve geomantic figures to the twelve Houses of Heaven on an astrological chart.

As explained in the last chapter, the only fixed framework which marks out the sky in astrology is the House system, through which revolves the Zodiac and against which the planets move with complex motions. The Houses traditionally represent the departments of everyday life, and it is the Houses which contain the answers to the mundane questions with which geomancy deals—questions such as the number and sex of children, the outcome of a business deal, the success of a journey, and so on.

Therefore, the geomantic figures which have been derived by divination are to be put into this House grid system, and the figure which is allocated to the House most relevant to the question asked, becomes the major significator. With the addition of the seven planets and twelve Signs of the Zodiac to the House system, more information can be derived concerning the question.

The seven planets are the *forces* that act on human beings, the twelve Signs show *how* they act, while the Houses show *where* they act and in what department of life their action will be felt. In this manner the static answer of the plain geomantic divination is fleshed out with background information and associated causes and conditions.

Before considering the system for allocating the geomantic figures to the 12 Houses, let us look at the "department of life" and type of question relevant to each House, which we briefly touched upon in the previous chapter.

TABLE OF MEANINGS OF EACH HOUSE

1st House — The person himself, his life, health, behavior, habits, disposition, personal characteristics and apparent personality.

2nd House — Money, property, personal wealth, financial profit and loss, income and expenditure, and associated ideas of theft, loss or negligence.

3rd House — Brothers, sisters, blood relatives, news, letters, communication, short journeys, languages, writing, publicity, agencies, and similar Mercurial pursuits.

4th House — Home environment, fathers and grandfathers, inheritances, possessions, especially buildings, land and hidden treasure. It also gives details about thefts and thieves. Retirement, the grave, or the conclusion of any matter are also included in the significancations of this house.

5th House	Women, luxury, eating, drinking. Creation, recreation, procreation, love affairs, courtship, pregnancy and childbirth, children and the young in general, creative artistic work, amusements and pleasures, sexual compatibility, gambling or speculation.
6th House	Servants and employees, sickness and recovery, which parts of the body are most likely to suffer in illness or injury, aunts and uncles, and domestic animals.
7th House	Wedlock, prostitution and fornication, love, marriage, partnerships and associations. Public enemies, lawsuits, company business, war, conflict, opponents and controversies. Thieves, robbers, dishonor.
8th House	Deaths, financial matters connected with death such as wills, legacies, the estate of the deceased, or business connected with death such as undertakers, executors or spirit mediums. Poverty.
9th House	Long journeys, voyages, relations with foreigners. Science, philosophy, the Church, religion, art, visions, dreams and divinations.
10th House	Fame or notoriety, reputation, rank, honor, trade or profession, authority, employment, and worldly position generally. Also signifies the mother.

11th House	Friends, acquaintances and social contacts, hopes and wishes. Also patronage by the rich or well placed. Philanthropic or altruistic organizations.
12th House	Sorrows, fears, punishments, imprisonment, intrigue, enemies in secret, servants, prostitutes, institutions, asylums, orphanages, hospitals, prisons, secret societies, unseen dangers, restrictions, and misfortune generally (for details refer to the Sixth and Eighth Houses).

Before using this system, it is necessary to understand the terms Angular, Succedent and Cadent. They refer to the three types of Houses. Those on the angles, that is the horizon in the east and west and the Houses at the Midheaven and directly below the earth, are the strongest Angular Houses and are the 1st, 4th, 7th and 10th. Those Houses following or succeeding the Angular Houses are called Succedent Houses and are the 2nd, 5th, 8th and 11th Houses. Finally those farthest from the first mentioned Angular Houses are called Cadent, and are the 3rd, 6th, 9th and 12th Houses. (See Illustration 10.)

Now, there are several systems for allocating the geomantic figures derived in an ordinary divination to the 12 Houses of astrology. It has often been said that the correct method of allocation is the real secret of geomancy which has never been published. Even Aleister Crowley, who was in the habit of "telling everything like it is," admitted that a major key had been left out of his explanation of the technical side of astro-geomancy. That key was the House allocation system. Among the systems outlined in this book is the major key which was omitted. For the present we will simply use the House allocation system prescribed by the Golden Dawn. In Appendix III you will find the alternative systems. You may find, with practice, that one of those systems gives you more consistently accurate results. It is up to you to choose one system and stick with it.

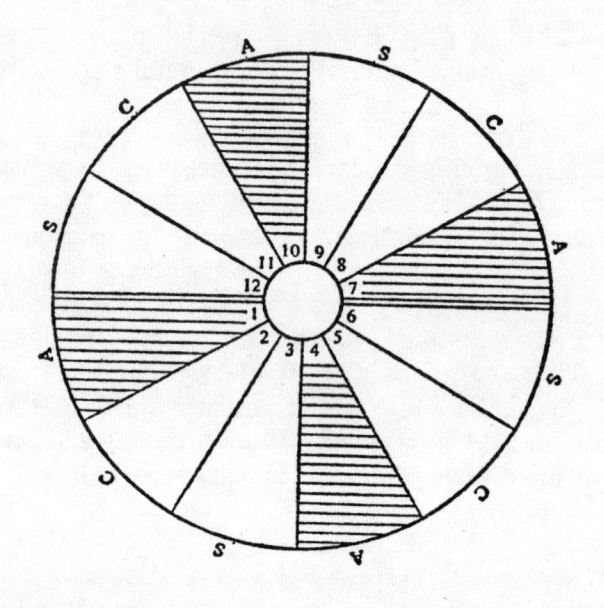

Illustration 10: Angular, Succedent and Cadent Houses

THE GOLDEN DAWN SYSTEM OF HOUSE ALLOCATION

Mothers:	I	House 10	⎫
	II	House 1 (or Ascendant)	⎬ Angular Houses
	III	House 4	⎪
	IV	House 7	⎭
Daughters:	V	House 11	⎫
	VI	House 2	⎬ Succedent Houses
	VII	House 5	⎪
	VIII	House 8	⎭
Nephews:	IX	House 12	⎫
	X	House 3	⎬ Cadent Houses
	XI	House 6	⎪
	XII	House 9	⎭

The system relies on the Mothers, the primary geomantic figures, being placed at the 4 so-called Angular Houses (the Houses at the east and Midheaven and their opposite points, i.e. Houses 10, 1, 4 and 7). The secondary figures, the Daughters, are given to the Succedent Houses, that is the next House round in an anticlockwise direction from each of the Angular Houses (Houses 11, 2, 5 and 8). Finally the 4 remaining or Cadent Houses are allocated the 4 Nephews (Houses 12, 3, 6 and 9). The reasons for the allocation are not important—what is important is the above table.

To illustrate this method of allocation let us take the example we used in Chapter 7 and apply it to the House framework. Look at the Geomantic Chart. To avoid having to go back, we have repeated it again here.

GEOMANTIC CHART

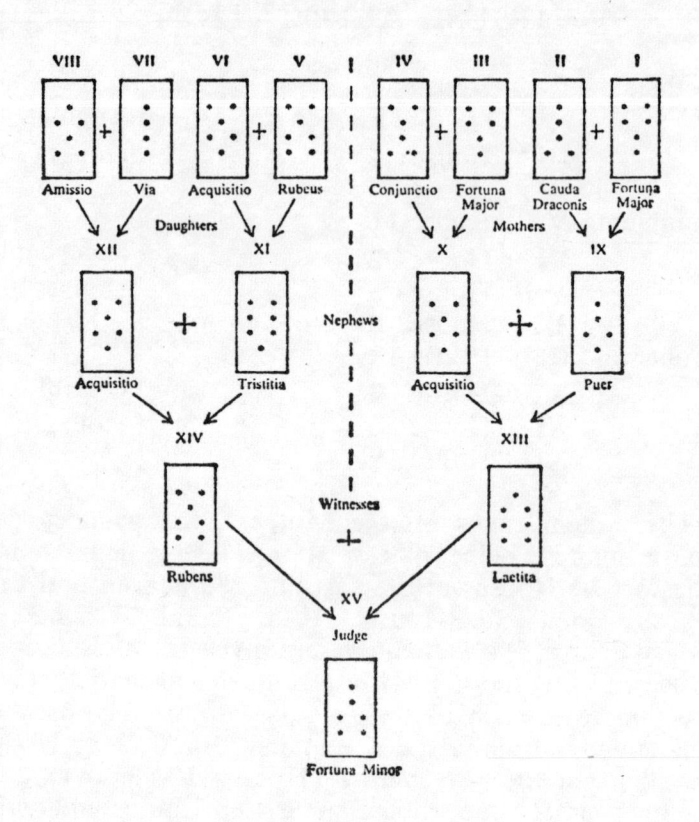

VIII	VII		VI	V	IV	III	II	I
Amissio	Via		Acquisitio	Rubeus	Conjunctio	Fortuna Major	Cauda Draconis	Fortuna Major

Daughters   Mothers

XII   XI   X   IX

Acquisitio   Tristitia   Acquisitio   Puer

Nephews

XIV   XIII

Rubens   Laetita

Witnesses

XV
Judge

Fortuna Minor

Using the Golden Dawn system of allocation we have:

Mothers: I   * *   allocated to House 10
                     * *
                     *
                     *

        II   *   allocated to House 1
                     *
                     *
                  * *

       III   * *   allocated to House 4
                   * *
                    *
                    *

       IV   * *   allocated to House 7
                     *
                     *
                  * *

Daughters: V   * *   allocated to House 11
                     *
                  * *
                  * *

       VI   * *   allocated to House 2
                     *
                  * *
                     *

       VII   *   allocated to House 5
                     *
                     *
                     *

       VIII   *   allocated to House 8
                  * *
                     *
                  * *

Nephews:			
	IX	* * * * *	allocated to House 12
	X	* * * * * *	allocated to House 3
	XI	* * * * * * *	allocated to House 6
	XII	* * * * * *	allocated to House 9

Now place the first Mother, Fortuna Major, into the 10th House. Then mark in the second Mother, Cauda Draconis, in the 1st House or Ascendant. Follow through anticlockwise with the rest of the Mothers in order, then the Daughters and Nephews. (See Illustration 11.)

One word of warning here, whichever House system you decide to use, the ordinary or the esoteric, remember always that if Rubeus or Cauda Draconis fall in the 1st House or Ascendant, the chart is *not fit for judgment* and it should be destroyed without any further calculation or consideration. You should not attempt divination again concerning this question, for at least a couple of hours and preferably not for a day or so. Presumably the question is important for such a result to have happened, and therefore you should think about it very seriously before re-attempting the divination.

Why such an extreme reaction? Well, Cauda Draconis in the 1st House means a short life and bad fortune, in fact impending death for the person asking the question. Rubeus in the 1st House means the same, and it became

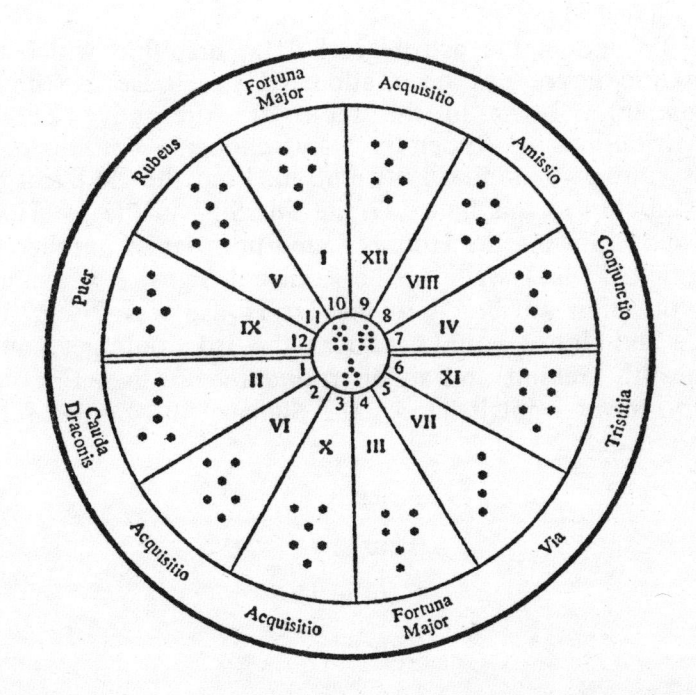

Illustration 11: The Geomantic Figures distributed among the twelve Houses of Heaven

the practice to destroy these two answers which occasionally crop up, on the principle that with these two particularly nasty outcomes, it is as well not to tempt fate by examining them in detail.

You will notice that only the first twelve figures are used in astrological geomancy, that is, the Mothers, Daughters and Nephews. You may if you like, place the two Witnesses and the Judge in the central circular space to remind you of the general interpretation of the geomantic layout.

Having inserted the geomantic figures into the House framework it is now necessary to translate them into astrological terms of reference.

Zodiacal Signs

To add in the astrological data, first find which geomantic figure has been allocated to House I (the Ascendant). Look in the table of Alternative Zodiacal Attributions in Appendix I and choose a column to use as your own standard attribution. Find the Zodiacal Sign attributed to this figure. Write this Sign in the 1st House. Then following the Houses round in order of number (i.e. anticlockwise) write in the Zodiacal Signs. For example, if the Sign attributed to the 1st House was Pisces, then the 2nd House would get Aries, the 3rd would get Taurus, the 4th Gemini and so on round the Zodiac. For those who haven't got it handy, the Signs of the Zodiac follow the order:

Aries	♈
Taurus	♉
Gemini	♊
Cancer	♋
Leo	♌
Virgo	♍
Libra	♎
Scorpio	♏
Sagittarius	♐
Capricorn	♑
Aquarius	♒
Pisces	♓

Returning to our example (Illustration 11) look in the first House and you will see that it contains Cauda

Draconis. Now, although a chart with Cauda Draconis in the 1st House should not be used, let us continue for the moment with this just to illustrate the method. Look up Cauda Draconis in Appendix I and, using column 2 for example, we find that Cauda Draconis = Scorpio (♏). Therefore place Scorpio in the 1st House.

Now take the Signs in order, placing Sagittarius in the 2nd House, Capricorn in the 3rd House, and so on until we have filled in the whole chart, as in Illustration 12.

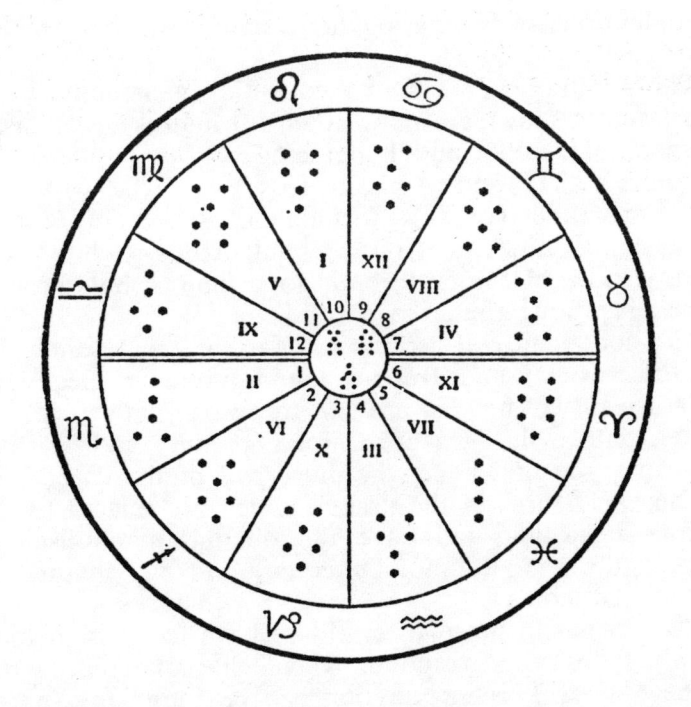

Illustration 12: Zodiacal attributions (using column 2 of Appendix I for House 1, then following anticlockwise in Zodiacal order)

259

Planets

The ascription of the planets to the geomantic figures is quite straightforward but first let us recap on the astrological attributions:

The greater and lesser Fortunes are ascribed to the Sun; Fortuna Major when the Sun is above the horizon and astrologically dignified, Fortuna Minor during the night when the sun is below the horizon or placed in lesser dignities.

The Moon rules Via (street or way) and Populus (people or crowds) during her waxing and her waning respectively.

The Jupiterian figures of Acquisitio (gain and profit) and Laetitia (joy) are both bountiful figures respectively of material success and happiness.

Puella (girl) and Amissio (loss) are the fortunate and retrograde (or less fortunate) aspects of Venus. Similarly, Conjunctio (union) and Albus (white) are the two sides of Mercury, both good figures, but the first more propitious than the second.

The good and evil aspects of Mars are represented by the Puer (boy) and Rubeus (red) figures respectively.

Saturn's two figures are by the very nature of the planet, both evil. They are Carcer (prison) and Tristitia (sorrow); the first being the more evil of the two.

The two figures of the dragon which are related to the Moon's head and tail have the obvious symbolism of good in the head (Caput Draconis) and evil in the tail (Cauda Draconis).

Now to put in the planets all we have to do is to look up which figure corresponds to which planet and write in the planet. This information can be found in Appendix I (or in Chapter 6, page 70-71). In our example:

In the 1st House, Cauda Draconis corresponds to itself ☋
In the 2nd House, Acquisitio corresponds to Jupiter ♃
In the 3rd House, Acquisitio corresponds to Jupiter ♃
In the 4th House, Fortuna Major corresponds to Sun ☉

In the 5th House, via corresponds to the Moon ☽
In the 6th House, Tristitia corresponds to Saturn ♄
In the 7th House, Conjunctio corresponds to Mercury ☿
In the 8th House, Amissio corresponds to Saturn ♄
In the 9th House, Acquisitio corresponds to Jupiter ♃
In the 10th House, Fortuna Major corresponds to Sun ☉
In the 11th House, Rubeus corresponds to Mars ♂
In the 12th House, Puer corresponds to Mars ♂

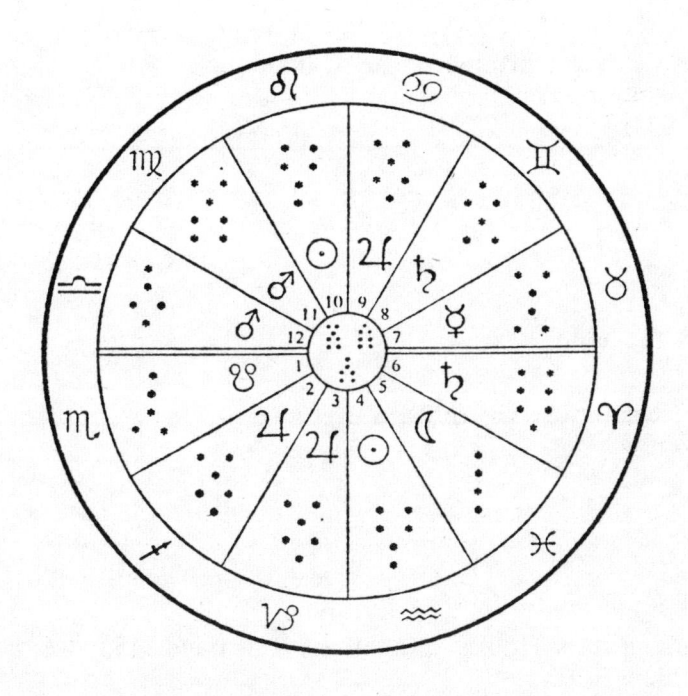

Illustration 13: The complete Astro-Geomantic Figure (including the planetary equivalent of each geomantic figure)

Example

To make sure that the method is clear let us go through another example. Suppose that the initial lines produced these four Mothers:

IV	III	II	I
*	* *	* *	*
*	*	*	*
* *	* *	*	*
*	* *	* *	*

These in turn produced the Daughters:

VIII	VII	VI	V
*	*	*	*
* *	*	*	* *
* *	* *	*	* *
*	* *	*	*

And the Nephews:

XII	XI	X	IX
* *	* *	*	*
*	*	* *	* *
* *	*	* *	* *
*	* *	*	*

1. Using the House allocations on page 253 we can place:

Mothers: I   *   in House 10
                       *
                       *
                       *

II	* * * * * *	in House 1
III	* * * * * * *	in House 4
IV	* * * * *	in House 7
Daughters: V	* * * * * *	in House 11
VI	* * * *	in House 2
VII	* * * * * *	in House 5
VIII	* * * * * *	in House 8
Nephews: IX	* * * * * *	in House 12

```
X        *            in House 3
       * *
       * *
         *

XI       * *          in House 6
         *
         *
       * *

XII      * *          in House 9
         *
       * *
         *
```

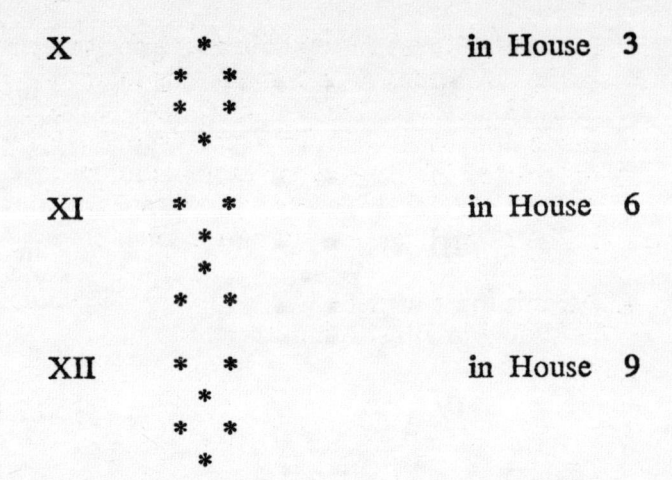

2. Then to determine the Zodiac Sign in the 1st House, look at Figure II which is

```
       * *
        *
        *
       * *
```
Conjunctio

and goes in House 1. The Zodiacal Sign corresponding is Virgo. Therefore write ♍ Virgo in House I (the Ascendant). Now going in an anticlockwise direction, write Libra ♎ in House 2, Scorpio ♏ in House 3, Sagittarius ♐ in House 4 and so on until you reach Leo ♌ in House 12.

3. Now translate each geomantic figure into its planetary equivalent (again using Appendix I) as follows:

In the 1st House Conjunctio corresponds to Mercury
In the 2nd House Via corresponds to the Moon
In the 3rd House Carcer corresponds in Saturn
In the 4th House Rubeus corresponds to Mars
In the 5th House Fortuna Minor corresponds to the Sun

In the 6th House Conjunctio corresponds to Mercury
In the 7th House Puer corresponds to Mars
In the 8th House Carcer corresponds to Saturn
In the 9th House Acquisitio corresponds to Jupiter
In the 10th House Via corresponds to the Moon
In the 11th House Carcer corresponds to Saturn
In the 12th House Carcer corresponds to Saturn

4. All this must now be laid on the astro-geomantic chart as shown in Illustration 14.

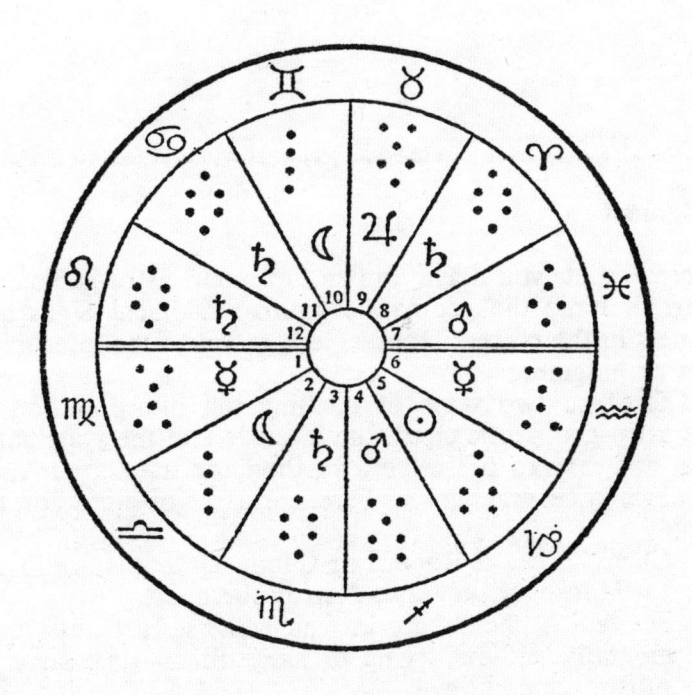

Illustration 14: Example of Astro-Geomantic Chart

CHAPTER 11

ANSWERS FROM SKY AND EARTH

Judgment

Now that you have drawn up your astro-geomantic chart, entered the geomantic figures, Zodiacal Signs and planets in the correct Houses, let's go on to the interpretation or judgment.

There are two ways of tackling the interpretation of this astro-geomantic chart, the intuitive and the systematic. It is not easy to prescribe a method for the former as it develops with practice, so here are a set of steps for the latter:

1. Check to see if Rubeus or Cauda Draconis are in the 1st House. If they are, destroy the chart.
2. See which planets are in which Signs. Just note them mentally without trying to judge them—just so your subconscious knows.
3. Check the Witnesses and Judge (as in ordinary geomancy) to see if the latter is favorable or otherwise. Write this down also.
4. Note which geomantic figure falls in the House relating to the question and write it down along with its accompanying Sign and planet.

5. See if this figure occurs anywhere else in the chart. If it does, note the House or Houses down. Consider what things are listed under this House to see if they affect the answer in any way. For example, in a question concerning stolen money, if the figure in the 2nd House (money and movable possessions) is also found in the 6th House (servants and employees) it might indicate that the thief was a servant or employee. Write down the details.
6. Locate the Index (or if it is a question of money, the Part of Fortune). This is done by calculating the total number of dots originally formed in the sand or with the pencil, and dividing this amount by twelve. The number remaining after this division indicates the House in which the Index (or Part of Fortune) will be found: the geomantic figure in this House is the Index. This Index is rather like the astro-geomantic equivalent of the Judge, and if it is a money question, the Part of Fortune often indicates a possible source of ready cash.
7. Look in the "Table of Geomantic Figures in the Houses" (given later in this chapter) to see the significance of the geomantic figure that falls into the House of the question under consideration. Write this down in full, or at least that part of it which appears to relate to the question.
8. Check the "Table of Essential Dignities" (also given in this chapter) to determine the strength of the figure in that House. This will tell you how much weight to give any factor in the final analysis.
9. Add the meaning of the figure in the 4th House which denotes the conclusion or outcome of the matter in question.
10. Check to see if the same geomantic figure as Figure XV, the Judge, (which has not been placed in a House but in the center of the chart) actually turns up anywhere else. If it does, then the House it appears in is highly significant.
11. It is possible if the divination is still not clear at this point to form a new Reconciler figure by adding together the points of the Judge and the figure in the House of the question, by geomantic addition.

12. You should now have quite a mass of written data. Read it through several times to get the feel of the balance of the answer, that is, if it tends towards a bad or good answer. If necessary mark each piece of data as "g" or "b" to establish the balance. Underline what appears to be major points. From them form your opinion, being careful to look at each scrap of data you have written down.

Questions of Money

As money is such an important factor in life and perhaps the most subject to vicissitudes, astrologers have in

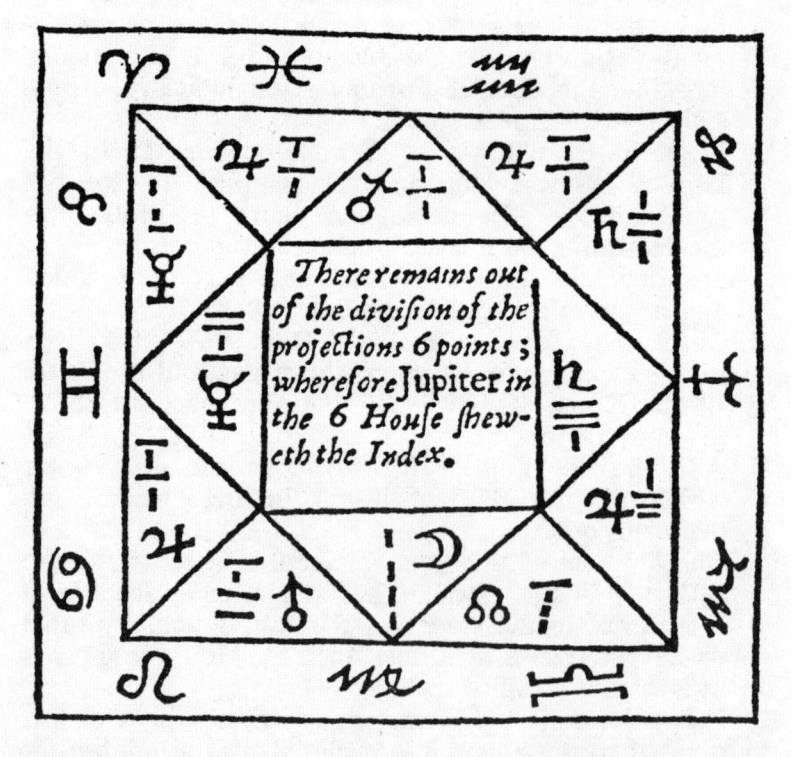

Illustration 15: A typical astro-geomantic chart from Cornelius Agrippa's *Of Geomancy*

the past devised a special calculation and symbol for ready money, or easily available cash belonging to the person asking the question. This is called the Part of Fortune and symbolized by a circle with a cross dividing it into quarters.

For geomantic purposes, it is not necessary to perform the astrological calculations to find the Part of Fortune. It is just necessary to add together all the points of the first twelve geomantic figures, that is the total points of the four Mothers, four Daughters and four Nephews.

Divide your total by twelve and note down the remainder. The number of the remainder will give you the number of the House in which the Part of Fortune is to be found. If there is no remainder, it goes in the 12th House. This has already been explained in Step 6 of the instructions for judgment.

What does that tell you? Well the nature of the House it falls in tells you the direction from which ready cash might come, or could be obtained. The geomantic figure, the Sign and the planet in the House, give you details of the likelihood of the ready cash turning up (geomantic figure) and the sequence of events involved in its appearance (the planets).

Relative Strength of Figures in Houses

Sometimes the interpretation of the meaning of an answer given by an astro-geomantic chart is difficult because a number of competing pieces of information can be extracted, but it is difficult to see the overall picture because of apparently conflicting items in the chart.

To give a simple example, you may find Acquisitio in the 2nd House, boding very well for gain of money or property. However the same figure, Acquisitio may also turn up in another House, for example House 6—illness and employees. In principle you know that Acquisitio is "acquisition as a result of your own effort" and that employees are unlikely to be part of the work indicated, while illness could even be a strong factor preventing you exercising this effort. However, this still leaves you with an uncertainty as to whether that effort is going to be strongly baulked by the effects of House 6 or only mildly retarded. To assess this, providing there is not a clear indication elsewhere in the chart, it is necessary to have some measure of the relative strength of one influence versus another. This measure of strength is given in Illustration 16, and relies on the "essential dignity" of the planets and their associated geomantic figures. Acquisitio is *strong* in the 2nd House but at its *weakest* in the 6th, therefore fortunately the influence of the 2nd House will prevail.

The essential dignity of a figure in a particular House is a measure of its strength, the degree to which it will influence the judgment. It could in fact be invoked as a "tie-breaker."

The term, "essential dignity" means the strength of a figure when found in a particular House. A figure is, therefore, strongest when in its own House, very strong when in its Exaltation, very weak in its Fall; and weakest of all in its Detriment. A figure is in its Fall when in a House opposite to that of its Exaltation, and in its Detriment when opposite to its own House.

Terms, terms and yet more terms! You *don't* have to understand these terms, and they are only given by way of explanation to those who like to know the underlying astrological reasons. "Essential dignity" is the term which covers the various gradations of strength and weakness. It is sufficient to merely use the table to determine which of two apparently conflicting situations shown in a chart is the stronger and therefore the most likely to overcome the other. The numbers refer to the House in which the geomantic figure is strong or weak. (See Illustration 16.)

The table shows the five categories of essential dignity, ranging from the strongest to the weakest. The planets appear only as a guide, and the main use of the table is to settle judgments made complicated by several factors. Thus if Puer was in the 1st House and the 4th House, looking at the first line of the table, it is obvious that Puer

TABLE OF ESSENTIAL DIGNITIES

Geomantic Figure	Corresponding Planet	Strongest: Ruler of Own House	Very Strong: Exaltation	Strong: Triplicity	Very Weak: Fall	Weakest Detriment
Puer	Mars	1, 8	10	5	4	2, 7
Amissio	Venus	2, 7	12	9, 11	6	1, 8
Albus	Mercury	3, 6	6	4, 10	12	9, 12
Populus	Moon	4	2	12	8	10
Fortuna Major	Sun	5	1	8	7	11
Conjunctio	Mercury	3, 6	6	4, 10	12	9, 12
Puella	Venus	2, 7	12	9, 11	6	1, 8
Rubeus	Mars	1, 8	10	5	4	2, 7
Acquisitio	Jupiter	9, 12	4	1, 2, 7	10	3, 6
Carcer	Saturn	10, 11	7	3, 6	1	4, 5
Tristitia	Saturn	10, 11	7	3, 6	1	4, 5
Laetitia	Jupiter	9, 12	4	1, 2, 7	10	3, 6
Cauda Draconis			9		3	
Caput Draconis			3		9	
Fortuna Minor	Sun	5	1	8,	7,	11
Via	Moon	4	2	12	8	10

Illustration 16: The five categories of essential dignity

has a much stronger significance in the 1st House (in connection with the nature and characteristics of the person himself) then in the 4th House (where it shows the outcome of the matter or the nature of the home environment or property owned by the questioner).

Remember that although this section appears complex, it is not another step in the divination but merely a simplification aid designed only to be used when there is some doubt as to the balance of the various aspects making up the answer.

Now for every combination of geomantic figure and House we have the following tables:

TABLE OF GEOMANTIC FIGURES IN THE HOUSES

FORTUNA MAJOR

1st House: Gives long life, and frees from diseases. Man of noble nature, magnanimous, of good manners, medium height, complexion ruddy, hair curling.

2nd House: Signifies riches and manifest gain, good fortune, and the gaining of anything lost or mislaid; the taking of a thief, and recovery of things stolen.

3rd House: Signifies brethren and kinsmen, nobles, and witty conversationalists; journeys to be prosperous and gainful. Men are faithful and their friendship is unfeigned.

4th House: Represents a noble father, of good reputation, and known by many people. He becomes wealthy in cities, and inherits legacies, and discovers hidden treasures. In this House it also signifies theft, and the recovery of everything lost.

5th House: Joy of children who attain great honors. Position obtained with some difficulty. Rumors are found to be true. Man becomes very famous after his death. A woman bears a male child.

6th House: Diseases are cured in a short time. The physician administers good medicine of which there ought to be no suspicion. Servants and ministers are faithful. Horses.

7th House: A wife rich, honest, well-mannered, loving and pleasant. He overcomes strifes and contentions. But if the question be concerning them, the adversaries will be very powerful and great favorites.

8th House: The person about whose death one inquires, still lives. It also signifies a painless and natural death, honors after death, legacies and a great dowry belonging to one's wife.

9th House: Signifies long and prosperous journeys. The return of those that are absent; men of good faith, religious and constant in their intentions. Dreams come true; true and perfect sciences.

10th House: Great honors, public offices, honors in the courts of princes; judges to be just, and not corrupt; a cause to be easily and soon expedited; kings to be powerful, fortunate and victorious; victory to be certain; a noble mother of long life.

11th House: True friends and profitable; a rich and liberal prince makes a man fortunate.

12th House: If a question be proposed concerning the power of enemies, they will be powerful, noble and difficult to oppose. But if the question concerns any other condition of the enemies, it means a lucky escape from their treacheries. It signifies faithful servants; escape from prison. Also it indicates horses, lions and bulls; dangers are either mitigated or taken away.

FORTUNA MINOR

1st House: Gives long life with various troubles and sickness: a person of short stature, a lean body, having a mole or mark on his forehead or right eye.

2nd House: Money, but squandering; lavish expenses; the thief remains hidden; stolen articles are not recovered at all, or with great trouble.

3rd House: Discord among brethren and relatives; danger in a journey, but escape. Reliable men but reserved and uncommunicative.

4th House: Loss of legacies and inheritances; conceals treasuries; things lost cannot be regained except with great difficulty. An honest father, but a prodigal spender of his estate, leaving small portions to his children.

5th House: Only few children; a girl is to be born; honorable positions with but little remuneration. Small honors, little fame.

6th House: Sanguine and choleric disease; the patient is in great danger but will recover; faithful servants, but lazy and unprofitable.

7th House: A wife of a good family, but many troubles with her; love is anxious and inconstant; prolonged contentions and tedious lawsuits, but final success.

8th House: A good death but in a strange place, or on pilgrimage; legacies to be obtained through lawsuit and with difficulty, the portion of a wife's dowry to be obtained with difficulty, but easily spent.

9th House: Dangerous journeys; someone absent slowly to return; men to be occupied in offices of religion; sciences to be unaccomplished; but constancy in faith and religion.

10th House: Kings and princes who gain their power with war and violence; banished men shall soon return: honors, great offices and benefits, but for which you shall continually labor and strive, instability of fortune. A judge shall not favor you; lawsuits and contentions are prolonged; a father and mother shall soon die; and always to be affected with many diseases.

11th House: Many friends, but such as are poor and unprofitable, and not able to relieve your necessities; it ingratiates you with princes, giving great hopes, but small gains; no security in any position or office bestowed by a prince.

12th House: Enemies are crafty, subtle, and fraudulent; to a prisoner a long captivity but final freedom. Useless servants. Frequent changes of fortune from good to evil and vice versa.

PUER

1st House: Life not very long but full of trouble; men rise to great fame through military endeavor; a person of a strong body, ruddy complexion, a fair countenance and black hair.

2nd House: Money obtained from other men by plundering, rape, confiscation, military laws, and such like; the thief escapes and the thing stolen is not returned; he finds no treasure.

3rd House: A man is honored above his friends and is feared by them; journeys are dangerous; persons of good reputation.

4th House: Dubious inheritances and possessions; a father achieves his wealth through violence.

5th House: Good children, who will attain honors and dignities; a woman will give birth to a boy; honors and great fame to be acquired by military discipline.

6th House: Diseases and infirmities caused by violence, such as wounds, falls, contusions, bruises, but the sick are easily cured because the physician and surgeon are good; employees are good, strong and profitable.

7th House: Causes a wife to be a virago, headstrong, truthful, but one who rules the house; difficulties and adversaries, which are scarcely restrained by justice.

8th House: The person inquired about is alive; death not painful, or laborious, and caused by some hot humor, by iron or the sword; no legacies or other inheritance.

9th House: Journeys not to be undergone without peril and danger of life, but nevertheless accomplished prosperously and safely; dangerous but successful voyages; a person neither very religious nor conscientious; considerable learning in natural sciences, medicine and the arts.

10th House: Powerful princes, famous for warlike achievements, but their fortunes are changeable because of the fortune of war; judges are cruel and unmerciful; law to be exercised by fire and sword; a mother's life endangered.

11th House: Noble friends, such as frequent the courts of princes, and follow after warfare; many adhere to cruel men: nevertheless much favor from those in high places but their favor is to be suspected.

12th House: Enemies are cruel and pernicious; those that are in prison shall escape and avoid many dangers.

ALBUS

1st House: A person troubled with continual ailments and serious diseases; a man of a short stature, broad chest, large arms, curly hair, a broad full mouth, a great talker and "blabbermouth," but still a jolly and popular fellow.

2nd House: Gain from things that serve for amusement, sports, plays, vile and base arts, but such as are pleasing and delightful; plays, pastimes, dancing and laughter; the thief, and the things stolen are discovered; treasure is not found.

3rd House: Only few relatives; few but difficult voyages; a great deal of cheating.

4th House: Little or no inheritance from the parents; the father is well known but employed in a menial job.

5th House: No children, or if there are any, they will die soon; servile woman; miscarriage or birth of deformed children; rumors are false; no honors to be expected.

6th House: Tedious diseases. Fraudulent and dishonest employees. Diseases of livestock are mortal; the patient mistrusts his physician.

7th House: A beautiful and beloved wife, but who will bear no children. Few but long-lasting lawsuits.

8th House: The person inquired after will die; the dowry of the wife is small, and will be the cause of a lawsuit.

9th House: Voyages bringing but little profit; obstacles for the absent person who will not return; a superstitious man, adhering to false sciences.

10th House: Princes and judges are malevolent; unpleasant and lowly positions; the mother is a whore, or suspected of adultery.

11th House: Dissembling and false friends; varying fortunes and inconstant love.

12th House: Vile but impotent and unsophisticated enemies; the prisoner shall not escape, a great many and various troubles.

CONJUNCTIO

1st House: A prosperous life; a man of a medium size with a long face, plain, fair, small beard, long fingers and thighs, liberal, amiable, and a friend to many people.

2nd House: No riches but free of poverty; the thief is caught and the things stolen are returned; acquires hidden treasure.

3rd House: Various journeys with various successes; reliability of character.

4th House: Average fortune from parents; a good and intelligent father.

5th House: Intelligent children. The expected child is a son. Self-acquired honors, great fame, good reputation; news and rumors found to be true.

6th House: Long and tedious diseases. An experienced physician; faithful and blameless servants; animals profitable.

7th House: A very obedient and intelligent wife, dutiful to her husband; difficult lawsuits with crafty, subtle and malicious adversaries.

8th House: The person inquired after is dead, and some gain is to be derived by his death; a wife shall not be very rich.

9th House: A few journeys, but long and tedious; one that is absent shall return after a long time; of benefit to various arts, sciences and mysteries of religion; gives a quick, perspicuous and efficacious wit.

10th House: Makes princes liberal, affable and benevolent towards those learned in various sciences and secret arts; upright judges who are perspicacious and easily discern the truth of the matter; appointments connected with letters, learning, sound doctrines and sciences; an honest, intelligent and prosperous mother.

11th House: Many friends and especially great favors from high personages.

12th House: Wary and quick-witted enemies; the prisoner remains in prison for a very long time; escape from many dangers.

AMISSIO

1st House: The sick will not live long; a short life; a man of disproportionate limbs, and of a wicked life, spiteful, and marked with a noticeable disability, either lame or maimed.

2nd House: Loss or squandering of money. Poverty. That which is lost or stolen will not be restored; the thief will escape. No luck in finding hoped-for fortune, but loss or damage incurred in seeking it.

3rd House: Death of relatives, or the lack of them, and of friends; no journeys; one is deceived by many people.

4th House: The utter destruction of one's inheritance; the father is poor, and the son will die.

5th House: Death of children, many sorrows; a woman not pregnant or else a miscarriage; no fame or honors; false rumors dispelled.

6th House: The sick recover soon; loss and damage through employees and livestock.

7th House: An adulterous and quarrelsome wife, who, however, will die soon.

8th House: A man is dead; the wife's money is soon used up; no inheritances or legacies.

9th House: No voyages, or if there are any they will cause great loss; a person of vacillating mind, changing his belief frequently, ignorant in every respect.

10th House: Unfortunate nobles, ending their lives in exile and banishment; judges are wicked and corrupted by bribes, positions that will cause loss and harm the reputation; death of a mother.

11th House: Few friends; friendship easily lost; friends become enemies; no influence with those in high places, who may be harmful.

12th House: The enemies will be annihilated. The prisoner will be long in captivity, but is otherwise safe.

PUELLA

1st House: A short life and a weak constitution, medium sized, little fat, but fair, effeminate and luxurious, and one who will incur many troubles and dangers in his lifetime for the love of women.

2nd House: No increase of riches nor greater poverty; lost or stolen things will not be restored; the thief has not left the city; there is no treasure.

3rd House: More sisters than brothers; agreeable voyages; pleasant social surroundings.

4th House: The inherited fortune is small; the harvest will be good.

5th House: The expected child is a girl. No messages; much success with women, and some favors obtained through their influence.

6th House: The patient is very feeble, but will speedily recover. The physician is ignorant and inexperienced, but commonly held in great respect. Useful servants, employees and livestock.

7th House: A beautiful and agreeable wife, living in peace with her husband, but being of an amorous nature desired by many men; no serious lawsuits of any kind, but some minor arguments.

8th House: The person believed to be dead still lives. The dowry is small, but the man is satisfied with it.

9th House: Very few journeys; a religious-minded man without great talents, except for music and singing.

10th House: Not very powerful rulers; govern peaceably and are respected by their neighbors and subjects; they are affable, mild and courteous, enjoying mirth, plays, and hunting; judges are good, godly and merciful; appointments with women of rank.

11th House: Many friends, success with women.

12th House: Few enemies, but trouble with women; prisoners will obtain their freedom through the intercession of friends.

LAETITIA

1st House: Long, prosperous and happy life; a man to outlive and be more successful than all his relations; a tall man with a broad forehead, large teeth, handsome face.

2nd House: Riches and many gains, but great expenses and various changes of fortune; anything lost or stolen is recovered and returned; the thief has fled.

3rd House: Agreeable but short-lived relatives; good voyages; fidelity and sincerity.

4th House: Considerable parental fortune; possessions; a noble father honored by a high appointment; good fortune to be found where expected, but of less value than expected.

5th House: Obedient and good-natured children. A daughter will be born. A good appointment. Rumors and news found to be altogether true; fame after death.

6th House: The sick will recover; reliable employees; profitable livestock.

7th House: A beautiful and young wife; overcoming problems resulting in good fortune in love affairs.

8th House: Legacies; a wife from a wealthy family; the person inquired about is still alive.

9th House: Very few journeys, but those that are undertaken are either matters of diplomacy or pilgrimages; a man of a religious character, not very learned, but intuitive.

10th House: Kings and princes famous for maintaining peace during their times; judges are cruel and severe; honorable positions in the church schools or in law. If the mother is a widow, she will marry again.

11th House: Many friends among the high. Protection.

12th House: Victory over enemies; useful servants; freedom for the prisoner, protection against evils.

ACQUISITIO

1st House: A long life and prosperous old age; a man of medium size with a large head, a distinguished countenance, long nose, large beard, curling hair and fair eyes, who spends much on his meat and drink, but in all other things is sparing and not liberal.

2nd House: Very great riches; thieves caught, whatsoever is lost is recovered.

3rd House: Relatives who are wealthy; many gainful journeys; a man of good faith.

4th House: A large inheritance, many possessions and good harvests; a hidden treasure shall be found; a rich, but covetous father.

5th House: Many children of both sexes, but more males than females; a pregnant woman will give birth without danger; if a question be asked concerning any sex, the answer is masculine; profitable offices and messages; fame does not last long after death; rumors found to be true.

6th House: Many long and serious diseases; danger of death; but an experienced physician. Many servants and profit.

7th House: A rich wife, but either a widow, or a woman of a mature age; long lawsuits and arguments; love and marriage will be affected by chance.

8th House: The person inquired after is dead. Quick death after a disease of only a few days' duration. Profitable legacies. A wife with a rich dowry.

9th House: Long and profitable journeys; if anyone is absent, he shall soon return; a gain from ecclesiasts and scholars; a true scholar.

10th House: Rulers gain new lands; a judge favorable to your cause but he must be bribed; appointment to be very profitable; a rich and happy mother.

11th House: Many useful and profitable friendships. Favors from high personages.

12th House: Many powerful enemies; return of absconding agents and lost livestock; the prisoner will not be released.

POPULUS

1st House: Life of average duration with various diseases and changes of fortune. A fat person of medium stature, perhaps with a mark about his left eye. If a question is propounded concerning the figure of a man, and if there be joined to this figure any of the figures of Saturn or Rubeus, it shows the man to be monstrously and congenitally deformed; but if in the fifth House, and surrounded by malevolent aspects, then that monstrous deformity is in the future.

2nd House: Moderate fortune, obtained with much trouble. The stolen property will not be recovered, nor will that which has been lost or hidden be restored. The thief has not escaped, but is lurking within the city.

3rd House: Few friends, or relatives. Journeys, but with labor and trouble; notwithstanding some profit may accrue from them. A man unstable in his faith; loss by being cheated.

4th House: A sick father with a difficult life, his earthly possessions and inheritances to be taken away; profit to be gained by water; treasure not to be hidden; or if there is any hidden treasure, it will not be found; an inheritance that is difficult to keep.

5th House: Untruthful messages through the mail or by courier; false rumors are exposed which appear to have some truth; a barren woman; pregnancy aborted; an inglorious funeral, and ill report after death.

6th House: Illness, cold chiefly affecting the lower parts of the body; a physician is careless and negligent in administering medicine; and the sick are in danger of death, and scarcely recover at all; the servants or agents are deceitful; bad omen for cattle.

7th House: A fair and pleasant wife, but one that will have many affairs; her love is feigned; weak and impotent adversaries soon to cease lawsuit.

8th House: Sudden death without any long sickness or anguish, often death by water; no inheritance or legacy from the dead; and if there is one, it will be lost by some intervening contention; the dowry of a wife is small or non-existent.

9th House: Deceptive dreams; a vulgar and coarse person; in clerical matters low positions; a person indifferent towards religion and lacking a conscience.

10th House: Kings and princes may be deposed, or suffer continual trouble; appointments connected with water, the navy, bridges, fishing, shores, meadows, and similar things; judges variable and slow in expediting cases; a sick mother will not live long.

11th House: Few friends, and many flatterers; princes give neither favor nor fortune.

12th House: Weak and ignoble enemies; one in prison will not be delivered; danger in water and watery places.

VIA

1st House: A long and prosperous life; a stranger, lean, tall, fair of complexion, having a small beard, liberal and pleasant, but slow and little inclined to labor.

2nd House: Increase of fortune and riches; recovery of anything that is stolen or lost, but the thief leaves the city.

3rd House: Many brothers and relatives; many prosperous journeys; men that are publicly known, honest and of good conversation.

4th House: An honest father; increase of fortune inherited from the father; good harvest; gain in the quarter expected; anything lost is recovered.

5th House: Numerous male children; a son will be born; honorable positions in foreign countries; he becomes well known in many countries.

6th House: Protection against diseases; the patient will quickly recover; useful servants and animals.

7th House: A beautiful and agreeable wife; lasting happiness in marriage; favorable progress of lawsuits; adversaries to be easily overcome, and they shall willingly submit their controversies to the arbitration of good men.

8th House: Death from phlegmatic diseases; to be honest, and of good report; a great legacy, and rich inheritances to be obtained by the dead. If any one has been reported to be dead, he is in fact alive.

9th House: Long journeys by water, especially by sea, very great gains to be acquired thereby; priesthoods, and profits from ecclesiastical employments; men of good religion, upright and constant of faith; true dreams, whose meaning shall suddenly appear; philosophical and grammatical sciences flourish, and those things which appertain to the instruction and bringing up of children.

10th House: Kings and princes happy and fortunate, if they maintain continual peace with their allies; friendship among many princes by diplomacy; public honors and appointments among the common people, or about things pertaining to the water, journeys, or about gathering taxes; judges are just and merciful, and that shall quickly dispatch cases; denotes a respected mother, healthy and of long life.

11th House: Many wealthy and faithful friends in foreign countries, who will help; ingratiates persons with profit and truth among princes who appoint him to positions which will cause him to travel often.

12th House; Many enemies, but such as are not to be feared; profitable agents, servants and animals; whosoever is in prison will escape, or speedily be delivered from thence; preserves a man from the evil accidents of Fortune.

RUBEUS

1st House: A short life and an evil end; a filthy and lazy man with an evil, cruel and malicious face, having some noticeable scar on some part of his body.

2nd House: Poverty; thieves and robbers; people securing a livelihood by using false, wicked, evil and unlawful arts; aids thieves and conceals theft; no treasure to be concealed or sought after.

3rd House: Relatives full of hatred, unpleasant to one another, showing their bad manners and disposition; journeys are very dangerous; treachery.

4th House: Lost and dispersed inheritances; destruction of harvest by bad weather. The father meets a quick and sudden death.

5th House: Many children, who will be wicked and disobedient, or afflict their parents with grief, disgrace and infamy.

6th House: Mortal wounds, sicknesses and diseases; he that is sick shall die; the physician makes mistakes; treacherous servants; danger from livestock or wild animals.

7th House: A wife of ill-repute, publicly adulterous and quarrelsome; enemies are treacherous, and will endeavor to overcome you, by draft and circumvention of the law.

8th House: A violent death by capital punishment, the execution of public justice; the person inquired after is certainly dead; the wife has no dowry.

9th House: Difficult and dangerous journeys with a likelihood of thieves and robbers; a man of heretical opinion who will often deny his faith at every temptation; false and deceitful sciences.

10th House: Cruel and tyrannical princes, who will come to an evil end, being either murdered by their own subjects, or taken captive by their conquerors and put to an ignominious and cruel death, end their lives in prison; judges and officials are corrupt and addicted to usury; the mother shall soon die, leaving a bad reputation behind her.

11th House: No true or faithful friends but men of wicked lives who cause a man to be rejected from the society and conversation of good and noble people.

12th House: Enemies are cruel and traitorous; the prisoner shall come to an evil end; a great many obstacles and perversities.

CARCER

1st House: A short life; a vicious, ugly, and unclean person, who is an object of hate and contempt.

2nd House: Extreme poverty; the thief will be captured; and the thing stolen will be regained; no treasure to be hid.

3rd House: Hatred and dissention amongst relatives; unfortunate journeys; evil company.

4th House: Of no possessions or inheritances, a father to be a wicked man, and to die a sudden and evil death.

5th House: Many children; a barren woman persuades those that are pregnant to have an abortion, or kills the child; no honors; dispels false rumors.

6th House: Long sicknesses; wicked and useless employees; the physician is ignorant.

7th House: The wife is hated by her husband; lawsuits are badly concluded.

8th House: Death by some fall, mischance, or false accusation; men shall be condemned to prison or capital punishment, or they will commit suicide; the wife loses her legacy.

9th House: He that is absent shall not return, having met with an accident on the way; person devoid of religion, conscience or learning.

10th House: Very wicked princes when they are established in their power, becoming wholly addicted to every voluptuous lust, pleasure and tyranny and thereby coming to a bad end; unjust and false judges, the mother is cruel, infamous and adulterous; he obtains no positions except those that are obtained either by lying, or through theft and cruel robbery.

11th House: No friends, nor love, nor favor among men.

12th House: Enemies, detained in prison; many evils.

TRISTITIA

1st House: The life is not necessarily short, but full of trouble; a good-natured person, but solitary and slow in everything; one that is solitary, melancholy and avaricious.

2nd House: Great riches, but they that have them will not enjoy them, but instead hide them, and appear not to be able to afford food; treasure will not be found; the thief escapes and the stolen goods are not restored.

3rd House: Few relatives, who will all die before the questioner. Unfortunate voyages.

4th House: Fields, possessions and inheritances are destroyed; a long-lived and avaricious father who is a miser.

5th House: There are no children, or, if any, they will die young; the expected child is a girl; no honors or fame.

6th House: The sick shall die; employees are good but slothful; stock of low value.

7th House: The wife shall soon die; very painful lawsuits, judgment given against you.

8th House: Death after a long and painful sickness; legacies; the wife has a dowry.

9th House: The absent person is dead and has met with an accident on his journey; unfortunate voyages; a devout man and a profound scholar.

10th House: Severe but just kings; slow but just judges; the mother will be honest and have a long life but with various troubles; the positions obtained are important but not of long duration; occupations connected with water or agriculture, or with theological or philosophical matters.

11th House: Scarcity of friends, and the death of friends; little love or favor.

12th House: No enemies; the prisoner will be condemned; a life with many difficulties.

CAPUT DRACONIS

1st House: Long life and good fortune.

2nd House: Increased riches; a thief concealed and saved treasure hidden.

3rd House: Many relatives; journeys; good faith and credit.

4th House: Wealthy inheritances; the father attains old age.

5th House: Many children; the expected child is a girl or it is likely there will be twins; great honors and fame; the news and rumors are true.

6th House: Increasing sickness and diseases; the physician is learned; many employees and possessions.

7th House: A man shall have many wives; there are many adversaries and lawsuits.

8th House: Death is certain; legacies and inheritances; prospects of a wealthy wife.

9th House: Many journeys; wide-ranging knowledge and faith; those that are absent shall soon return.

10th House: Celebrated rulers; respected judges; important affairs and remunerative occupations.

11th House: Many friends, and the favor of all men.

12th House: Many enemies and many women; the prisoner is detained and heavily punished.

CAUDA DRACONIS

1st House: Short life and bad fortune.

2nd House: Poverty; thief is caught; treasure not hidden.

3rd House: Few relatives; bad reputation.

4th House: Poor legacies; the father dies young.

5th House: Few children; the expected child is a boy; few honors and no fame; rumors are false.

6th House: Good health but an ignorant physician; few possessions.

7th House: No marriage prospects; few enemies.

8th House: Death is not imminent; no legacies; poor wife.

9th House: Few journeys; lack of faith and intelligence; those absent will not return.

10th House: Insignificant rulers and judges; poor job prospects.

11th House: Few friends, unpopular.

12th House: Few enemies; few affairs of the heart; the prisoner is freed without punishment.

CHAPTER 12
SILKWEAVERS AND BONAPARTE'S BOOK OF FATE

Let us take an example and try to judge it thoroughly by using the twelve steps outlined in the last chapter. Suppose we were to ask: Will the proposed business partnership be a success for me?

As before, we generate the four basic Mother figures from the sixteen lines of dots, getting:

```
     *           —  9 dots
     *           — 13 dots
    * *          — 14 dots
    * *          —  8 dots
    ─────────────────────
    * *          — 10 dots
    * *          — 10 dots
     *           —  7 dots
     *           —  7 dots
    ─────────────────────
    * *          — 12 dots
     *           —  7 dots
    * *          —  8 dots
     *           — 11 dots
```

```
        * *        — 12 dots
         *         —  9 dots
         *         —  5 dots
         *         —  9 dots
         ─────────────────────
                   151 = total dots in all
```

Now these become the Mothers, and in the by-now-familiar fashion, are generated the Daughters, Nephews, Witnesses and Judge:

Mothers

IV	III	II	I
* *	* *	* *	*
*	*	* *	*
*	* *	*	* *
*	*	*	* *

Daughters

VIII	VII	VI	V
* *	* *	*	*
*	*	* *	* *
*	* *	*	* *
*	*	*	* *

Nephews

XII	XI	X	IX
* *	* *	* *	*
* *	* *	* *	*
*	*	*	*
* *	*	* *	*

Witnesses

XIV	XIII
* *	*
* *	*
* *	* *
*	*

Judge
XV
```
 *
 *
* *
* *
```

These in turn can be translated to the astrological chart form placing the figures I-XII in the 12 Houses, with the Witnesses and Judge in the center. Let us again use the Golden Dawn system of figure to House allocation:

Mothers:	I	House	10
	II	House	1
	III	House	4
	IV	House	7
Daughters:	V	House	11
	VI	House	2
	VII	House	5
	VIII	House	8
Nephews:	IX	House	12
	X	House	3
	XI	House	6
	XII	House	9

Now the figure in the 1st House is Fortuna Minor, which (again using the Golden Dawn attribution) is Leo ♌, therefore the Zodiacal Signs may be inserted from the 1st House as Leo, in their proper order, through the 2nd House as Virgo, 3rd House as Libra and so on to the 12th House of Cancer.

The planets, of course, are simply the translation of each figure into its appropriate planet (Appendix I). The end result and astro-geomantic chart is shown in Illustration 17.

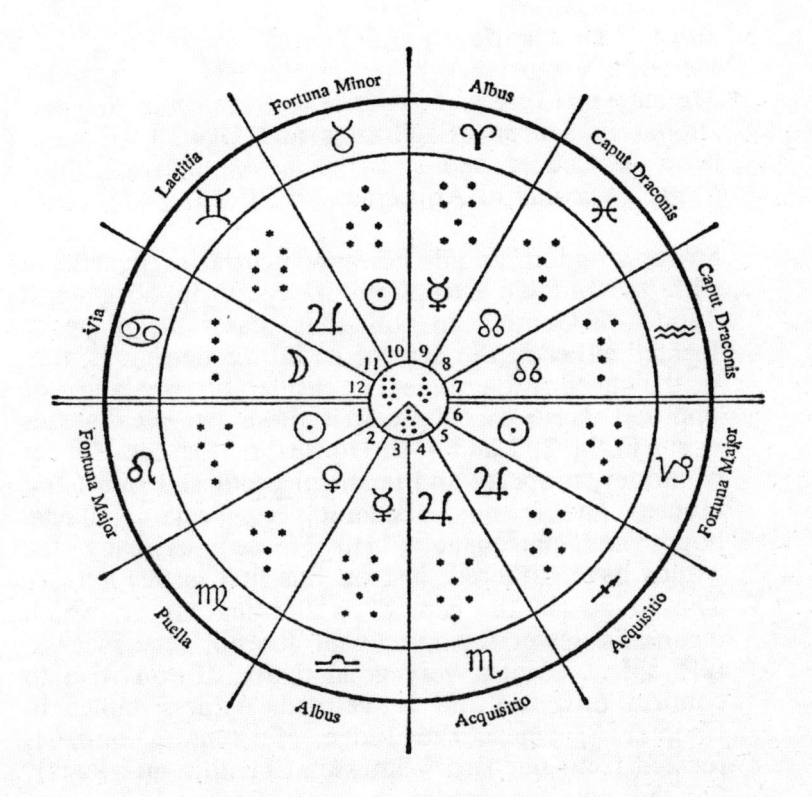

Illustration 17: Will the proposed business partnership be a success for me?

Now we can begin the judgment, taking our interpretation step by step, as in the last chapter. Look at the chart as you go through the following steps.
1. First, neither Rubeus nor Cauda Draconis are in the 1st House, so the figure is safe to proceed with.
2. Noting planets in Signs we have:

Sun in Leo, Capricorn and Taurus
Venus in Virgo
Mercury in Libra and Aries
Jupiter in Scorpio, Sagittarius and Gemini
Moon in Cancer, and
Caput Draconis in Aquarius and Pisces.

So far so good, as all these are neutral or beneficent with the notable exception of Venus in Virgo and Jupiter in Gemini. In both these cases the planet is located either in the Sign of its fall or detriment, that is, the effect of the planet is considerably weakened or opposed. Note especially that these two weaknesses occur in the 2nd and 11th Houses, that is, the Houses of money, property and financial profit and loss (2nd House) and friends, acquaintances, social contacts, hopes and patronage (11th House). Already the clouds have gathered, just on this first inspection.
3. The Judge (in the center) is Fortuna Minor, which means the lesser fortune, lesser (or not very successful) aid . . . not a very good figure. If you wish to confirm this, use the Judge and Witness tables in Chapter 8, where the Judge (Fortuna Minor) is formed from our two Witnesses (Tristitia and Puer). Of the possible range of questions used in these tables, question No. 4 (How will the undertaking end?) seems the most appropriate. The answer as given on page 148 is "the end is of no use," another strong warning against the proposed partnership.
4. Now let us look in the Houses relevant to the question. These are:

House 2: money, property, personal wealth, financial profit and loss, income and expenditure.

House 7: partnerships, among other things.
House 11: friends, acquaintances and social contacts, hopes and wishes, and patronage.

Interestingly we find the same two Houses that sprang to our attention when we examined the planet and Sign combination (step 2). This is a typical example of the way in which a successful geomantic divination begins unmistakably to "fall into place." Again and again the same elements come to our attention confirming and strengthening our verdict.

But, to continue, as we have identified the three relevant Houses, let us look in the tables printed at the end of the previous chapter to interpret the meaning of the geomantic figures found in these three Houses. (See "Table of Geomantic Figures in the Houses.")

Puella in House 2: (Venus in Virgo) No increase of riches nor greater poverty.
Caput Draconis in House 7: (in Aquarius) There are many adversaries and lawsuits.
Laetitia in House 11: (Jupiter in Gemini) Many friends among the high, protection. (This might be interpreted that either your partnership is with someone well placed or that you may escape the worst results of such a partnership by appealing to friends in high places.)

Again the picture is one of warning against the partnership: it will not be profitable and may involve you in costly lawsuits.

5. Of the three geomantic figures in the three relevant Houses, only Caput Draconis appears elsewhere or "springs into" another House. Puella and Laetitia only occur once each in the whole figure.

Caput Draconis "springs into" House 8 where its meaning is: "death is certain; legacies and inheritances; prospects of a wealthy wife." Those parts relevant to financial matters indicate that legacies (inheritance due to someone's death) or a financially advantageous marriage are more likely to be of Profit than the Proposed business Partnership. This may indicate that the venture is better financed from family money rather than that of the partner, although this possibility would involve a second complete reading in itself.

6. To determine the Index (or as it is a money question, the Part of Fortune) add up the total number of dots originally inscribed to form the Mothers. In this example, the total comes to 151 dots. Dividing by 12 gives an answer of 12 with a remainder of 7. The remainder is significant because it places the Part of Fortune in the 7th House. Again we have the 7th House (of the twelve possible Houses) cropping up to reinforce the reading of Caput Draconis in the 7th House, which was: "There are many adversaries and lawsuits." Again our answer is confirmed: don't enter the partnership.
7. We have already discussed the implications of the figures in Houses 2, 7 and 11 under step 4, so we can move on to the next step.
8. As the interpretation so far has been in complete accord with itself there is no need to use the "tiebreaker" table of essential dignities, but just for practice look it up (Illustration 16, page 271.)

Puella in the 2nd House
Caput Draconis in the 7th House
Laetitia in the 11th House.

The first is listed as the strongest possible combinations, while Laetitia and Caput Draconis are neither strong nor weak. This confirms the inadvisability of the partnership without offering much hope of it being salvaged by high-placed friends. Here it is useful to have an assessment of the weight to place on each piece of the interpretation, and the message of Puella and Caput Draconis is unequivocal: don't do it!

9. The outcome, which is the 4th House, shows Acquisitio. In the tables given in Chapter 11, it reads: "A large inheritance . . . a hidden treasure shall be

found; a rich, but covetous father." This harks back to the earlier remarks that in this case inheritance is a more likely source of wealth than the business partnership, and in fact confirms that this will be the eventual outcome.
10. Although the occurrence of the Judge (Figure XV) elsewhere in the figure is a very minor indication, here we will follow it up, just to be complete. Figure XV does in fact appear in House 10, so we can look it up, Fortuna Minor in House 10, where we find a wealth of detail. The only relevant material suggests the death of the parents (the idea of inheritance again) and lawsuits and contentions (outcome of the partnership if undertaken).
11. A Reconciler is not necessary as we already have a wealth of confirmation.
12. The answer is clear, such a partnership would result in no profit, but lawsuits and contention. It is better not to enter into it and money will come from an inheritance instead. How much greater clarity could you expect?

An interesting example of the application of geomancy to political prognostication is to be found in an article entitled a "Singular Fulfilment of Predictions respecting the Spitalfields Silk-weavers," which was published in the early nineteenth-century magazine known as *The Straggling Astrologer*.

This geomantic figure was cast on the earth in Kensington Gardens to ascertain the result of the Bill pending in Parliament in 1824 concerned with the regulation of the Spitalfields silk-weavers: the latter were petitioning against it. The same techniques of interpretation could just as easily be applied to twentieth-century politics. (You will note in this case that the allocation of figures to Houses differs from the one we have been using so far, but is included in Appendix III.)

The interpretation ran as follows: "By examination of the scheme, it will be found that Amissio and Venus rule the 1st House, or Ascendant of the silk-weavers, and admirably represent this business in hand, while Tristitia, a figure of Saturn in the 10th House, is symbolical of a

FIGURE OF GEOMANCY MADE MARCH 20, 1824, 2H. 10M. P.M.
(on the earth in Kensington Gardens)

1st House	2nd House	3rd House	4th House
* * * * * * * * I	* * * * * * * II	* * * * * * * * * III	* * * * * * * * * * * * IV

5th House	6th House	7th House	8th House
* * * * * * V	* * * * * * * * * * * * VI	* * * * * * * * * * VII	* * * * * * * * VIII

9th House	10th House	11th House	12th House
* * * * * * * IX	* * * * * * * * * X	* * * * * * * XI	* * * * * * * XII

```
Right
Witness  * *
         * . *    XIII
         * * *
```

```
Judge  * * * * *
       * * * * *   XV      Reconciler  * *
                                       * . *   XVI
                                       * * *
```

```
Left
Witness  * *
         * . *    XIV
         * * *
```

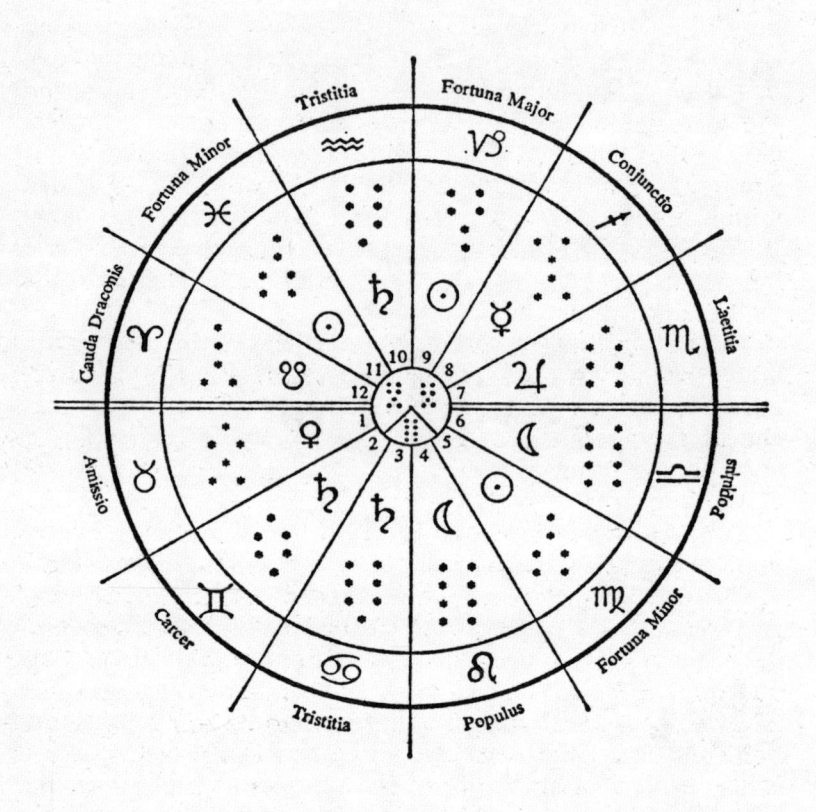

Illustration 18: Figure of geomancy made March 20, 1824, in chart form

decline and falling-off in this trade; and Carcer in the house of wealth and gain (2nd House), a most evil figure, likewise governed by Saturn in his most malevolent debilities, sufficiently indicates great loss both to the workmen and their masters. Part of this evil has already taken place, but much more, unfortunately, remains to come.

"As we were required by several scientific gentlemen to give our opinion whether the bill, then pending, would be passed, or thrown out altogether; we gave it as our decided opinion, that the opponents of this industrious and numerous class of manufacturers, would be the likeliest to gain the victory; but as the two witnesses are ruled by Mercury [both being Albus], and Populus the Judge . . . while the 16th figure [the Reconciler, formed from Figures I and XV] moves into the Ascendant [i.e. is the same as the figure in House I, Amissio], we expected that the bill would receive a partial alteration favourable to the petitioners against it."

As history has recorded, every part of the prediction was verified. To continue with this prediction, it is interesting to see the wide range of details derived from this chart by the geomancer.

"There are several other topics relative to the above class of persons, which may be gathered from the figure: —as, for instance, Fortuna Major in the 9th House, shewing success in this manufacture to foreigners. Cauda Draconis in the 12th house, denoting coolness in the petitioners' friends, and many secret enemies; and Populus, in the 4th house, denoting the depreciation of the article in question; while the fixed nature of several significators are likely to cause the whole of these evils to be of long duration, and upon the increase. Conjunctio in the 8th house is also typical of short life to the principal agitators of the bill and its supporters, which is yet to be fulfilled, although not many seasons will elapse before this will be verified!"

Politics might be all the richer for such deliberations, and a whole new element would be added to polling!

Interestingly, the magazine *The Straggling Astrologer* in which this divination first appeared was edited by Robert Cross Smith, who was the first astrologer to use the pseudonym "Raphael," and was also not above a little chicanery when it came to promoting his magazine's circulation. Ellis Howe, the astrological historian, says of Smith that, he "was in the habit of 'discovering' pseudo-Napoleonic manuscripts, and was as assiduous in attributing occult interest to Napoleon as a later generation was in connection with Adolph Hitler." Two years before the publication of the magazine, Smith had published a book called *The Philosophical Merlin*, which purported to have been Napoleon's bedside oracle which helped him win more than half of Europe, and gave him counsel in each of his battles.

In the same year as *The Philosophical Merlin* came out, another book appeared, edited by Herman Kirchenhoffer, also purporting to have belonged to Napoleon: it was called *Napoleon's Book of Fate*. Both books make use of geomantic figures, but both are quite different in style. The first, the *Philosophical Merlin* which is reproduced in Appendix IX is a fairly orthodox geomantic text, while the second (which ran through many editions) is not detailed here because it relies on a form of geomancy in which the figures each have *five* lines of odd or even dots rather than the traditional four. Anyway the latter is easily available in Richard Deacon's *The Book of Fate*, (published, London 1976). It even appeared as recently as 1962 disguised as *The Ladies Oracle* and erroneously ascribed to "Cornelius Agrippa, being an infallible prophet of the male sex"; enough to make the original Agrippa turn in his grave!

The Book of Fate by Kirchenhoffer claims an Egyptian origin and was allegedly discovered by Napoleon in a royal tomb near Thebes during his Egyptian campaign in 1798. It was then supposed to have been translated out of the hieroglyphics into French by a Copt (about a thousand years after the knowledge of the meaning of the hieroglyphs had died out among the indigenous Coptic population, and almost a quarter of a century before Champollion *re*discovered their meaning). The manuscript was then translated into German (for saftey!) and in this form found its way in Kirchenhoffer's hands. Unfortunately the book is simply an extension of geomancy, with a simplified system for generating one Mother figure, and is almost certainly a translation from some earlier German book on geomancy. It consists of a series of questions to which a long list of possible answers are appended, appropriately glamorized by the addition of Napoleon and Egyptology, both of which were the rage at the time.

As Richard Deacon says of it: "*The Book of Fate* became a talking point at fashionable London dinner parties, for the moment that Napoleon died a fickle British public turned him from an ogre through which they threatened recalcitrant children into a romantic legend of chivalry and genius. They became eager to learn every possible scrap of gossip about the man who so very nearly became Master of the World. The book itself was sometimes used, as *The Fashion Gazette* had suggested, for party games and refined but shy young ladies surreptitiously consulted it in the privacy of their bedrooms to find out what kind of husbands they could expect. There were plenty who scoffed, of course, but they were outnumbered by those who actually consulted the book."

Both *The Book of Fate* and the *Philosophical Merlin* claim that the manuscript belonged to the French Emperor and was lost by him at the battle of Leipzig, after which (of course) he was never again completely victorious. It is however rather difficult to see how he won battles using the technique described in either book, for *The Book of Fate* specializes in questions like:

> "Inform me of any or all particulars relating to the woman I shall marry.
> Shall I live to an old age?
> Shall I have to travel far by sea or land, or reside in foreign territories?
> Shall I make or lose my fortune by gambling?
> Will the patient recover from illness?
> Does the person whom I love, love and esteem me?
> Have I any, or many enemies?
> Will my name be immortalised and will posterity applaud it?
> Will my beloved prove true in my absence?
> Shall I ever recover from my present misfortune?"

The Philosophical Merlin however is not constructed in the same manner, and consists of an interpretation of the sixteen traditional geomantic figures; it seems, however, to be equally as useless for determining military strategy! For details of its method of operation and complete copies of its table of geomantic figures, refer to Appendix IX.

Such were some of the manifestations of geomancy in the nineteenth century: masquerading as Napoleon's bedside book or as the secrets of an ancient Egyptian papyrus. As we have already seen, Europe knew the secrets of geomancy long before either Robert Cross Smith or Napoleon.

Illustration 19: Typical Renaissance Astro-geomantic Chart (From Gerard Cremonensis *Of Astronomical Geomancy*)

CHAPTER 13
GERARD OF CREMONA'S ASTRO-GEOMANCY

There is yet another method of astrological geomancy described by Gerard Cremonensis, or Gerard of Cremona, a medieval translator of Ptolemy's classic astronomy and astrology.

Gerard spent his early years in the great Moorish schools of Toledo, that eerie city high up on the cliffs above the Tagus river not far from Madrid. In those days it was the capital of Spain and one of the main intellectual capitals of Europe.

Here where magic was taught as a university subject and lectured to large groups of students by the most respected teachers of the day, both Moslem and Spanish, Gerard thrived, and absorbed Latin and Arabic at a prodigious rate. Early in his career he determined to devote the rest of his life to translating Arabic scientific and magical treatises into Latin, the common language of the rest of Europe. His most important translation was Ptolemy's *Almagest* which together with Ptolemy's other work, the *Tetrabiblos*, formed the base of the whole structure of astronomy and astrology in medieval Europe for centuries to come. He translated at least sixty-six other treaties, of which his treatise on astrological geomancy, translated from Arabic in the late twelfth century, forms the main source of this chapter.

The method is quite simple, but requires a good knowledge of the character of the various planets and Signs. Enough detail of the nature of the planets has already been given to use the system, although study of standard texts on astrology such as Margaret Hone's *Text Book of Modern Astrology* would also be helpful.

Before we begin, it is necessary to draw up a blank map of the heavens with the same House grid as we used before. Now for the method.

Ascendant

Again it is not necessary to consult the Ephemeris for mathematical details of the Ascendant, because the Ascendant is determined by geomancy.

First, four lines of dots are made in the usual manner. These generate a geomantic figure. Look this up in Appendix I to determine its corresponding Zodiacal Sign which becomes the Sign in the Ascendant or 1st House.

(The Sign corresponding with the figure can be determined from the table in Chapter 6, which is based on Golden Dawn ascriptions, or if you wish to be consistent with Gerard of Cremona's usage, then refer to Appendix I and use column 5.)

In the 2nd House put the next Zodiacal Sign, in the 3rd House the Sign after that, following the order of the Zodiac right around the twelve Houses. For example, if the geomantic figure derived from the four lines is Conjunctio, then Virgo should be marked down in the Ascendant, or House I. Now proceeding anti-clockwise you should mark in Libra in House 2, Scorpio in House 3, Sagittarius in House 4, and so on.

Planets

Next, make another set of four lines of dots to determine the position of the Sun, as you did to ascertain the

Ascendant. Count off these dots in groups of twelve until you are left with twelve or less. This number will indicate the House in which you should put the Sun.

Repeat this process for the other planets but be sure always to do them in this order: Sun, Moon, Venus, Mercury, Saturn, Jupiter, Mars, Caput Draconis and Cauda Draconis. Remember that the last two, although the names of geomantic figures, are also positions on the map of the heavens, and for the purposes of deciding their House, should be treated as if they were planets. Now, write each planet, including Cauda and Caput Draconis in its appropriate House.

And that is the sum total of the mechanics. Easy, isn't it? However what Gerard makes easy in terms of the mechanics of constructing the chart, he makes up for in terms of interpretation, as it is here that your knowledge of the astrological meanings comes to the aid of your interpretive ability.

Before going on any further let us recapitulate the sequence of steps:

1. Make four lines of dots. These give you the figure which determines which Zodiacal Sign goes into the 1st House or Ascendant.
2. Write this Sign into the chart, then taking the Zodiacal Signs in their normal order, write in the 2nd, 3rd, and 4th House's Sign, through to the 12th House.
3. Now for the planets. Draw four up lines of dots for each. Count off twelves until there is a remainder indivisible by twelve. This gives you the House number for that planet. If the remainder is zero, then put the planet in the 12th House.
4. The planets should always be caluculated in this order:

Sun	☉
Moon	☽
Venus	♀
Mercury	☿
Saturn	♄
Jupiter	♃
Mars	♂
Caput Draconis	☊
Cauda Draconis	☋

5. Interpret the resulting chart. Let's illustrate this by taking a particular example.

Example

You might wish to know if a particular person will recover from an illness. You draw out your four random lines of dots while concentrating on the question.

If for example the top line of dots is even, the next is odd, the third is even and the bottom line odd, then the figure formed is Acquisitio. By Gerard's table of Zodiacal attributions this is Aries ♈, so you put Aries in the 1st House or Ascendant.

(If you had been using the Golden Dawn table, you would have to put Sagittarius in the Ascendant. The idea is to select one attribution system and stick to it. In this case we are using Gerard's atttributions because it is his particular method.)

Next we again draw four lines of random dots for the Sun and in counting off sets of twelve we are left with nine. Therefore the Sun ☉ is inserted in the 9th House.

Again we mark down the dots, and after division, a remainder of two is left. Now take the next planet in order the Moon ☾, and place it in the 2nd House. By the same process:

Venus ♀ goes into the 12th House

Mercury ☿ goes into the 7th House

Saturn ♄ goes into the 8th House

Jupiter ♃ goes into the 12th House

Mars ♂ goes into the 8th House

Caput Draconis ☊ goes into the 5th House

Cauda Draconis ☋ goes into the 1st House, or Ascendant.

As you can see, in this system of astrological geomancy

it is possible for more than one planet to go into the same House: in this case, Venus and Jupiter are both in the 12th House, while Saturn and Mars share the 8th House. The figure when drawn up is shown in Illustration 20.

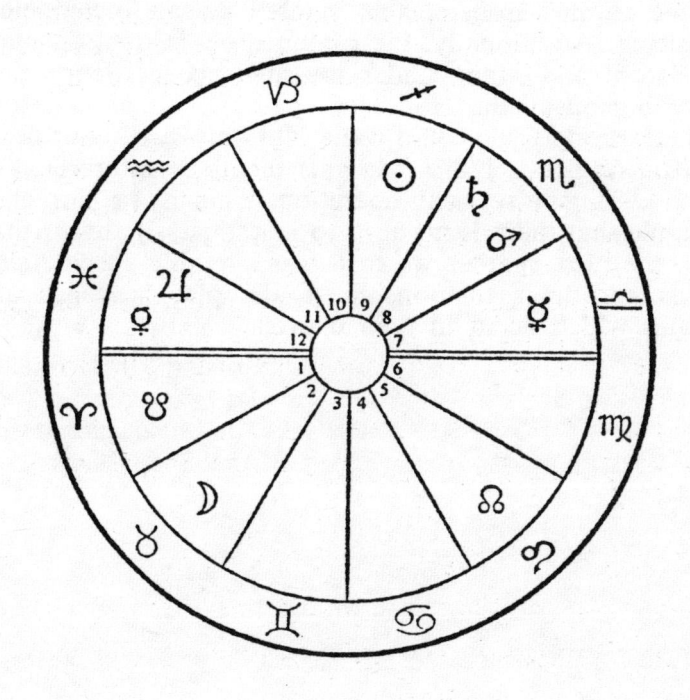

Illustration 20: Modern astro-geomantic figure

Interpretation

In this case there is hardly any possibility of the patient recovering. The presence of Cauda Draconis, the dreaded tail of the dragon, in the crucial 1st House or Ascendant is a very bad sign. As the 1st House symbolizes the person himself, then the prediction is "the lower threshold" or death. Also in the tables of geomantic figures in the Houses, this symbolizes an incompetent physician. Additionally, the presence of the malefic planets Saturn and Mars, under the influence of Scorpio, in the 8th House (the House of death) is about as strong an indication as you could want. Not only death, but death by iron or fire is indicated. This might be interpreted as death during a surgical operation. This is such a clear example that there is no need to investigate it any further.

In the next chapter we turn to examining specific situations and their relationship to the planets, Signs and Houses which occur in their charts.

CHAPTER 14

QUESTIONS FOR ALL THE HOUSES

This chapter is a practice chapter, where sample questions are interpreted not strictly according to the formal technique already outlined, but in a rather condensed form designed to highlight the most important astrological aspects. This chapter is in fact for the student who has already used the previous techniques to the point where he is totally familiar with them and wishes to go on to slightly more difficult interpretation which demands a more thorough astrological knowledge. It is also for the student of astrology who wishes to apply his existing knowledge more closely to astro-geomancy, to bring both more technical knowledge into play and also to broaden his ability to use his intuition in weighing the material so derived.

Now for practice, take one question from the selection of questions in the latter half of this chapter and apply it to someone or something you wish to know, then:
1. Cast the astro-geomantic chart as already described.
2. Interpret it in the usual manner.
3. Tabulate the following:

a) House number of the question.
b) All planets in this House.
c) The astrological Sign in this House.
d) The planet ruling this Sign or Lord of the Sign. (from the table of planetary rulers on page 233).
a) Look in the geomantic chart to see if the planet written down in d) above shares the House it is actually located in, with any other planets. If it does, write these down.

4. Look up the question in this chapter and read off the answer by comparing it with your answers in step 3 above.

As many other factors as there are combinations of Houses, Signs and planets can be taken into account according to your degree of practice and desire for detailed information, but in most cases the above salient points should be enough to form your judgment, and by comparing them with the question, your interpretive ability will be exercised and expanded. After a while you can incorporate these added tests into your ordinary divinations. Remember that this chapter is just experimental and not a new set of rules: it is designed for *practice* not theory.

Before considering each House in detail, it is necessary to remember which planets are "friendly" with one another and which are not. Planets are said to be friends, when they agree in one quality, as Mars and the Sun because both their natures are hot and dry; Venus and the Moon agree because they are both cold and moist; or when planets agree in substance and nature, as Jupiter and Venus are friends; or when the House of one is the exaltation of another, or vice versa.

More simply put, the planets can be divided into "malefic," "benefic" or "neutral." The Sun and Moon are often referred to as the "two luminaries," the first of the day the second of the night. Mercury of course is the tricky messenger of the gods flirting with both good and evil, scholars and thieves. Traditionally, Venus and Jupiter are the two benefics, the "Lesser Fortune" and the "Greater Fortune," fortunate or "lucky" planets; Mars and Saturn are the two malefics, the "Lesser" and "Greater Infortune," "evil" or "unlucky"; Sun, Moon and Mercury are "variable," becoming "good" or "bad" according to their positions and the other planets that are combined in any way with them.

Malefic		Benefic		Neutral	
Mars	♂	Venus	♀	Sun	☉
Saturn	♄	Jupiter	♃	Moon	☾
				Mercury	☿

In the rest of the chapter examples of possible interpretations are given for each House. Obviously, there are millions of combinations possible, but the following questions and their interpretations should provide you with enough examples to put you on the right track.

QUESTIONS OF THE 1ST HOUSE

If You Wish to Know How Long Anybody Will Live

Find the planet which is ruler of the Sign in the 1st House(the Ascendant). If this planet is in an Angular House (the 1st, 4th, 7th and 10th) then the person will have a long life. If the planet is in a Cadent House, (the 3rd, 6th, 9th and 12th) he will have a short life. If however the planet is found in a Succedent House (the 2nd, 5th, 8th and 11th) his lifespan will be between the two other extremes.

For example, if the Sign Taurus is in the 1st House, then its ruler is Venus, so you look in the chart for Venus. In this case, Venus is in the 9th House which is a Cadent House. From this you can judge that the life expectancy is short, especially as Saturn is in the 1st House itself. (See Illustration 21.)

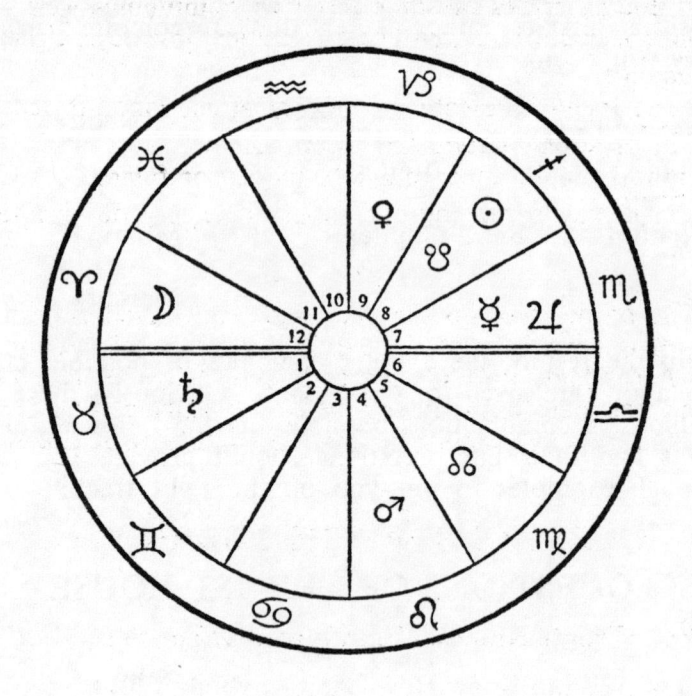

Illustration 21: Life expectancy in the 1st House

To Discover the Nature of the Question Being Asked You by Somebody Else

Again examine the Ascendant (the Sign in the 1st House). Write down the planet ruling it. The nature of the question being asked will be related to the nature of this planet (as the 1st House governs the questioner himself). For example, if the planet is:

<u>Sun</u>: the question could concern his health or possibly a fear he has of someone else.
<u>Venus</u>: it may concern matters of love or something connected with the arts.

Mercury: it may indicate an inquiry about something lost, illness, books or some letter or communications.
Moon: it could be a matter of emotions, journeys, dreams or change.
Saturn: it may indicate an inquiry about land, property, death, or some particularly deep sorrow.
Jupiter: it might concern a job, money or fame.
Mars: it may be an inquiry about an enemy or disagreement.

The scope is of course very wide, but given a certain degree of sensitivity plus the evidence of the planet ruling the Ascendant, it is often possible to tell someone else what their question concerns before actually getting down to answering it. Facility in this comes only with practice.

QUESTIONS OF THE 2ND HOUSE

If You Want to Know a Man's Financial Position

Pick out the Sign in the 2nd House and identify its ruling planet. Find this planet elsewhere in the chart. If this planet shares its house with a good planet (Venus, Jupiter or the Sun) and there is also a good planet in the 2nd house itself then the person is rich.

Conversely, if the reverse is true and the planet ruling the Sign in the 2nd House shares its House with Saturn, Mars or Cauda Draconis, then the person is poor. For example, if the 2nd House contains Cancer and you find its ruler, the Moon, elsewhere in the chart sharing a House with Saturn, then the person concerned is certainly broke. (See Illustration 22.)

Whether You Will Have a Loaned Possession Returned to You

Again use the planet ruling the Sign in the 2nd House to determine the advisability of a loan.

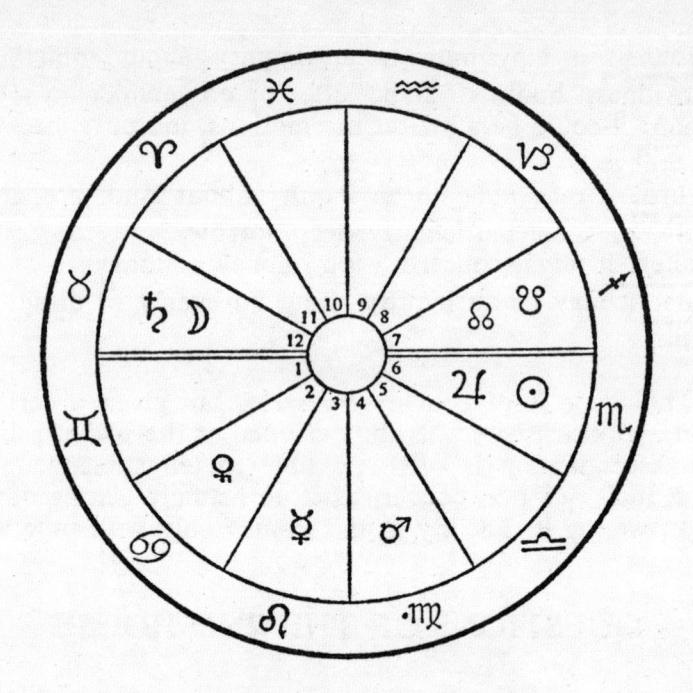

Illustration 22: Finance in the 2nd House

If you are thinking of lending money to someone you know, and a benefic planet occurs in the 2nd House while the ruler of the Sign in the House occurs in the 4th House with Jupiter then the loan seems feasible. On the other hand, if the 2nd House has Scorpio, whose ruler is Mars (conflict) and Mars is located in another House, with Saturn, in opposition (i.e. 180° away) to the 2nd House, then there is no way you should lend this money. (See Illustration 23.)

QUESTIONS OF THE 3RD HOUSE

These include questions concerning study, writing, publicity agencies and similar Mercurial activities as well as neighbors and family. For this House then it is imperative that the position of Mercury be carefully assessed,

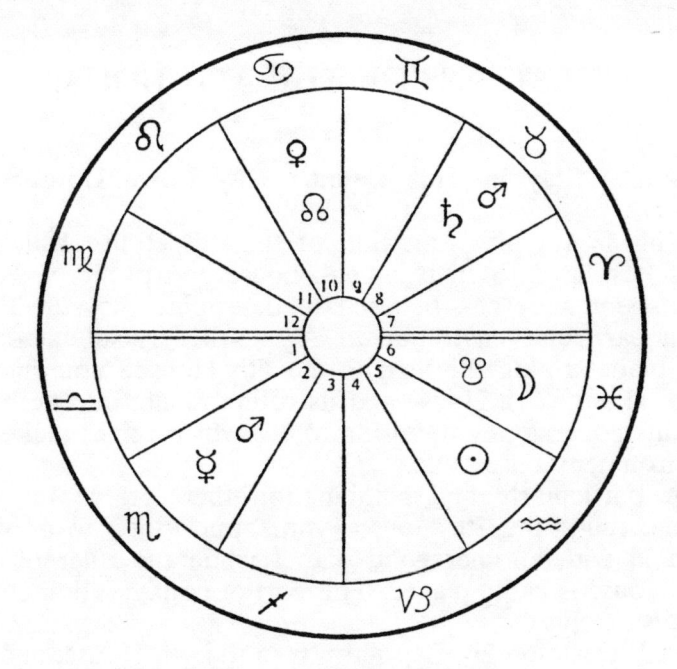

Illustration 23: Loans in the 2nd House

along with the usual considerations of the planet ruling the Sign in this House, and its location elsewhere in the chart.

Often in this House, because it is the House of family, planets may indicate individual family members (rather like a significator in a Tarot divination).

Mars, Sun, Saturn, Jupiter or Caput Draconis may indicate a male member of the family, while Moon, Venus or Cauda Draconis may indicate a female member of the family. Mercury is sexually ambiguous but may indicate predominantly male characteristics when near masculine planets or located in a masculine Zodiacal Sign (Aries, Gemini, Leo, Libra, Sagittarius or Aquarius). The reverse is true of proximity to female planets or female Zodiacal Signs.

QUESTIONS OF THE 4TH HOUSE

Should I Stay in This Country/City/Town/House?

This is a typical question of the 4th House which is closely related to environment, house and property. Here astro-geomancy can be used to determine the suitability of a particular environment. Again the crucial factor is the planet ruling the Sign in the 4th House. You should also take the 7th House and its ruling planet into account as this governs any opposing forces which might make an environment unsuitable.

A particularly bad combination therefore is for the planet ruling the 7th House (your opposition) to be well located with another good planet while the ruler of the 4th House is badly placed. This sort of configuration could be disastrous.

In Illustration 24, Capricorn is in the 4th House, and its ruler (Saturn) is in opposition to it and joined with that particularly evil sign, Cauda Draconis. The ruler of the 7th House however is Mars and it is well placed to its own House and shares the 11th House with the Sun, showing that opposition is strong and well favored. You would probably do better in a new environment.

If You Want To Know When an Absent Person Will Return

Here it is difficult to judge the time factor from the chart, as in any form of prediction, but on the whole if the planet ruling the 1st House is located in an Angular House, then the person should return within the year. If the ruler of the 4th House is in his own House, then the travelers' return is imminent.

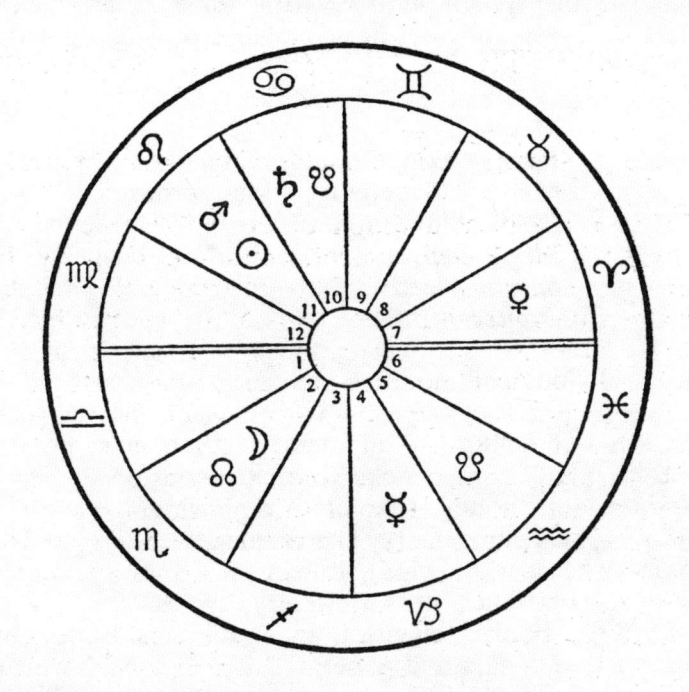

Illustration 24: Location in the 4th House

Whether There Is To Be a Glut or Shortage of Any Particular Commodity.

Questions concerning the conditions of markets of various sorts can be asked of the 4th House, but a word of warning first. If you hope to speculate on the information gained here, be very careful. For example, if your divination showed a likelihood of a shortage of sugar, you might decide that it would be worthwhile buying some of that commodity in anticipation of a consequent price rise. However, as there is no *time* indication you might find that a fall in the price comes before a later rise, and the rise might happen next week or next year.

Generally however, the presence of the relevant planet in an Angular House might mean a scarcity of that commodity. In contrast, the Cadent Houses tend to indicate a glut or plenty. Of course, with some items such as metals, it is very obvious which planet provides the right indication.

> *Mars*—iron
> *Venus*—copper
> *Mercury*—mercury, brass, bronze
> *Sun*—gold
> *Moon*—silver
> *Saturn*—lead
> *Jupiter*—tin

Less obvious commodities include:

Saturn—agricultural equipment, leather, nuts, potatoes and corn, bricks, cement, houses.
Jupiter—oil, honey, silk, cloth and wine.
Mars—meat, machinery, armaments.
Sun—wheat, wine, cloth, horses.
Venus—perfumes, furs, jewelery, wines.
Mercury—books, television and radio sets, barley, millet, cars and paper.
Moon—dairy products, poultry, eggs, pearls, water.

Be careful to take into account the Signs in which the planets appear as this will strengthen or weaken the indication. The "Table of Essential Dignities" (Illustration 16, page 271) will help to indicate if a shortage or a glut is pronounced enough to show up in major price changes and also indicate the duration of the trend.

QUESTIONS OF THE 5TH HOUSE

To Discover If a Woman Is Pregnant or Not

This house governs children generally and can be used to predict the number of children a woman might have, or the outcome of a particular pregnancy. Testing for pregnancy is better left to a doctor, but in the Middle Ages geomancy often took the place of physical examination (even doctors resorted to it) and the 5th House was often consulted in an age of non-existent or uncertain contraception. The aspects most likely to indicate pregnancy outnumber those indicating the reverse. They include:

a) Planet ruling the Ascendant located in the 7th or 5th House.
b) Planet ruling the 5th House located in the 1st House.
c) Planet ruling the 5th House located in the 7th House.

And so on for another seven or more possible combinations. The only really definite contra-indications are the presence of Leo or Virgo in the 1st or 5th House.

Will the Woman Miscarry?

The possibility of miscarriage is indicated traditionally by a number of configurations but as the incidence of miscarriage is considerably lower these days, only something as drastic as Cauda Draconis in the Ascendant (or 1st House) or Mars together with either the Moon or Saturn in the 1st, 7th or 10th House could indicate this possibility. A mutable Sign (Gemini, Virgo, Sagittarius or Pisces) in the 1st House will accentuate this possibility.

Will the Child Be a Boy or Girl?

This age-old chestnut can only be cracked by geomantic divination if the Signs are unmistakably male or unmistakably female.

Check the ruler of the Sign in the 1st House. If this planet is masculine (Mars, Jupiter, Saturn, Sun) and is located in another part of the chart in a masculine Sign, then the chances are the child will be a boy. If the vast majority of the planets are in masculine Signs then this clinches it. The reverse of course is true of a female planet in a female Sign.

Will the Child Be Legitimate?

This is another tricky question which the old writers on geomancy thought was answered in the negative if Saturn, Mars or Cauda Draconis appeared in the 5th House, or appeared elsewhere but in the same house as the planet ruling the 5th House.

Are the Rumors I Hear True or False?

The principle behind the interpretation of this question is rather strange, for if a malefic planet (Saturn, Mars or Cauda Draconis) appears in the 1st House then the rumors are false, but if a benefic planet (Sun, Jupiter or Caput Draconis) appears in this House, then the rumors are true.

Mercury being god of communications and of liars is a key witness for this question: if it is in the 1st House then the news is untrue. The Moon in the same place attests that the news is true.

Will My Absent Friend or Lover Return and When?

The planets ruling the 1st and 5th Houses and their placing with respect to each other and the rest of the planets are the key to this question.

QUESTIONS OF THE 6TH HOUSE

If a Sick Person Will Recover

Although this question is appropriate to the 6th House, it is important to also consult the 1st House, for if Saturn, Mars or Cauda Draconis are found in the latter, then rapid recovery is not indicated. If the same malefic planets are found in the 8th House (the House of death) then recovery is unlikely.

Again, if benefic or malefic planets are located in the Angular Houses (1st, 4th, 7th and 10th) then the chances of recovery are increased or reduced respectively, as the Angular Houses have a much stronger bearing on any question than the Succedent or Cadent Houses.

A rapid recovery would be indicated by such a chart as the following, where benefic planets are found in the 1st, 6th and 8th Houses (being the Ascendant and the Houses of sickness, respectively). Also the ruler of the 1st House (Venus ruling Libra) is *not* located in the 8th House, thereby not connecting the Ascendant with the House of death. Further, Venus also rules the 8th House indicating benefic influence here. (See Illustration 25.) Similar configurations, where the benefics were located in the Angular Houses and the ruler of the 1st House is

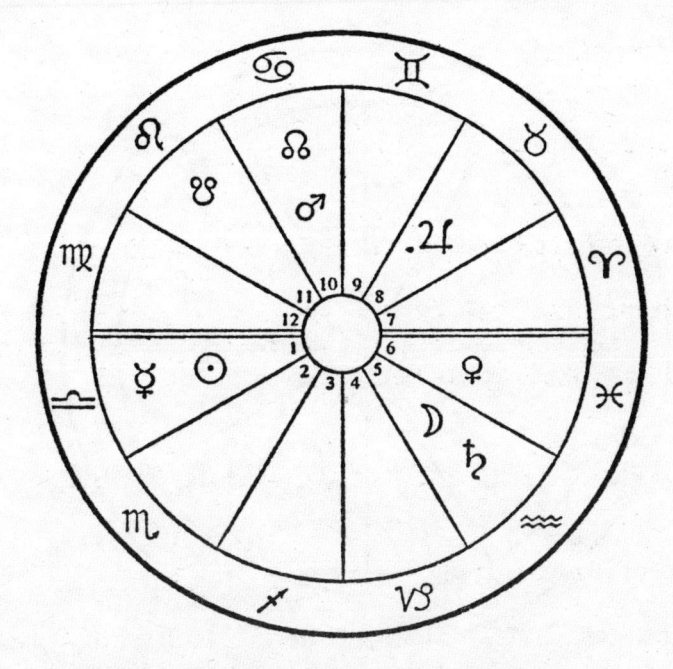

Illustration 25: Illness in the 6th House

not associated with the 8th House also bode for a quick recovery.

How Will a Sick Person Be Cured? How Could the Treatment Be Improved?

With questions of illness you can allocate the 1st House to the physician, the 10th to the sick person, the 7th to the illness, and the 4th to the medicine or treatment prescribed, to determine which if any of the factors is responsible for the failure or success of a treatment.

Here simply the presence of malefic or benefic planets in any of the above Houses, indicates where the work needs to be done or changes made (malefic planets in the relevant Houses) or where success and a cure is likely to come from (benefic in the relevant Houses).

For example, in Illustration 26, the doctor is on the

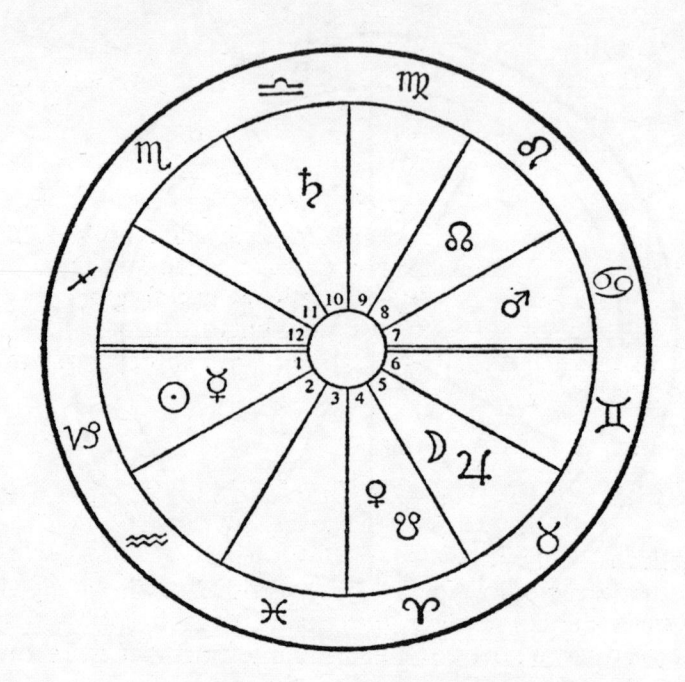

Illustration 26: Medication in the 6th House

right track (1st House) but the patient is not responding to the treatment (in the 10th House, Saturn is a planet of inertia). The illness is of a feverish nature (Mars disagreeing with Cancer in the 7th House) but the treatment is not able to cope with it (Venus weakened by Cauda Draconis in the 4th House) and should be stronger (Mars being the ruler of Aries which is the Sign in the 4th House).

In Which Part of the Body Does a Sick Person Suffer?

From Illustration 26, it can be seen that the illness (7th House) has the Sign Cancer which is attributed to the stomach, so it is likely that the illness is based here. The other Signs correspond to the body as follows:—

♈	Aries	head and face
♉	Taurus	neck and throat
♊	Gemini	shoulders, arms, lungs, nervous system
♋	Cancer	stomach
♌	Leo	spine, back and heart
♍	Virgo	Bowels and fingers
♎	Libra	kidneys, lumbar region and skin
♏	Scorpio	genitals and excretory organs
♐	Sagittarius	hips, buttocks and thighs
♑	Capricorn	bones and knees
♒	Aquarius	ankles and circulatory system
♓	Pisces	feet

QUESTIONS OF THE 7TH HOUSE

Thieves seem to be an intrinsic part of life both now and in the Middle Ages. Consequently, a whole barrage of questions concerning the thief, the thing stolen and their recovery can be found in many books of geomancy.

Shall My Stolen Property Be Returned To Me?

In this case, you would examine the planet ruling the Sign in the 7th House. If it is located in the 1st House, then the goods will be recovered. If the reverse is true, then a considerable time will elapse before they are seen again. Other combinations of aspects or of the positioning of these two planets give a greater or lesser chance of recovery.

In Which Direction or To Which Country Has The Thief Escaped To?

Check out the planet ruling the Sign in the 7th House. Find the planet elsewhere in the chart and note which Sign it resides in.

If it is in Aries then the thief has escaped towards the east and so on as below:

Taurus	—	SE
Gemini	—	SW
Cancer	—	N
Leo	—	NE
Virgo	—	SW
Libra	—	W
Scorpio	—	NW
Sagittarius	—	NE
Capricorn	—	S
Aquarius	—	NW
Pisces	—	NW

If You Wish To Know Whether a Marriage Will Take Place

This could be a useful piece of information, and can be ascertained by taking the planet ruling the 1st House as symbolic of the person making the inquiry, while the planet ruling the 7th House symbolizes the prospective partner.

Now if either of the planets representing both parties fall in the same House, or if either falls in the 7th House, the marriage will certainly take place.

Originally the early geomantic texts only made provision for inquiries initiated by the man, but in this era of sexual equality the technique has been modified to suit the needs of either party. In the early texts, the Moon symbolized the man's ideal partner, and its location in a House with the planet representing his prospective partner was a very good sign. The reverse of course is true, that the Sun indicates the woman's ideal partner.

Does My Wife Mistress Have Another Lover?

The 7th House which rules marriage and other partnerships is the obvious House together with the 5th (recreation and procreation) to look for an answer to this and associated questions.

If you find Mars in the 7th House, she does not have another lover. However if Saturn is located in this House the reverse is true; she in fact loves someone else, but has not made love with him yet! Cauda Draconis (the lower threshold) in this house indicates that they are in fact sleeping together. Jupiter indicates that she barely escapes being chaste while Venus on the surface indicates whorish behavior but may in fact be deceptive and indicate the opposite. Mercury being fickle and changeable indicates, when in this House, a past but not current liaison. The Moon likewise indicates the possibility of an affair in the future. The two strong indications of virtue in these matters is the presence of either the Sun or Caput Draconis in this House.

Shall the Friendship or Partnership That I Desire Take Place?

Here general indications such as benefic planets in the 1st and 7th House will provide the clue while malefic planets in these locations suggest that such a partnership is best not entered into.

Which of the Friends or Partners Shall Gain Most From the Union?

This is a usefully specific question to ask when about to contract a partnership. Look at the 2nd House and the planet ruling the Sign therein for an indication of the degree of gain of the questioner, and in the 8th House and the location of the planet ruling its Sign for the degree of gain of the other party to the contract. The degree of strength and the malefic or benefic nature of each of these will indicate whether the questioner or the other party will find the contract most profitable.

If You Want to Know If Two People Will Love One Another?

This is easily completed by examining the planets ruling the Signs found in the 1st and 7th Houses respectively. If they are compatible (i.e. both benefics) then the two people will get on well, but if the planets are not of a similar nature then the two people concerned will also not be compatible.

Who Will Win the War?

Strangely enough the 7th House is also concerned with matters of warfare and straightforward questions such as who will win the war? can be answered by reference to the 1st House (representing the questioner) and the 7th House (representing his adversary), and their ruling planets will provide you with information on the relative strengths and likelihood of victory of both sides.

QUESTIONS OF THE 8TH HOUSE

How Shall I Die?

This House concerns death and all the professions connected with it. It is also said to specify the type of death which may befall the questioner.

The traditional answers to the geomantic interpretation of this House are not as relevant today, as for example the number of people who "shall die by a beast" at least in the Western world has diminished to almost non-existence, while deaths attributable to various "mechanical beasts" from the car onwards is soaring yearly.

Traditionally, Leo or Scorpio located in the 8th House indicates death by a wild animal, while Saturn in the 8th House or with the planet ruling its Sign, in Scorpio, Cancer or Pisces means death by water. Death by fire is indicated by the presence of Mars, Saturn or Cauda Draconis in the 8th House or in another House with the planet ruling the 8th. Presumably the latter could also indicate death by car, especially if sharing the House with Mercury, god of transport. Opposed to these less pleasannt exits, Jupiter, the Sun, Caput Draconis and Venus located in the 8th House indicate a natural death.

QUESTIONS OF THE 9TH HOUSE

Questions of this House concern journeys both geographical and metaphysical, including matters of philosophy, law, science or theology.

Shall I Go On a Long Journey?

In an era where a journey from say England to Rome might have taken as long as a year, and involved many adventures or even the possibility of being involved in a war, or attacked by brigands of one description or another, this was a most important question. Nowadays as the number of travel risks are considerably diminished, only the strongest contra-indications should be heeded.

Thus if there is a malefic planet, particularly Mars or Cauda Draconis in the 9th House and the ruler of the Sign in this House is in another House which is not of a similar nature, together with a malefic planet, then perhaps the journey should be postponed.

Mercury, being the patron of travelers, if well positioned in the 9th House or with the ruler of this House, then the journey should be very rewarding.

Shall I Return from My Journey With My Mission Successfully Accomplished?

The Moon plays a critical part in the success or otherwise of the journey, as she shares with Mercury the function of influencing travel. Consequently, examine the position of the Moon in the chart, especially with reference to the 9th House, its ruler, and the planets in the same House as the Moon itself.

The Moon in Cancer, Taurus or Pisces is a good indication, these being respectively her rulership, exaltation and strength, while the Moon in her detriment (Capricorn) or Fall (Scorpio) is a bad indication.

QUESTIONS OF THE 10TH HOUSE

If You Want to Know Whether Any Honors Will Be Bestowed on You by People of High Rank

Here the House of patronage, fame, notoriety or profession gives the key to this question. The questioner is again represented by the 1st House, and fame represented by the 10th, so that if the planet ruling one House is found in the other or sharing a House with a benefic planet, then the omen is good. A mutual exchange of benefic planets ruling the 1st and 10th Houses indicate the highest honors for the questioner.

Whether Honors Will Come To You in Your Own or a Foreign Country?

Here the division of Houses into Angular, Succedent and Cadent again comes into play, with respect to the planet ruling the 9th House. Although "a prophet is without honor in his own country" the occurrence of the planet ruling the 9th House in an Angular House suggests that the questioner is better off trying for fame and fortune at home.

If the ruler is in a Succedent House then travel farther afield is indicated, and if in a Cadent House, then fame is to be attained overseas.

QUESTIONS OF THE 11TH HOUSE

This House governs questions of social position, friends, acquaintances and membership to societies, especially those that are altruistic or philanthropic. Interpretation of questions of this House depends as before on the position of the planet ruling the Sign in the House, and as the question concerns your relationship with other people, the ruler of the 1st House is almost as crucial.

QUESTIONS OF THE 12TH HOUSE

Here questions might range from the inner life, to secret societies and those rather Saturnian institutions, prisons, asylums, orphanages, hospitals and similar institutions. Internment in or escape from such places can be interpreted from the relative positions of the rulers of the 1st and 12th Houses and their relations to Saturn (unchanging, fixed) and the Moon and Mercury (movement or escape).

The conspiracy of enemies, intrigue—political and personal, and your fantasy or dream life are also included in the functions of this House.

Well, by now, you should have developed quite a feel not only for geomancy but also for astrology. The basic concepts of astrology that have been delineated in chapter 9 will stand you in good stead if you wish to go on exploring astrology at greater depth. If you were already interested in astrology when you came to this book, you will find that the geomantic interpretations of the combinations of Signs and planets will help to bring your astrological interpretations down to earth, by forcing you to apply it to practical problems rather than just getting caught up in the fascination of the system itself.

CHAPTER 15
GEOMANCY TODAY

Throughout this book geomancy has been explained as a practical system, one for use both in divining the answers to questions that logic and reason cannot give, and to help develop your own intuition. If you have persevered and mastered first the simple system of geomancy, and then have gone on to the more complicated forms of astro-geomancy (keeping a thorough record of each of your experiments) then I am sure you will find that not only do you have a powerful divinatory technique, an oracle which will supply concrete answers to concrete questions, but you will also find that your own innate problem-solving ability will have improved immensely.

The oracle of geomancy, based as it is firmly on the ground, ranks together with the Tarot, the I Ching and astrology as one of the great classical forms of divination. In this book we have brought together all the basic information about geomancy, and as much of astrology as is needed to interpret astro-geomancy, for the first time since the Middle Ages. It is also only the second book in the English language devoted wholly to divinatory geomancy.

We began with the Pope and Ptolemy ranged against

the theories of Copernicus and Kepler, we took the older world-view and looked back for the roots of this oracle, divination by earth in the classical world, the world of Islam, and its roots in the world of African magic and divination. We saw how the sixteen eyes of Fa are used in the divination of the witch doctors of Dahomey. We saw how the ancient Romans plotted, planned and predicted their new emperors, how Alexander the Great used his sword, and how the sands of the Sahara are used even to this day for *raml* divination.

Coming closer to the modern day the "master magician," Cornelius Agrippa, shared with us his knowledge of the oracle, and of the planets, sigils, times and figures of geomantic divination. We discovered how to manipulate the family of figures, from the Mothers, through the Daughters, Nephews, Witnesses and Judges, and in Chapter 5 the whole system was summarized. The next three chapters explained judgment, gave examples of divination and a system for deriving quick answers.

In Chapter 9 we entered upon the astrological dimensions of geomancy, and here the forms of the stars added their influence to the forms of the earth, and the symbols above were matched with the symbols below. Each question was categorized in a particular House and many details beyond the initial inquiry extracted from this generous oracle. Even Napoleon appears to have used this oracle, and politics too fell prey to divination.

Gerard of Cremona provided an even simpler form of geomancy and in the last chapter many questions of various sorts were answered by the interpretation of the interaction of the earth figures with the appropriate astrological figures. Needless to say, many of the questions which were relevant in the Middle Ages, to people like Gerard, are now of little or no interest, and so this last chapter has been updated to the present day so that it is possible to discover by astrogeo-mancy as many things as your ingenuity can determine. From an interpretation of the figures (for after all, both the geomantic figures and the astrological ones are archetypal and universal) you can apply the answers you derive to any sort of problem, now or in the future.

Whatever your profession or position, the oracle has something to say to you!

APPENDIX I
ALTERNATIVE ZODIACAL ATTRIBUTIONS OF THE GEOMANTIC FIGURES

* * * * * *	* * * * * *	* * * * * * *	* * * * * * *	* * * * * * *	* * * * * * *	* * * * * * *	* * * * * * *	* * * * * * *
Cauda Draconis	Caput Draconis	Laetitia	Tristitia	Carcer	Acquisitio	Rubeus	Puella	Conjunctio
♋	♌	♃	♄	♄	♃	♂	♀	☿
♋	♌	♓	♒	♑	♐	♏	♎	♍
♏	♑	♐	♒	♑	♓	♏	♉	♍
♑	♎	♓	♐	♓	♈	♋	♋	♎
♐	♍	♉	♒	♓	♈	♓	♎	♍
♐	♍	♉	♏	♓	♈	♓	♎	♍

ALTERNATIVE ZODIACAL ATTRIBUTIONS

	Planet	1 Golden Dawn	2 Agrippa By Ruler	3 Agrippa	4 Franz Hartmann	5 Gerard of Cremona
Puer ∵∴	♂	♈	♈	♏	♈	♏
Amissio ∴∵	♀	♉	♎	♐	♎	♋
Albus ∵∴∵	☿	♓	♓	♌	♋	♌
Populus ∴∴∴∴	☾	♋	♋	♒	♑	♑
Via ∵∵∵∵	☾	♋	♋	♍	♌	♌
Fortuna Major ∴∵∵	☉	♌	♌	♉	♒	♒
Fortuna Minor ∵∴∴	☉	♌	♌	♉	♉	♉

Column no. 1: Golden Dawn ascriptions derived from the rulership of the planets as follows:

☉	rules	♌		
☽	rules	♋		
♀	rules	♉	and	♎
☿	rules	♍	and	♊
♃	rules	♐	and	♓
♄	rules	♑	and	♒
♂	rules	♏	and	♈

Column no. 2: Agrippa's first attribution in Book IV is also drawn from the above rulership of the planets but with some differences in the case of joint rulership. There is a misprint in Agrippa, as Puer is omitted from the series so the only remaining Sign, Aries, has been inserted here.

Column no. 3: A second attribution of Agrippa's given as traditional but "vulgarly used," in other words these attributions though common in books on geomancy, are not the initiated version.

Column no. 4: This system is derived from Agrippa Book II (except that the latter gives Scorpio to Tristitia), and was used by Franz Hartmann in his book on geomancy. However it labors under the disadvantage of using some Signs several times (other than the more obviously logical duplication of Leo and Cancer).

Column no. 5: Was used by Gerard of Cremona in his system of astrological geomancy.

These alternative zodiacal attributions have been tabulated here for the sake of completeness, but the first two columns are the most workable.

APPENDIX II

ELEMENT ATTRIBUTIONS OF THE GEOMANTIC FIGURES*

Arrangement / Element	1 Golden Dawn According To Sign	2 Agrippa According To Sign	3 Agrippa According To Planet & Figure	4 Agrippa "Esoteric Arrangement"
Fire △	Puer ♈ Fortuna Major ♌ Acquisitio ♐ (Fortuna Minor ♌) Cauda Draconis ☋	Puer ♈ Fortuna Major ♌ Laetitia ♐ Fortuna Minor ♌	Puer ♂ Fortuna Major ☉ Amissio Rubeus ♂	Fortuna Minor Amissio Rubeus Cauda Draconis
Air 🜁	Albus ♊ Puella ♎ Tristitia ♒ (Fortuna Minor ♌)	Albus ♊ Amissio ♎ Tristitia ♒	Conjunctio ☿ Puella Laetitia ♃ Fortuna Minor ☉	Conjunctio Acquisitio Laetitia Puer
Water ▽	Populus ♋ Rubeus ♏ Laetitia ♓ Via ♋	Populus ♋ Rubeus ♏ Acquisitio ♓ Via ♋ Cauda Draconis ♏	Populus ☾ Acquisitio Via ☾ Cauda Draconis	Populus Albus Puella Via
Earth 🜃	Amissio ♉ Conjunctio ♍ Carcer ♑ Caput Draconis ☊	Puella ♉ Conjunctio ♍ Carcer ♑ Caput Draconis ♑	Albus Tristitia ♄ Carcer ♄ Caput Draconis	Fortuna Major Tristitia Carcer Caput Draconis

Column no. 1: The Golden Dawn elemental attributions follow the Golden Dawn arrangement of Zodiacal attributions. Fortuna Minor being an exception: as it is Leo it belongs with Fire, but could pass for Air for the sake of even division.

Column no. 2: Agrippa's attributions are likewise based on *Agrippa's* Zodiacal arrangement.

Column no. 3: This arrangement brings into consideration the shape of the figures, (e.g. the two upward pointing triangles of Amissio suggesting Fire) or of the divinatory meaning (e.g. Rubeus belonging in Fire because of the red color). Interesting for its not being as mechanical as the other systems.

Column no. 4: Agrippa says of this arrangement that "this order is also far more true and rational than that which vulgarly is used." With the exception of Puer which is placed in Fire, this is the same arrangement as used by Franz Hartmann.

APPENDIX III

ALLOCATION OF THE GEOMANTIC FIGURES TO THE HOUSES

Ordinary House Allocation

The simplest method of allocating the geomantic figures to the 12 Houses is simply to take the Mothers, Daughters and Nephews and allocate them in order.

Mothers:	I	House	1
	II	House	2
	III	House	3
	IV	House	4
Daughters:	V	House	5
	VI	House	6
	VII	House	7
	VIII	House	8
Nephews:	IX	House	9
	X	House	10
	XI	House	11
	XII	House	12

The Witness and Judge (Figures XIII-XV) are placed in the center of the chart, not in any specific House.

Esoteric Method of House Allocation

Although this system of House allocation was often used, there is another and more secret method for combining the divinatory techniques of geomancy and astrology. It relies on the division of the Houses into Angular, Succedent and Cadent as explained in Chapter 10.

To allocate the geomantic figures to the Houses by this method it is merely necessary to place them in turn as follows:

>   Mothers   4 Angular Houses
>   Daughters   4 Succedent Houses
>   Nephews   4 Cadent Houses

Laid out in full the 12 Houses contain these figures.

	Figure		Houses
Angular	I	Mother	1
Succedent	V	Daughter	2
Cadent	IX	Nephew	3
Angular	II	Mother	4
Succedent	VIII	Daughter	5
Cadent	XII	Nephew	6
Angular	III	Mother	7
Succedent	VII	Daughter	8
Cadent	XI	Nephew	9
Angular	IV	Mother	10
Succedent	VI	Daughter	11
Cadent	X	Nephew	12

Apart from the straightforward methods of allocating the geomantic figures to the Houses given earlier in this book, there is a variation on the "esoteric" method which although the same for Angular and Succedent Houses, has a more complex approach to deriving the geomantic figures for the Cadent Houses. The geomantic figure for each Cadent House is drawn from the addition of the figures from the two other Houses of the same element.

Thus the figure for Cadent House 3 is drawn from the

addition of the figures of House 7 and 11 because Houses 3, 7 and 11 are all Houses attributed to Air. Similarly, the Cadent House 6 is drawn from the addition of the figures in Houses 2 and 10, all being Houses of the element Earth. Cadent House 9 is drawn from the Fire Houses 1 and 5, and lastly Cadent House 12 is drawn from the Water Houses 4 and 8. The allocation of geomantic figures looks something like this:

4 Mothers are allocated to the 4 Angular Houses.
4 daughters are allocated to the 4 Succedent Houses.

Figure drawn from House 7 & 11 allocated to Cadent House 3.
    "   "   "   "   2 & 10   "   "   "   "   6.
    "   "   "   "   1 & 5   "   "   "   "   9.
    "   "   "   "   4 & 8   "   "   "   "   12.

Laid out in full the 12 Houses contain these figures.

Figure			Houses	Figure
Angular	I	Mother	1	
Succedent	V	Daughter	2	
Cadent			3	—generated from Air Houses 7 & 11 by adding III & VI
Angular	II	Mother	4	
Succedent	VIII	Daughter	5	
Cadent			6	—generated from Earth Houses 2 & 10 by adding IV & V
Angular	III	Mother	7	
Succedent	VII	Daughter	8	
Cadent			9	—generated from Fire Houses 1 & 5 by adding I & VIII
Angular	IV	Mother	10	
Succedent	VI	Daughter	11	
Cadent			12	—generated from Water Houses 4 & 8 by adding II & VII

APPENDIX IV

TIMES OF PLANETARY DAYS AND HOURS

Obviously quite often questions cannot wait but if it is at all possible it is useful to consult the oracle on the planetary day suitable to the question in hand. For instance, all questions concerning agriculture or mines should be asked on the day of Saturn, all questions regarding love and marriage on the day of Venus, etc. The planetary days are:

Monday	questions	of the	Moon
Tuesday	"	"	Mars
Wednesday	"	"	Mercury
Thursday	"	"	Jupiter
Friday	"	"	Venus
Saturday	"	"	Saturn
Sunday	"	" the	Sun

If you wish to be very careful and take all possible precautions with your divination you can even select the correct planetary hour in which to consult the oracle.

If so, find out the time of sunrise and sunset from an ephemeris or the daily newspaper and count up the number of minutes in the day between these two times. Only on two days of the year (on the Equinoxes) will the number of daylight hours actually come to twelve.

Divide the length of the day by twelve to give you the exact length of a planetary "hour," which will be less than sixty minutes in winter but more than sixty minutes during the summer.

Counting off each "hour" (calculating according to the number of minutes in the planetary hour) you find that the first and the eighth "hour" of each day is dedicated to the planetary ruler of that day as in the table above. For example, the first and eighth hour of Monday is sacred to the Moon, while the first and eighth hour of Friday is dedicated to Venus.

If you wish to choose an appropriate night hour, again count the number of minutes of darkness from sunset to sunrise. Divide this by twelve to get the length of a planetary night "hour." Then counting of these "hours," take the third and the tenth "hours" of the night. Thus the third and tenth "hours" of Monday night are dedicated to the Moon, while the third and tenth night hours of Friday are dedicated to Venus, and so on.

APPENDIX V

CONSTITUENTS OF EACH LINE OF THE GEOMANTIC FIGURES

		Mothers		
I	II	III	IV	
A	E	I	M	heads
B	F	J	N	necks
C	G	K	O	bodies
D	H	L	P	feet

If we take the four Mothers which are the original figures from which all the other figures come and allocate 4 letters for each figure, we can lay out the generation of the other figures like this:

	Daughters		
V	VI	VII	VIII
A	B	C	D
E	F	G	H
I	J	K	L
M	N	O	P

Nephews

IX	X	XI	XII
A + E	I + M	A + B	C + D
B + F	J + N	E + F	G + H
C + G	K + O	I + J	K + L
D + H	L + P	M + N	O + P

Witnesses

XIII	XIV
A + E + I + M	A + B + C + D
B + F + J + N	E + F + G + H
C + G + K + O	I + J + K + L
D + H + L + P	M + N + O + P

Judge

XV

A + E + I + M + A + B + C + D
B + F + J + N + E + F + G + H
C + G + K + O + I + J + K + L
D + H + L + P + M + N + O + P

If we rearrange the letters in each line and add together the same letters, rationalizing this figure, it will be seen that the only possible combinations that could make up the Judge are the four symmetrical pairs

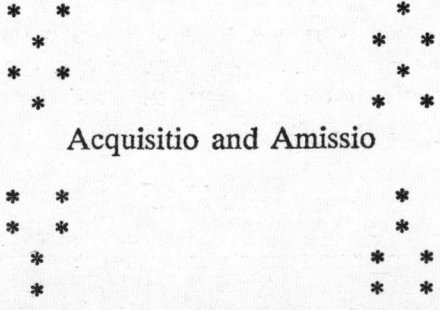

```
 * *           *
  *           * *
 * *           *
  *           * *
```
Acquisitio and Amissio

```
 * *           *
 * *           *
  *           * *
  *           * *
```
Fortuna Major and Fortuna Minor

351

```
* *                    *
* *                    *
* *                    *
* *                    *
      Populus and Via

* *                    *
 *                    * *
 *                    * *
* *                    *
      Conjunctio and Carcer
```

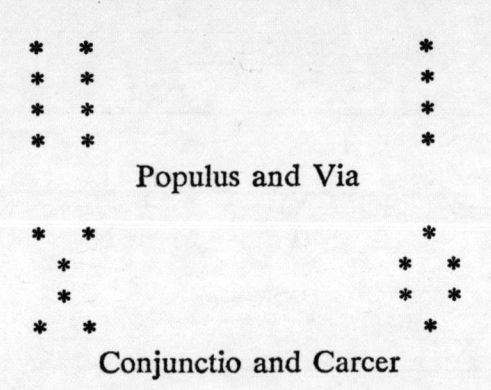

APPENDIX VI

GENERATION OF THE GEOMANTIC FIGURES

The sixteen possible figures generated by dots in the earth or on paper consist of four "layers." Each "layer" is positive or negative as it contains one or two dots. Thus the figures can range from

```
    *              * *
    *              * *
        through to
    *              * *
    *              * *
```

with every combination in between. As there are four "layers" to each figure and two possibilities for each layer, this results in 2^4, or sixteen, combinations.

As you can see, the sixteen figures cover every possible combination rather like the sixty-four hexagrams of the I Ching which cover every possible combination of Yang (———) and Yin (— —). The only difference is that the I Ching uses lines, while geomancy uses dots, also the hexagram has six layers not four, and has consequently 2^6 possible combinations, the sixty-four hexagrams. Laying out the possible geomantic combinations, we can produce the "Table of the Generation of the Geomantic Figure," in which we show how they are generated.

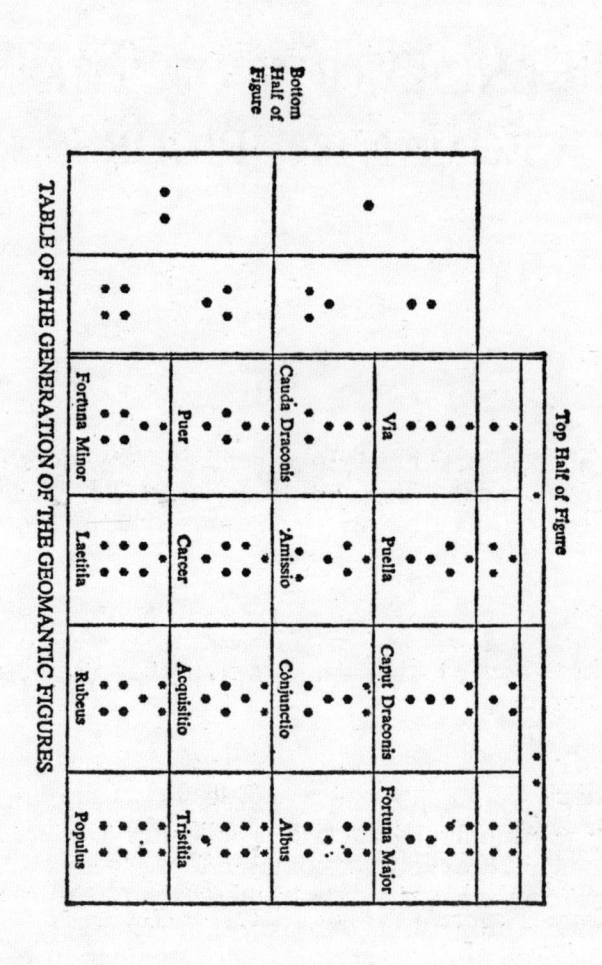

APPENDIX VII
LOGICAL GROUPINGS OF THE GEOMANTIC FIGURES

The following groupings are set out for their suggestive value in comparing or memorizing the sixteen figures of geomancy.

Inversion

Pairs of figures which become one another when turned upside down are:

Puer	—	Puella
Albus	—	Rubeus
Amissio	—	Acquisitio
Fortuna Major	—	Fortuna Minor
Tristitia	—	Laetitia
Caput Draconis	—	Cauda Draconis

Via, Populus, Conjunctio and Carcer, being symmetrical are unchanged.

Transmutation

Pairs of figures which become one another if all their layers with two dots are changed into one dot, and vice versa:

Via	transmutes into		Populus
Puer	"	"	Albus
Amissio	"	"	Acquisitio
Fortuna Major	"	"	Fortuna Minor
Conjunctio	"	"	Carcer
Puella	"	"	Rubeus
Tristitia	"	"	Cauda Draconis
Laetitia	"	"	Caput Draconis

APPENDIX VIII
NAMES OF THE 16 GEOMANTIC FIGURES IN LATIN, ARABIC, HEBREW, AND MALAGASY
(From a work published in 1665)

ALTERNATIVE LATIN NAMES AND THEIR MEANINGS

FIGURE	LATIN NAME	MEANING
populus	congregatio	assembling together, union, society
via	iter	way, street, going, journey, march
conjunctio	coadunatio collectio	add together, collecting, gathering together, collection
carcer	constrictus	fetter, confine, to draw together, bind together
fortuna major	auxilium majus auxilium intus tutela intrans	interior aid or assistance (interior change, guard or protection)
fortuna minor	auxilium minus auxilium foris tutela exiens	exterior aid or assistance (exterior change, guard or protection)
acquisitio	comprehensum intus	interior comprehension or interior seizing or laying hold of.
amissio	comprehensum extra comprehensum foris	exterior comprehension or exterior seizing or laying hold of.
tristitia	damnatus transversus diminutum	condemn, blame, transverse, oblique, athwart, diminution.
laetitia	sanus barbatus ridens	bearded, laughter, healthy, sane
rubeus	ruffus	red, ruddy
albus	candidus	shining white, glittering, dead white
puella	mundus facie (faciei)	pretty, pure form, figure or face
puer	gladius erigendus (imberbis) flavus	(beardless) upright sword (i.e. a boy), golden-yellow
caput draconis	limen intrans (intus) limen superius	interior threshold, upper threshold
cauda draconis	limen exiens (foris) limen inferius	exterior threshold, lower threshold

FIGURE	ARABIC NAME	MEANING
populus	jamā'a	group of people, band, party, gang
via	tarīq	way, road, highway, trail
conjunctio	ijtimā'	meeting, get together, gathering, social life, conjunction
carcer	'ugla	knot, knob, node, joint or articulation, knuckle, layer
fortuna major	nuṣra el-dākila	interior, inside, inmost, hidden help or assistance
fortuna minor	nuṣra el-khârga	external, outer, outside, foreign, exterior, help, aid or assistance
acquisitio	gabḍ el-dākil	gripping, grasping, taking possession, receiving, receipt, from the interior
amissio	gabḍ el-kharge	receiving from the exterior, from outside
tristitia	(mankūs)	upside-down, to fall, inverted, reversed, relapsing or suffering a relapse
laetitia	(janūbi fariha? = liḥya?)	southern happiness (happiness in the South?), rejoicing, gladness, bearded (i.e. grown up?)
rubeus	ḥumra	redness, red implying a bad omen, danger, erysipelas (St. Anthony's fire)
albus	el-bayāḍ	whiteness, or writing paper, or blank space in a manuscript, barren, desolate, wasteland

FIGURE	ARABIC NAME	MEANING
puella	naqīy ḵadd	clear cheek (complexion), pure, clean, immaculate, unstained, free of dirt or impurity
puer	(jūd lahu') kausaj	literally "generosity is for him," openhandedness, liberality. Kausaj is a swordfish (variety xiphias gladius)
caput draconis	el 'ataba el-dāḵila	the interior threshold (the step to go inside)
cauda draconis	el 'ataba el-khârga	the exterior threshold (the step to go outside)

FIGURE	HEBREW	MEANING
populus	kehila	congregation (from the same root in Bible kohelet = Ecclessiastes)
via	derech	way
conjunctio	chibur (kibbutz)	collection (collective) (the verb is "to tie")
carcer	beit hasohar	prison
fortuna major	kavod nichnas	honor or fortune enters (incoming)
fortuna minor	kavod yotze	honor or fortune exits (goes out)
acquisitio	mamun nichnas	monetary fortune enters (incoming)
amissio	mamun yotze	monetary fortune exits (goes out)
tristitia	shefel rosh	main humiliation (poverty)
laetitia	nisho rosh	main joy (wife)
rubeus	(ha) adom	the red one
albus	ha laban	the white one
puella	bar halechi	the one with the (clear) cheek
puer	nilcham	the fighter
caput draconis	sof nichnas	enters threshold
cauda draconis	sof yotze	exits threshold

FIGURE	MALAGASY
populus	jama
via	taraika
conjunctio	aditsimag
carcer	alokòla
fortuna major	asoravavy
fortuna minor	asoralahy
acquisitio	molahidy
amissio	mikiarija
tristitia	adikizy
laetitia	alezany
rubeus	alemora
albus	adibidjàdy
puella	kizo
puer	adikia sajy
caput draconis	saka
cauda draconis	vontsira

APPENDIX IX

THE GEOMANTIC FIGURES OF *THE PHILOSOPHICAL MERLIN*

The Philosophical Merlin . . . , *a Valuable Manuscript Formerly in the Possession of Napoleon Buonaparte* is a curious little tract which was published in London in 1882 by Robert Cross Smith and G. W. Graham. It uses the sixteen geomantic figures to outline disposition, auspicious colors, favorable hours and days, and inherent qualities, much like astrological Sign descriptions.

The Philosophical Merlin was much less sophisticated in its divination techniques than those already outlined in this book. One arrives at the figure by making only eight lines of random dots: the instructions suggest that each random line should have at least twelve dots in it. These lines of dots generated two figures in the usual manner (each odd line gave one dot, each even line, two dots).

Then these two figures are joined together by ading each line (odd and even in the usual fashion) until you are left with your final figure.

For example if you took your pen and marked down eight lines of dots or points, without counting them (there ought to be at least twelve in each line—but don't try counting them as you do them) you right get

```
* * * * * * * * * * * * * *
* * * * * * * * * * * * * *
* * * * * * * * * * * * *
* * * * * * * * * * * * *

* * * * * * * * * * * * * * *
* * * * * * * * * * * * * * * *
* * * * * * * * * * * * *
* * * * * * * * * * * * *
```

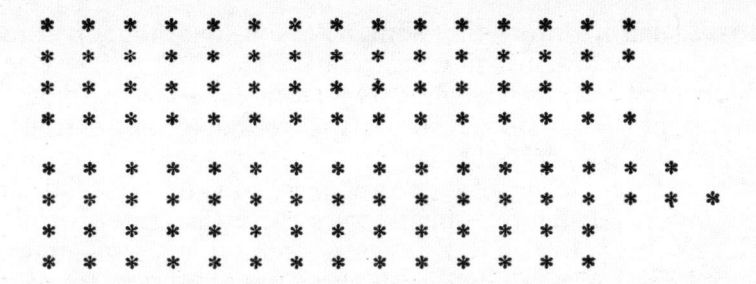

Then counting up each line you will find that they add up to:

    odd   *
    odd   *
    even * *
    odd   *

    even * *
    odd   *
    even * *
    even * *

Then placing these figures side by side, add them together to get the final figure:

    *
  * *
  * *
    *

You are then supposed to look up the relevant geomantic figure and see if the answer appears to coincide with your fate and fortune. If it does, well and good—the rest of the text gives you all the details you need.

If it doesn't then the experiment should be repeated up to three times in all, with a delay of at least an hour between each try. The manuscript goes on to explain that:

"It is necessary for the Reader to observe that, if on trial, the answer does not correspond with the *known* part of his fate, (and particularly the disposition and bodily marks;) he may be sure that some mistake has been made by him in the process . . . This being the case, (which sometimes will necessarily happen), let him, if during the Summer Season, wait during the full space of an hour and a half, and if during the Winter Season, one hour, before he again makes his divining points. The Editor has also discovered from repeated trials, among his Friends, that it would be better for each person to make *three* trials, (after the proper time has intervened), and if *two*, out of the *three* trials, produce similar *figures*, let him choose *that particular* figure, which comes *twice* the same, for his Horoscope. (In 1822 this word did not *only* mean an astrological chart). But if all three are different, let him choose that which corresponds with his own ideas, and bodily marks or moles, as described in the Work."

The text occasionally refers to people "being born under one symbol" or another, thus betraying the fact that this material was obviously "borrowed" from an earlier work of astro-geomancy rather than from Napoleon's bedside. Nevertheless the interpretations of each geomantic figure are quite unique, even if the modus operandi is somewhat oversimplified.

When one particular geomantic figure is finally settled upon, then look at the appended passage for details of your most favorable astrological influences, qualities of mind and body, particular fads, fantasies or phobias, favorite color, financial fortune, crucial ages, and fortunate times and hours. The details of the sixteen figures follow, and you will recognize among them our old friends, the sixteen geomantic figures, interpreted in a rather unique manner.

AMISSIO

```
  *
 * *
  *
 * *
```

THEY who have this *figure* of Geomancy, arising, are under the spirits of the watery regions, and chiefly under the Moon and Venus. They will be of a studious, melancholic, patient, firm, and laborious disposition, rather inclined to obstinacy, and very amorous, votaries of Venus. —Part of their life, will be much fatigued, with getting riches; which they shall obtain; but often lose again, and that suddenly, without great caution is used.—However, as they sink into the vale of years, fortune shall again smile on them; and they shall again re-gain, even more than they lost; seeing their most bitter enemies utterly subjected, and cast down, while they shall descend to the silent tomb, surrounded by happiness.

They shall have moles on the neck, throat, arms, and breast; are subject to scorbutic and hereditary diseases, heart-burn, liver complaints, and hypochondria; but generally enjoying good health.

In the south angle of their horoscope, they will have the sorrowful figure Tristitia, of the airy Triplicitie, chiefly governed by the cold and rigid Saturn; which will make them remarkable for having dreams of dead things, sepulchers, church-yards, ghosts, and terrific, yet unnatural appearances; and of lofty places, troubled and muddy waters, and destruction. Their dreams shall indeed, for the most part, be ominous, and troublesome. Let them beware of disappointments, when they dream of money—and of deceit, after having dreamed of flattering notice.

They shall be fortunate in finding hidden, and lost things, and shall at some period of their life, discover a treasure. In their gait, they shall generally appear stooping, and looking, as if towards the earth. They shall arrive to great honor, and dignity, and experience great favor, and friendship, from rich and noble persons, bearing rule in public affairs or offices, and fortunate in the science of hydraulics, and in liquids and fluids in general. —They will be successful in houses, lands, gardens, and earthy things, and should reside in low, crowded and dark places, where they are much frequented.

They will be in danger from an ox, and from other beasts, chiefly those who ruminate, to violent blows and falls, they will be much subject, especially at the ages of *five* and *eight* years. They must be careful of water, at the ages of *nine* and *thirty-six*.

In the west angle, will be found the deceitful and violent figure *Rubeus*, which will cause them at times to be very enviously accused, in some measure through their own seeking, as they shall at times, court hostility, but though not very courageous shall overcome their adversaries. This figure also gives many false friends, with danger of law suits, or public contentions, and will cause them during some period of their life to appear before a Court of Justice, either on the offensive or defensive.

At *ten, fifteen, twenty-one, thirty*, and *forty-six* years of age, they will meet with changes and good fortune, removals, or journeys. At *two, four, five, seven, eleven, sixteen, twenty-eight, thirty-five*, and *forty-two* years of age, they will meet with sickness and trouble; at *eighteen* or *twenty-eight* take a long voyage, or go to reside near the water. They shall marry well, but to persons of hasty temper, occasionally devoted to Bacchus, but rigidly careful. At *nineteen*, if a woman, she shall be in love, and marry previous to *twenty-four* years of age. They shall have more than one marriage, and bury their first child.

In the north angle they will have *Fortuna Major*, belonging to the region of the fire, foreshowing a legacy, or some considerable property—trifling gain by the lottery, or games of chance,—they shall be fortunate in *white, purple, red,* and *citron* colors,—and in bay horses.

They shall have much trouble through their relations, and survive the greatest part of their kindred,—they will be liable to stings from insects, and especially bees or wasps,—they will generally however, die an easy death.

If they travel, let it be by land, and not on horseback, but in some conveyance, let them also beware of fair women, on their travels.

Friday, is their fortunate day, and chiefly about sun-setting, they will prevail. Let them also chose the Moon in *Taurus*, if they would overcome any obstacle, and going to the *full*.

If born in the night time, they will be more fortunate, and successful, than those who are born between sun-rising and sun-setting.

The name of this Angel, or Tutelary Spirit is *Anael*.

PUER

```
     *
     *
   *   *
     *
```

THEY who have this *figure*, arising, are born under the spirits of the fiery Trigon; and under the influence of

Mars and the Sun. They will be bold, romantic, ambitious, and very aspiring; filled with warlike ideas; flourishing in youth; having either *few* brethren, or *few* to survive.

They will be much subject to a mutable and inconstant fortune, wasting their paternal estate, and suffering through usurers, or money lenders; but often recovering their losses, and turning them into gain. They will, at times, appear to have an excess of liberality; and displease some by too much freedom, bestowing their benefit for the most part upon very ungrateful persons, without scarcely ever meeting a return. They will be much subject to pains in the head and face, tooth-ache, lethargy and eruptions, subject to hurts by fire and sharp instruments, and shall receive a bite of injury from a dog,—or horned cattle they must also take care. They will be liable to scalds and cuts, having moles on the face, loins, feet, and arms; chiefly fortunate in white and red colors, and in martial and surgical things.

In the south angle they will have posited the figure *Carcer*, shewing that they will attain to many honorable acts, and through invincibility, and flattery, gain some eminent office, chiefly in public employment, most probably naval, military, or relating to the fire and metals, especially steel and iron; they will also be much concerned in religious matters, likewise their whole life shall be markedly open, and exposed to public gaze, seldom any thing in domestic concerns remaining hid—except that which they perform on the day of the new Moon, which may possibly be kept secret, though not availing. Many, who are born under this horoscope, are desirous of prying into the secrets of nature, and make excellent philosophers, chemists and mathematicians, optical instrument makers, engravers, and artists. They will prosper in war, and in games of chance. In merchandizing with women they shall prosper; but much subject to vexation and anger. At some time or other of their life they shall meet with much trouble, or be near imprisonment through relatives or deceptive friends,—from old persons they will generally attain much honor.

At the ages of *fifteen* years, at *twenty-two* years, and at *forty-four* years, they shall travel or meet with changes in advancement; at *four* years old they will have sickness, also at the ages of either *eighteen*, or *twenty-eight;* at *twenty*, a journey, at *twenty-one*, much vexation, at *thirty*, a long voyage.

In the west angle will be placed, *Puella*, which will increase greatly, the mutability of their fortune; and give many public opponents. They shall be in danger of being cast down from the elevation to which they may arrive, and for a length of time be much troubled,—envy fighting against their happiness, if in public life, the worst. They shall succeed in law suits, and gain favor from the Judge.

They shall also generally recover lost or stolen property. —Fair women will be their favorites, especially the younger sort, and in an inferior capacity, such as servants and minors—and those of free and open manners. If a woman, she shall marry a fair man, rather effeminate; if a man, his first love shall not be his wife—let them also beware of illegitimate offspring.

In the north angle, will be found, *Populus*, governed by the watery element, and chiefly under the full Moon, which gives many enemies in their own house; they shall live where many people usually frequent, and will do best in the most populous and busy part. They will be fortunate as buyers and sellers of lands and heritages. Seeing the death of their father, and generally of both parents: they shall be the heir to vast legacies and have money left them. At the age of *forty-five* let them beware of the water. They shall visit distant parts, and receive good from the East and West. They will during youth be fond of noise, bustle, quarrelling and contest, careless of their persons, but in old age given to religion.

In books, letters, new clothes, or new articles, they will be very unfortunate, and receive injury through mercurial men.

In small cattle, and dogs, they may be fortunate, but if born in the day time, and if in the morning, especially from eleven to twelve, they will meet with more success than if born in the night. If born exactly at midnight, they will be lawyers or divines.

Tuesday, is their fortunate day, and in their undertakings let them choose the Moon in *Capricorn*, and in her first quarter, if they would prevail.

They are under the Tutelary Spirit, called *Samael*.

POPULUS

```
* *
* *
* *
* *
```

THE native born under this figure, *Populus*, a symbol of the watery Triplicitie, is chiefly under the Moon, and Jupiter, but if born in the day time, under the Moon alone. They will be of a mild, quick, subtil, and ready wit, doing most things with moderation, subject to anger, but as soon calmed; swift in journeys, and voyages. Fond of mystical and supernatural things; having remarkable and curious dreams, and ominous forebodings, generally given to flattery; and fond of novelties, travelling, and curiosities. If born in the night, the women have a dread of water. If a man he will be in some public employment, or office, also an excellent navigator, seaman, or merchant; also fortunate in dealing in colors and liquids. They who are born under this *figure*, are tinged with melancholy, and the spleen; cold and phlegmatic, subject to pains in the left side, and gnawings of the stomach.—If females, having fair children. They will have much vexation through their kindred, and will be in danger by fire and water. They will be greatly obnoxious to insects, of the meaner kind, and have a great hatred to spiders, beetles, and crawling things; but fond of dogs, cats, horses, and beasts; also of hunting, wrestling, running, and athletic sports.

They will have moles on the breast, arms, and other parts, and a dark mole near the loins. They will also be remarkably subject to colds and coughs.

In the south angle will be the figure, *Puer*, of the nature and property of Mars, in the constellation, of the celestial *Ram*, of the fiery Trigon; denoting them to be fortunate in green, russett, and sparkling, or glistening colors. They shall arrive to martial, and public renown, famed for heroic deeds, whether deserving or not.

They shall also inherit a strange fanciful imagination, hereditary, and no less eccentric than undefinable. If a woman, she will be much followed by the male sex.

In riches, their greatest gain will often be loss, being subject to a very mutable fate. Suffering also at times through a too conceited opinion of themselves and actions. Being rather given to obstinacy.

They shall travel much and change their residence often; likewise their whole life will be very strange and romantic.

If born in the day they will be more fortunate than in the night; they will also rise to much greater eminence if born in April or July. They will be eminently successful at particular periods, especially at *eighteen*, *twenty-four*, and *thirty-six* years of age. During the first two years of life, they are much subject to sickness and accidents. At *thirty* years old, they may expect much trouble.

In the west angle, will be the figure *Carcer*, denoting the Native, if a man, shall suffer much through women, and be defamed unjustly. They shall meet with loss; by searching continually after vain, and unprofitable things—and must also avoid law suits.

Such is the contrariety of their fate, that even in trouble they will be popular, and will be the keepers of others secrets. If they get over the age of forty-five, they shall live to a great age and attain an honorable burial. They will be in danger of a troublesome marriage, but ending well. They seldom marry rich, or in a good family, but mostly obscure persons. Many born under this figure never marry.

In the north part of the *figure* will be *Amissio*, governed by Venus, denoting the first child to be a son, and long lived, being preferred before the others, remarkable for good intellect. The Natives should live, if possible, near a sea port town, or in a city, receiving the produce of the ocean.

North Britons, under this *figure*, generally rise to eminence, however let those who require their services be wary.

Monday is their fortunate day, and also *Thursday* night. Let them choose the Moon increasing, in *Cancer*, or *Pisces* in their undertakings, and let her be in good aspect to Jupiter. At midnight, and eight in the morning is their favorable hours. They are born under the Tutelary Spirit or Angel, *Gabriel*.

ALBUS

```
    *   *
    *   *
      *
    *   *
```

THEY who are born under this *figure* of Geomancy, called *Albus*, are under the spirits of the airy region; chiefly under the planets, Saturn and Mercury. Their life shall commence with great labor, and their early days be remarkable, for incessant fatigue, as well as quick action. They will obtain much prosperity and good fortune, through parents, kindred, and noble persons. They will be successful in public capacities, and make eminent clerks, accountants, stenographers, painters, embroiderers, architects, founders of buildings for public or private use, mechanics, engravers, horologers, astrologers, and artists. They will, like their patron, the fleet and winged Mercury, be clever and ingenious, inventing and re-inventing, but often losing the fruit of their labours through want of persevering patience, and unwearied assiduity. They will be eminent satirists, and volubie in speech; copious in writing; and expert in definition: much, however, they will lose, through keeping company with unfortunate and evil minded persons. They will be well calculated for business, and good arithmeticians. Nimble and mischevious as their patron, unless born on a Thursday, or Friday. If on a Saturday, they must be careful of their actions, or they will attract the notice of impartial justice. They will also be noted for giving the first cause in affronts, and for propagating reports, whether true or false; nevertheless they will be firm, and faithful in friendship; and in their promise be rigidly tenacious of performing what they intend.

They will have moles on the arms, thighs, feet, and legs, and be during infancy and youth much subject to falls, blows, and be very fond of climbing, adventuring, and bringing trouble upon themselves. At five years old, they will have a serious fall, or hurt, and lose a relation, either then, or at the age of ten years. They will bury both parents, but their mother the first.

In the mid-heaven will be found *Letitia*, denoting, or representing much dealing with naval concerns, or dwelling, or business, near the water. They shall at least, twice cross the ocean; in youth, being lost from their friends, for a time, or suffering through the carelessness of their friends. At *fifteen*, they will meet with changes, which will influence their whole life.

In books and writings they may be fortunate, also in mixed colors, especially red and white, light blue and azure. They will be fond of costly and expensive apparel, ornaments and decorations.

Their livelihood shall be in a great measure obtained by other men's endeavors, they will obtain eminence in two places, or else divide their patrimony. They shall take many short journeys, generally on a sudden, also chiefly towards the south and east.

In the west angle will be *Acquisitio*, denoting an amorous mind, having many admirers, and if a female, a coquette. Their mind will be much perplexed through enemies, mostly of their own causing, they being very fond of adulation. They will marry fair persons, good housewives, and having several handsome children, being also happy and fortunate in the marriage state. If a female her husband will be very fond of pleasure, and rather given to pernicious enjoyments. In high or mountainous places their fortune lays, therefore let them accordingly choose their residence.

In the north angle will be *Conjunctio*, of the earthy region, giving loss or suffering through brethren or sisters; a love of martial affairs, and remarkable hatred of oppression, but they will often be unjustly accused of oppressing others, when in reality they act entirely the reverse. They will be liable to the gravel, and if not careful diseased through females. At some particular periods of their life, they must be careful or they will be their own ruin. They will, however, be at times fortunate in games of chance.

They will inherit their father's estate, and would be successful in the secret and occult sciences, magic and necromancy. From distant relations, such as uncles, aunts, and others, they will have money or rich presents. Though fond of war, they will always do better by peace.

Wednesday is their fortunate day, and the first day of every week will be remarkable, in either loss or gain. Saturday, is to them, tolerable good. The spring of the year, and the Moon in Scorpio, is favorable, or else in the sign Aquarius, which at times will be better.

They are under the Angel, *Raphael*.

FORTUNA MAJOR

```
 *  *
 *  *
 *
 *
```

THEY who are fortunate enough to be born under this symbol, called *Fortuna Major*, of the fiery element, ruled by the Sun, and Jupiter, but in the day time by the Sun, alone; will arrive to great eminence, especially if born in the end of July, or from the beginning to the middle of August. Let them be born in what month they will, yet they will be persons of note, well known, public, and exemplary. They shall however be much subject to labor, and many dangers, much, and perpetually troubled with the business of other persons, very ingenious, fond of horsemanship, fond to a degree of flattery, even though the person who flattered them was a known enemy, also much liking those who either follow the same pursuits or coincide with them in opinion. They will be very aspiring, ambitious, and high-minded. Either travelling or much desirous thereof; bestowing much labor, time, and useless ingenuity, to give laws, and prescribe rules to other persons. They shall have moles on the back, legs and arms, be hairy and athletic, high fore-head, and generally gray eyes. They will be much inclined to royalty and loving grandeur, and too frequently ostentation, seldom however keeping a secret. They will be liable to inflammations, and fevers, head-aches and scurvy, liable also to danger by fire, kicks from a horse, and some slight danger by a fall, either from an high place, or by an accidental mistake.

In the mid-heaven will be posited *Amissio*, denoting much danger both in purse, property and health, through carelessness, or neglect. They will be very much in the employ of great persons, either in some place of public employ or trust, or in the church, in a public theatre, market, emporium for foreign produce, or else in some place where they shall bear great rule. They will lose at times, and very often through low persons, especially females, although through clowns and servants. They will lose much authority at times through a want of caution, and once in their life suffer imprisonment. They shall much lose by stolen property. If in any situation under royalty, they shall gain great favor from the heirs to the throne, and especially from the female branches and other illustrious persons. They will be amazingly fond of fair, bright, and clear weather, and fond of warm and heated things.

In the west angle will be found *Tristitia*, which shows they shall, if a man, refuse an honest and beautiful woman, and contract marriage with a low, servile, or obscure person; and unless they take great care nearly ruin themselves by marriage. If, however, they are careful, they may in a great measure mitigate the judgment. They will be either in love early, or else marry very early. They will have few children, but probably one daughter. They will during the early part of their life chiefly regard the matrimonial alliance for money: and indeed marry when they will, they will be prosperous thereby. If a woman, her husband shall be of proud and austere manners, and without him take extreme caution, the only thing for which she will condemn herself will be an evil marriage. They must beware of cards, dice and gambling, especially with elderly persons. In their amours the men shall much pride themselves, but once in a thousand, or thereabouts, they *may* meet with a virgin. They will notwithstanding be much given to illegitimate love, the natural consequences of which is severe trouble.

In the fourth house, they have *Rubeus*, which shews danger of imprisonment and restraint, with a mixture of loss and gain.— They shall be successful in metals, earths, liquids, poisonous, or corrosive acids, either in dealing in, or perfecting, for use in experiments or operations; also in sowing, tilling and planting; also in war or battle, mines, fortification, and implements of destruction, and famous for many new inventions, and in red and green colors. They shall suffer through treachery, and too much confidence; they will meet with much envy and be unjustly scandalized, but in old age, shall become rich.

If born at sun-rise they will be as a Prince among their household, and have as it were an army at their command. If born at the time of sun-setting, exactly, they will if no good aspect of Jupiter intervene, lose their life in battle or public strife. Let them always beware of explosions and sharp instruments.

Sunday, is their fortunate day, and the first and eighth hour thereof; let them choose the moon in *Aries* or *Sagittarius*, and in her first Sextile, and they will prevail.

The name of ther guardian Angel is, *Michael*.

CONJUNCTIO

* *
*
*
* *

THOSE born under this horoscope, are under the spirits of the earthy region, chiefly under Mercury and Venus; and if in the night, under Mercury and the Moon. They will be prone and apt to amorous incitements, desiring a perpetual friendship, and intercourse with the opposite sex.

They are skilful in dreams, ominous forebodings, and much given to prying after, and desiring an insight into the unfathomable depths of futurity. They will be lovers of the arts and sciences, diligent in business, of an excellent memory, though subject at times to defect of utterance, or else too much volubility, in either case very hurtful.

They will be expert at inventing and diligent in executing, especially in the sciences, of optics, acoustics, pneumatics, and the higher branches of experimental philosophy. Believers in animal magnetism, or very occult sympathy. If born at midnight, Astrologers, possessed of celestial and mystical knowledge, reading the Stars as easy and facile as an Epistle.

They will, if in inferior life, be excellent accountants, artists, lawyers, hydrographers and mechanics, expert in occular memory, and very fond of displaying their extraordinary faculties. They will subsist by their talents, and obtain much honor through tall thin persons, of scientific but studious habits.

In the mid-heaven will be the symbol, *Albus*, denoting them to be humane and courteous, but given to covetousness, or else very eager, and arduous, in their respective pursuits. Fortunate in buying and selling, and merchandize in general. If born at midnight, and the Moon in conjunction with the Sun, namely a *new Moon*, the dead in their graves shall scarcely rest for them, such will be their desire for mysterious intercourse, magic and necromancy. (The manuscript here relates that *Edward Kelly, Chiancungi,* and *Agrippa, were born under this horoscope, with similar configurations, one of which, the second, was crushed to atoms by infernal spirits.*) If they do not follow these arts, they will be expert in ancient things, Antiquities, Egyptian and hieroglyphical learning, translations, and become famous linguists.

They will have moles on the feet, knees and arms, of plain features generally, but voluptuous and warm in passion. Subject to falls, bruises and danger through experiments. In danger of breaking an arm, or leg; and if born on a *new* or *full Moon* in danger of drowning. If born in February, March, July, September or November, this judgment is still more certain; and they will not escape drowning or shipwreck, unless *Jupiter* be in the very degree ascending. They will be subject to head-aches, bowel complaints, and in old age to the gout and rheumatism. They will acquire an estate by some public or religious employment, and be the head of their house. They shall generally bear rule over others, and in old age be happy. *At ten, thirty,* and *forty-two,* they will have great changes. They will either be much conversant with exports or imports, or else take many journeys both by sea and land.

In the descendant will be *Laetitia*, denoting them to be much and publicly known, every twelfth year meeting with a change in life, and similar acquaintance. They shall much desire flattery and praise, though strictly worshipping *Plutus*. If a man, he shall marry a fair and affable woman, liberal, but a good housewife, a stranger by birth, and met by accident. If a woman, she will be much beloved by great persons. In either case, they may not expect much gain by marriage. The men will be so far amorous, as to desire the company of married persons. At *nineteen* and *twenty-four*, either sex will be near marriage.

In the north angle will be posited, *Acquisitio*, denoting easy performing of difficulties, good fortune through discovering hidden or lost things, and through secret science. Gain also by houses, lands, watery things or places, agriculture, and horses; also by chemical, metallic, and fiery things. A legacy from a middle aged person, fair complexion. Death of the children, or much illness to them, and loss thereby. Their end will be very happy.

Lofty places and the sea coast is their properest residence. They will be successsful in black and blue, spotted colors. Let them choose the Moon in *Cancer*, by day, and *Virgo*, by night, and both increasing, and in Trine to the Sun.

Wednesday is their best *day*, and also Saturday *night*. The name of their Genius is, *Raphael*.

PUELLA

*
* *
*
*

THOSE born under *Puella*, governed by the airy triplicitie, are chiefly under Venus. They will be skilful and ingenious, votaries of pleasure and curiosity. Subject to much sickness and many falls and casualties, especially from horses, and by the fall of old buildings. They will have many troubles, dangers, and adversaries, be near provoked to fight duels, and at times suffering through law suits and contentions. Their life will be at times very prosperous, but amazingly subject to mutability. Though timourous, yet they will be unconquerable, and when provoked, fiery in anger. Often those born under such a symbol, are enthusiastically religious, having singular and extraordinary dreams and visions. Having moles on the face, loins, feet and arms. In manners conceited and fond of praise, thereby often risking their own future fame, despising the intreaties and supplications of others, to their future detriment.

They will be ambitious, and particularly fond of fine apparel and outward shew. Particularly fond also of fine gardens, trees and aromatic shrubs. At the ages of *thirty* and *fifty-three*, they will be in great danger of their lives, and especially at the latter period.

In the zenith they will have the symbols *Via*, and *Populus*, which will make them famous, invincible and illustrious, rich and wealthy; they shall subsist by the gettings of others, and be high in office, but too often given to cruelty or oppression. In the law, or the church, they would succeed to a miracle.

Those born in the day time, and especially at sun-setting, and at noon, are the most fortunate, and will be employed under Kings. Those also who are born on the day of the *Autumnal equinox* are very famous, and will enjoy a posthumous reputation. Upon those born at the point of the *Summer* and *Winter solstice*, are eminent in war, battle, and destruction of their fellow men.

They will have in the seventh house, the symbol *Puer*, which will make them great travellers and voyagers, continually going amongst great companies of people. They will see the death of their mother, and of many other relatives. In the element of water, in Hydraulics, perfumes of a liquid nature, and Indian articles of luxury; they will be successful, but lose through endeavoring to pervert justice. Distinguished families under this symbol, arrive to great military and naval command. *(The Emperor Napoleon, himself was born under this horoscope.)*

Imprisonment they may expect to suffer, unless Jupiter, very favorably beholds the horoscope. It will, however, not be long in duration. They will also, if born in the day time, and in any other time except winter, be liable to attacks upon their life, and be much exposed to fraud and violence. They will also be much instrumental in their own death, if very strong testimonies do not intervene. They must beware of midnight and desert places. They will marry lively and shrewd persons, rich and powerful, probably noble.

In the north angle will be *Carcer,* denoting much danger by law suits, and public contentions; stout, short, and fair or ruddy persons will be great enemies. They will nevertheless profit much by their own industry and unremitting labors—and will be fortunate in dark crimson and purple colors.

At *forty-two,* much prosperity and public notice or advancement may be expected; attended, however, with much and eminent danger. They shall be unfortunate in their own offspring, and in houses, lands, and hereditaments, but never meeting much poverty.—They will much delight in splendid dwellings. Also in pomp, and outward shew, bestowing much time, labor, and expense, in ambitious pursuits; but in their old age, their former fluctuating fortune, shall give place to a settled and tranquil series of years; rendering their decline of existence, both rich and happy, especially if they attain to the age of *fifty-six.*

In their chief undertakings, let them choose the Moon, if possible, in Cancer or Capricorn, the latter if at night; and let her be applying to Venus, and near the last triangle with the Sun.

Friday is their fortunate day, and *Monday night.*
They are under the Genius *Anael.*

ACQUISITIO

```
  *   *
    *
  *   *
    *
```

THEY who are born under this symbol, are under the benevolent and auspicious rule of *Jupiter,* in the regal sign of the *Archer.* They will be of generous and free disposition, but very tenacious of rule, and bearing authority. They are born to the greatest good fortune, and if during the day time, arriving to immense riches.—Yet notwithstanding this, the horoscope is reckoned amongst those, which will during youth cause a sea of troubles, manifold perils and extreme dangers.

Their youth will also be laborious, and unsettled. They will have many adversaries, but have an estate most unexpectedly conferred upon them, without the least probability thereof. They will frequently travel into strange countries, commit themselves to the wide ocean, and great waters; or else be very conversant with the water, and fluids. They will be always doing things for the most public notice, and those generally *outrè*, and eccentric. They are of excellent parts, and superlative memory, wit, promptitude, and understanding, ingenious and skilful in all arts and sciences, following nature, and noted for both neatness and elegance. Most excellent horsemen, and particularly fond of athletic sports.

They are chiefly under the region of the fire, and have moles on the arms, thighs, neck and throat. Very subject to falls from horses, and high places, blows and contusions. Also to scalds and burns. They will also receive a bite from some carnivorous animal.

In the zenith is found, *Conjunctio*, of the earthy trigon, which denotes their being preferred to great power, and magistracy. They shall be obeyed by the common people, and regarded as a prince amongst their household; continually bearing away the palm of merit. From their public situations, many shall subsist by them, but generally those on whom they bestow their favors, will prove very ungrateful. In the law, or clerical affairs, they will meet with great preferment, but meet with uniform loss in martial affairs.

If a female, she will be much beloved and rule the tide of fashion, in her sphere of life, but let her beware of too much caprice; or it may be that her old age may suffer from it, chiefly through the rejection of good offers. In love and marriage, this judgment will be found very correct, and if born exactly at noon-day, they will refuse a coronet.

In the descendant will be placed the noted symbol

Albus, of the airy region, denoting a strange love for secret and hidden things, curious and mystical sciences, and ancient learning. They will be eminent teachers, and trainers of youth, especially in the polite arts. Also expert in the different branches of experimental philosophy. They will marry tall, fair, persons, generally, and will be liable to disputes and vexations in the marriage state. In early life they will have amours, but marrying before twenty-four years of age, for the most part. They may expect a numerous family, and very unruly, though some of the children will arrive to great honor and reknown. Although not exactly felicitous in wedlock, yet they will be much admired, courted and also followed by fair women, and by the sex in general. Females, born under this symbol, are lively, and well formed for the mysteries of Venus, and generally marry both rich and powerful persons. Most of the frail votaries, of the Cyprian goddess, are under this horoscope; as it is the symbol of mirth in love.

In the Nadir, or north angle is found *Letitia*, which will make them fortunate in blue, light green, olive and citron colors. Causing them also to be the keeper of others secrets, and not unfrequently to be ennobled. This causes much disaffection in the nuptial state, and often causes the native to marry an unchaste woman, (unless *Venus*, be well disposed, in the horoscope). At the ages of *ten*, *fifteen*, *twenty-one*, and *thirty-five*, great changes may be expected in their fortune, also a probability of journeys and voyages. They will have legacies left them, and be fortunate in discovering concealed things and lost treasure. Let them beware of poisonous and pernicious drinks, and corrosive liquids, also of two much revelling in the enjoyments of Bacchus. They will be continually subject to petty losses, but though at times unsuccessful, yet they will enjoy much prosperity in their old age, and laugh at the frowns of fortune.

If born during the end of November, and from thence to the middle of December, and especially if born in the *day*, at that time, they will be eminently successful, the highest personages admiring them. Thursday is their fortunate day, and at the hours of nine and twelve. Let them choose the Moon in *Pisces*, in trine to Jupiter or the Sun, and above all, let them *shun* the *new Moon*, in their undertakings.

The name of their Angel or Tutelary Spirit is, *Zadkiel*.

RUBEUS

```
 *  *
   *
 *  *
 *  *
```

The natives born under this symbol, *Rubeus*, a *figure* of the watery triplicitie, under the aquatic Genii, are chiefly governed by Mars, that fiery and warlike Planet, so much celebrated in mythological lore. They are generally very prone to anger, warm in passion, and fond of combats, fighting, and very revengeful. It were better to quarrel with an angry lion, and excite his tremendous fury, than to pointedly offend such persons, as they seldom or ever forgive an injury. (If born at the time the *Moon* is in evil aspect to the planet *Mars*, which may be known by an Astronomer, they are back-biters, perjured, cruel and malicious, and often murderers.) They have moles on the neck or throat, and concealed parts. They will be very fortunate as surgeons, chymists, apothecaries, manufacturers of acids, corrosives, poisonous articles used in dying, or coloring; also as sailors, fishermen and those subsisting by the ocean; painters, artists, and sculptors. Subject during infancy to perpetual falls, quarrels, blows and cuts. Invincible obstinate, never to be forced to anything, (even though the torture were used,) but soon won by flattery, and gentle persuasion. In youth, they shall be subject to many misfortunes, tossed to and fro, with many perils, whereby they will be almost driven to desperation, but afterwards, becoming rich and famous. They will be very high spirited, proud and conceited, perpetually running into danger, often through persuasion of false and wicked counsellors, and chiefly through great vigor of mind. They will be subject to bilious and liver complaints.

In the mid-heaven is the symbolical figure, *Fortuna Minor*, giving great fortitude and strength, but denoting that although they will be wearied with many labors, yet they shall obtain a place of honor and dignity under some great person, where they shall be much flattered and servilely applauded, by which means they will raise many others. They will also enjoy their paternal estate, and increase their hereditary property. By the good graces of eminent females, they will be advanced, also by the liberal and polite arts. At the age of *twenty-five* and *forty*, remarkable events, conducive to an entire change in life, may be expected. They will take several journeys, and travel over the ocean many thousand miles. If born on a *full Moon*, they will also be shipwrecked, or cast away upon some desolate island. Let them be born at what time they will, they will hardly escape imprisonment. Stout, fair persons will prove eminent friends, more especially if they are born in the month of August. If born at Sunrising, they will be severely stung, by some noxious insect, and have a perpetual dread thereof. If at Sun-setting, they will be in great danger of poison, especially if in the month of December. If they are born on a new Moon, they will escape without harm.

In the western horizon is found *Amissio*, which will give victory over enemies, both public and private; they will however, be subject to great loss through women and pleasure. They shall be very remarkable for the singular circumstance of twice in their life, being nearly beggars, but will die rich. Let them beware of becoming a surety for any one, or of being responsible for their words or actions.

They will much admire dark eyed women, and marry well, but never keeping to one person. If a woman, she is masculine, and scarcely waiting for the ordinations of nature, but will marry well. They shall lose several of their children, but retain their favorites. They will be successful in dark brown, and fiery red colors.

In the Nadir, will be the watery *Tristitia*, which signifies some danger by fluids or water, and evinces great ingratitude of friends, chiefly there, where much ought to be expected. If they go through life free from accidents, they will die of a gentle consumption.—They will have great difficulties to overcome, through the meanness of their family, and often lose thereby. They will also delight in ancient houses, castles and old buildings. They must beware of lawsuits with females, and must be also careful in lending money to the fair sex. In horses, especially those for war and battle, or for the use of noble persons, they would be fortunate in speculating; also in other generous animals.

Tuesday is their fortunate day, and the night of Friday.

Let them choose the Moon in *Cancer*, and approaching the *full*, if they would wish to be successful in their undertakings.

The name of their Tutelar Angel is, *Samael*.

TRISTITIA

* *
* *
* *
*

THEY who are born under the symbolical figure *Tristitia*, are under the spirits of the airy regions; and chiefly under the planets Saturn and Mercury. They will be of free and rather prodigal manners, fond of the arts and literature. They will have moles on the legs, arms and breast, and be subject to sprains, or slight injury to the extremities. This horoscope denotes that they shall waste, and lose, whatever they gain; but being born rather fortunate, they will again recover their losses. They will be great lovers of hospitality, and patrons to scientific persons, especially to the meaner sort; for this horoscope disposes them to be very just, liberal and humane. Let them be in what state they will, they will be in many dangers; but uniformly overcoming their difficulties, although at times they shall be almost driven to desperation. They will be much subject to calumny, and feel the shafts of envy most acutely, but in the end, seeing their most rancorous and malignant persecutors utterly destroyed.

In the zenith will consequently (from the nature of the scheme) be found *Rubeus*, of the aquatic region, causing them to be valiant and courageous, giving promotion, and good fortune, in divinity, law, or physic, but causing their life and actions to be laborious, and at times obnoxious to the meaner class of persons. This *figure* also denotes perpetual changing, and shifting from place to place, in the commencement of their lives, causing them to be in servile or laborious offices, but the result of all their actions to be prosperous.—They will be often troubled with sudden and unaccountable depression of spirits, and humid melancholy, proceeding from too great a redundance of phlegmatic moisture. They are from the same cause often pensive and shunning public company, and tinctured with a kind of austerity of manners, bordering upon pride. They will scorn control, although generally living under restraint, and love nothing so much as liberty. They will be very fortunate in recovering lost things, and discovering treasure, or lost rarities; also eminently attached to the study of antiquities, ancient curiosities, fond of the wonderful and romantic, hating sameness, and delighting in ancient armour, excavations, marine productions, geological rarities, details of sieges, battles and ancient warfare; but often the dupe of the designing. They will be eminently fortunate in buildings, especially in civil architecture, constructing aqueducts, bridges, public buildings and courts of justice. Tall, thin, dark persons, and mercurial persons will prove their friends. In combats, they will be nearly overcome at the first, but shall bear away the laurel at the end. They will be eminently skilful in fire-works, and uncommonly tenacious of ancient customs, rites and manners, believing themselves in these particulars superior to every other person. *(The Chinese are chiefly under this symbolical figure.)*

In the western angle is posited *Fortuna Major*, of the fiery regions, denoting ill fortune by his wife or children; and if a female, rather an evil marriage. They will marry with persons older than themselves, and will often times be at variance with their partners, as their husbands or wives shall promise much fidelity, but in reality love others better than themselves.

Their own household will also prove their enemies, too often, and assist their public oppressors, in injurious proceedings, to their great detriment. They also generally marry widows, or widowers, but rather wealthy. In their youth, they will be the uniform rivals of others, both in love and honor, but especially in the former. They will deal largely in beasts, articles for the fire, and foreign luxuries, being also very successful in aromatic perfumes, odours, and rich unguents; also in sky-blue and black colors.

They will be eminently successful in law suits and public actions, at times also fortunate in games of chance, especially if they venture while the Moon is in *Taurus* and *Virgo*, increasing, and in the night time. By day, they will not be so fortunate. Every twelve years they will be eminently successful in this and other chance speculations. Their friendships and enmities will be of very long duration.

In the verge of heaven, they will have the symbolical and terrene figure *Amissio*, which represents some considerable gain by legacy, or death of persons not related. They would be amazingly lucky in performing the last rites of the dead, and also as undertakers or cemetrians.

This promises riches in extreme old age, with eminent fame, from distinguished persons, but their youth shall be restless as the troubled ocean. One of their children shall arrive to great honors, and rule his brethren: but at thirty years of age, both parents and children will suffer imprisonment.

This *figure* promises the favor of a rich and distinguished lady, (if the native be male,) who shall delight in his embraces. They will entirely lose their patrimony, by the parents folly, but is as said above, acquire adequated compensation in contingent successes. If they who are born under this symbol are seamen or merchants, their vessels will be in danger from pirates, and be slow in their voyages. They will uniformly bury their parents, especially the father.

If born on a full Moon, they are more fortunate than at any other time, especially if it happens in the month of January or February.

Saturday is their most fortunate day, and especially at sun-rise. Let them also choose the Moon in *Capricorn* and in Sextile to the Sun.

The name of their Angel is called *Cassiel*.

CARCER

```
     *
   *   *
   *   *
     *
```

WHEN this symbolical figure, *Carcer*, arises, the persons are born under the spirits of the earthy region, and chiefly under Mars and Saturn. They are endued with a strange, mystical imagination, and strange fancy, naturally prone to see spirits and visions; and also to be soon terrified with supernatural noises or appearances. They are invincible in battle, and invulnerable as the Achillean armour, to any thing like fear, in war or strife; but in mystical and visionary things, mere cowards. Their imaginaton, naturally born to soar above the earth, and their mind, prone by nature to spurn every terrene obstacle, is notwithstanding perpetually tinged with an unaccountable gloom. They see objects as it were through a dense and distempered medium, and where the greatest trifler would enter unawed, they shrink back as they would from the icy touch of mortality, and their mind unconsciously bows in humble submission to an imperceptible influence, which they cannot define; but which is in reality the effect of planetary agency. They are much subject to danger and casualties, bites of carnivorous animals, vultures, and inhabitants of the desert. They will be great warriors, captains, and conquerors. *(Such as Hannibal the Carthagenian, Caesar, Edward the Black Prince, and last, though not least, Napoleon.)* With the eyes of eagles, and the foresight of an almost supernatural intellect, they will inherit the subtilty of the serpent; and in decision be swift as the winged lightning. Born to live as heroes, and die in the firm grasp of victory, yet at times, to remind them of their mortality, subject to losses, crosses and calamities.

If born at sun-rising, the world shall scarcely hold their vast designs, but can never contain their victorious actions. Their fame will be high and glorious as the bright and shining orb which gave it.

In the midst of heaven will be found *Puella*, denoting the persons under her influence to be merry, faithful, but rather crafty, of an eccentric life, and for ever exposed to public gaze. They will be true and sincere friends, much given to travel into strange countries, and relieve strangers, who will be generally ungrateful. They will be long lived, and arrive to great riches, studious in searching after secrets, and very ambitious. In love and marriage, as strange as in other things, and altogether remarkable.

In the western angle will be found *Via*, denoting greatly the love of women, and that they shall marry happy, but seldom keeping to one person. Their first child will probably be a son, but very sickly.

They will often be gainers through the misfortunes of others, especially inferior persons, but unconsciously and without injustice.—And be apt to travel much.

If born in the end of March, and from thence to the middle of April, they will receive a fall from an horse, or injury from a four-footed beast. They will also have a scar, or mark, in the head or face, and receive some injury in their feet. If born in the end of April or beginning of May, or until the first half of that month be past, they will be bit by a dog in the *twenty-eigth* or *thirty-fifth* year of their age.

They will marry fair persons, of mild, affable, but timorous dispositions, who shall receive immense wealth by legacies or fortuitous events. At *twenty* years of age, and at *forty-two*, they will bow as submissive victims to the powess of the Paphian goddess, and acknowledge the universal influence of all powerful love; although they generally separate for a time from their first wives; and if a woman, generally leaving her first husband.

They will be continually going into immense companies, and large concourses of people, of different habits, customs, and manners, or else, which has nearly the same signification, they will spend great part of their time on the stormy and turbulent ocean; in either case, appearing like Neptune with his Trident, majestically ordering, stilling and silencing the waves of public opinion, or of that tempestuous element, which so nearly resembles it.

In the Nadir, or north angle, is found *Puer*, denoting a variable and remarkable life, at times sinking (but never sunk,) into despair, yet quickly assisted by their good fortune, which will enable them to overcome every temporary difficulty. From the same cause they will enjoy good health and much felicity in their latter years, and like the renowned Hero of ancient times, be remembered when the very sepulchre which enclosd their mortal remains shall cease to exist.

Those in more inferior stations of life will be famed for original and curious inventions, or individual prowess, athletic force, or profound knowledge. They will do well to cultivate their knowledge of the arts, and would be eminently successful as mathematicians, geometricians, machinists, founders, searchers after ores, minerals or curiosities. They will be so far raised as to become rulers of the towns or villages where they reside; and thus in their sphere of birth, exercise authority, in a manner the same as those who are born in the higher stations of life.

Saturday is their fortunate day, and the night of Wednesday; generally about the first hours of each, that is, at Sun rising and Sun setting.

Let them choose the Moon in *Aries*, and in Trine to Jupiter, when they begin any thing of import, also let her be in equal degrees, and above all, let her not be in the Tail of the Dragon.

They are under the Angel *Samael*.

LAETITIA

```
      *
    *   *
    *   *
    *   *
```

THEY who are born under this figure, *Letitia*, are under the aquatic element, and chiefly under the planet Jupiter. If born at night, Venus will have some claim in their horoscope. They will be ingenious, prudent, faithful in friendship, but high-mind, and rather avaricious, or else extremely careful, and wishing to amass a sufficiency or surplus of the goods of fortune. They are generally witty, and having excellent memories, a fund of genuine sarcastic humour, and have great presence of mind, abhorring war and bloodshed.

They will make excellent musicians, painters, astronomers, and amateurs in the polite arts. Composers of music and attached firmly to the drama. Often, teachers of youth, and generally admirable for justice and piety. They are generally unbelievers in mystical appearances, and so much given to mathematical demonstration, as to doubt almost all which they cannot comprehend, but in their belief of Religion and of the Deity more firm; though even in this repeatedly changing their tenets, and following many new opinions.

They have an inward hatred to strife and warfare, but are rather given to craft and subtilty, and are not the firmest in unlimited things, when they have no control, being rather prone to conceal vice with the transient polish of flattery, especially when their interest is in any way much concerned.

They shall have many enemies, and be inclined to travel, voyage, and sojourn in foreign countries, or if abiding in their native land, yet having much to do with merchandize and foreign negociations.

They have moles on the feet and arms, and are subject to bilious or else phlegmatic complaints, redundancy of moisture, and inflammations. They will be at some time of their lives in great danger from water, and narrowly escape drowning, if born on a full Moon especially. But they will die a naturally and easy death, though in a strange and distant part to where they were born.

In the midst of heaven, the above figure causes the symbol *Acquisitio* to culminate, belonging to the fiery region, and ruled by Jupiter, giving many imminent perils, toils and dangers. Causing great variance with great and distinguished persons, law suits and contentions; they will also be subject to loss, through becoming surety for another person, whereby they shall lose the whole of their estate and possessions, but in the end, they shall obtain the dominion and possession of another's estate, and possess that to which they have no just claim. They will be fortunate in articles of the fire, and for common use, in steel, iron and metallic productions, extracts, tinctures, and pungent essences. In horses, menageries, and horned cattle, being also excellent sportsmen, anglers, fishermen, teachers of human exercises to docile animals, trainers of generous quadrupeds, and attached to all kinds of animals, birds, and remarkable productions. They shall succeed in pure white, and glistening or sparkling colors. In phosphoric or combustible ingredients, and in generous, exhilarating liquors; to which last, they will however be rather too much attached, for their personal and salific good. If born from the middle of May to the middle of June, they are more fortunate, but will receive a bite from a dog, hurt by a weapon, or fire, at twenty-three years old. If born from the middle of June to the same period of July, they will be amazingly fortunate after the age of twenty-six.

In the west angle, will be consequently found the symbol *Conjunctio*, ruled by the spirits of the earthy region; making them lovers of hospitality, hearty, but rather ostentatious, having many faithful secrets committed to their care, raising many friends by their help, but they always returning the favors conferred upon them by ingratitude. They will attain to riches and grandeur, but suffering much misfortune through marriage. If a man, he shall immoderately love, honor, and esteem his wife, and idolize his offspring, but they shall prove both treacherous and ungrateful, and requite for his love, hatred, and for his esteem, contempt; making his life thereby a chaos of misfortune. If they bury their first wife, the second promises more fair, but she will be of mean origin. At *fourteen*, *eighteen*, and *twenty-four*, they will bow to the shrine of Venus. At *twelve*, *twenty*, and *forty-one*, they will have a change in their whole life, probably taking strange residences, or laborious journies.

In the north angle, *Albus*, of aierial quality, promises much good fortune, and a never dying fame. But they will be troubled with a secret constitutional disease, which none can heal or even discover. They shall obtain an estate on a sudden, unlooked for, and unexpected. They will also be liable to sudden death, or to the apoplexy, unless born when Jupiter had great predominence in the eighth house of their horoscope. If born at the hours of *two* and *five* in the afternoon, and *twelve* at night, they are sure to be first of their kindred. If at *nine* in the morning, they will be secretaries to persons ruling under the government. They will suffer at times through law suits and tall, thin, women, of rather artful manners, and be more than once in danger of personal restraint, but in the end most assuredly overcome their enemies.

Thursday and Sunday are their best days.

Let them choose the moon in *Libra*, and in her first Sextile with the Sun, if possible, also in a Triangle with Saturn; and they will prevail.

They are chiefly under the Tutelar Spirits, *Zadkiel* and *Anael*.

VIA

*
*
*
*

THIS symbolical figure is termed *Via*. Those born under it, are under the spirits who rule the world of waters, and chiefly under the Moon. Partaking greatly of her nocturnal influence. They have moles on the breast, side, and shoulders; are of a peaceable, mild, but wavering disposition. Patient in their labors, noted for neatness, fairness and cleanliness, hating and abhorring oppression and tyranny. Loquacious, seldom retaining secrets, but although fickle minded, when once resolved, firm, and not to be changed from their purpose. They are much noted for strange and remarkable dreams. Filled with strange and unaccountable mysterious forebodings; prying unconsciously and unwittingly into the dread secrets of futurity; making use of oracles, visions, omens, traditions, occult testimonies, sayings, and all kinds of facile divination. Astutely and well managing their household concerns, tenacious to a degree of their name and fame, looking forward to the honors of posterity, and endeavoring to secure them. Subject to strange fancies in most things, and to surprising mental depression. They have a natural dread of water, and are often horror struck at the idea of drowning, or the sight of ponds, lakes or rivers. If a man, he will be an expert swimmer, but seldom venturing, after his youthful days, to tempt the deceitful element. In either case they will be in danger on voyages, from decayed vessels or carelessness of mariners.

Females born under this *figure* are fruitful, having lively children, but during pregnancy subject to pains in the side, and not entirely free from danger in child-bearing. They will be much followed by the male sex, especially dark persons, and those under the dominion of Mercury. In demeanor, the females are chaste and virtuous, void of voluptuousness, but well calculated to perform the mysteries of Venus. If born between midnight and morning, they will actually behold visionary appearances, and be firm believers in the secrets of the other world. They shall be fortunate in green colors.

At *fifteen*, *seventeen* and *twenty-two*, they will have amours or marriage. They will be very fond of animals, and also of solemn, mournful sounds, such as tolling of bells, and funeral elegies, also of shrill, piercing, and thrilling music. They are also continually apprehensive of death, and thereby destroying much of their own happiness, through fruitless and unnecessary vexation. They will be in danger from a spark of fire, and from a sudden or casual fall. If born on a full Moon, in the day time, they will arrive to great fortune, and be rich in their old age. Every twelfth year will prove nearly the same to them.

Monday night is their most fortunate time, and let them choose the Moon in *Capricorn* or *Virgo*, and avoid the day of the new Moon.

They are under the Angel, *Gabriel*.

(*This, and the other three remaining figures, have but one angle, from which they are judged.*)

FORTUNA MINOR

```
  *
  *
*   *
*   *
```

THEY who are found to have this figure, *Fortuna Minor*, arise, are under the nocturnal influence of the Sun. If born in the night, they are ambitious, romantic, and aspiring, and more fortunate than if born in the day time. If born in the month of April, they will become very rich, and amass great and sudden wealth. They are generally fond of adulation, great boasters, often beyond all bounds of probability, and skilful in philosophy or chemical experiments.—They have moles on the knees, legs and loins, are subject to scalds and burns, and in danger of personal injury from noxious effluvia or poisonous mixtures. They are fond of travelling, change and curiosity. They shall also, during the whole period of their lives, be well known and in public estimation. They will marry more than once, and generally prosper thereby, gaining much money by wedlock. They will have few or no children, but may expect an illegitimate offspring to provide for.

Let the men beware of dark women, and especially of those who come from a distant part. If females, let them beware of elderly men.

Those born under this *figure* will travel out of their native country, and cross the ocean more than once, perhaps several times. They will also live by the produce of foreign countries, or lend all their money to persons in a distant nation. They will be fortunate in articles of ornament, decorations, in gold and silver, precious stones, and luxurious rarities. But often losing through useless speculations. They will also be successful in mines, ores, and minerals.

If born from the middle of July to the same time in August, but more especially if in the beginning of August, they will be in great danger from fire and hot waters. But after the age of *twenty-one*, becoming suddenly wealthy. If from the middle of August to the same period of September, they will rise to great eminence in the world and be employed under a King or Prince. If a woman, she will marry young, and be violently in love at the age of *fifteen* years. But subject to many crosses and envious rivals. If born from the middle of September to the same period of October, they shall gain by rich perfumes and spices; and shall be interpreters of dreams and visions. If a woman marrying about the age of *twenty-three*, but liable to scalds and violent burns in youth, in old age becoming rich. Generally those under this symbolical *figure* gain by illicit love. Also, if born near to the period of the Sun reaching the ninth house of heaven, (which in summer is from noon-day till past two in the afternoon, and in winter from noon-day till half-past one,) they will be eminently successful in their public and private concerns; and wanting none of the luxuries of life. Nevertheless, they will *once* suffer a short imprisonment.

Saturday night, and Thursday at noon, are their most lucky times.

Let them also choose the Moon in *Leo* or *Pisces*, and increasing in light. They are under the Angel, *Michael*.

CAUDA DRACONIS

*
*
*
* *

THEY who have this figure, *Cauda Draconis*, arising are chiefly under the Spirits ruling the fiery region, and under the *South node* of the Moon, when she crosses the ecliptical line, *receding* from our hemisphere.

They are by no means born to riches, and although they will through the capriciousness of fortune, rise to eminent preferment, bearing rule and having many persons at their command, yet will they never be wealthy, but amidst all their greatness, acutely feel the want of money. If born at *sun-rise*, which then, may possibly favor them a little, they will be noted misers, penurious, and die wretched.

They will be much subject to hurts by fire, falls from horses, thrusts or attacks from beasts, danger from mines, explosions, suffocation, premature interment, danger from noxious vapors, and inflammable gasses, gun-powder, pyrotechnical experiments, and if visiting desert countries, be in danger of being devoured by wild beasts. If born on the new Moon, they will be imprisoned, and nearly ruined by false, and by perjured accusers, but overcoming in the end. If born in the night, they are more fortunate than if born in the day time, the surrounding darkness being a fit emblem of their bewildered fate. The north, with its frozen regions is their proper element. And the winter more successful to them than the summer.

Let them beware of sword fencing, and of sharp instruments, as they are born under a noxious and hurtful Constellation, and shall hardly escape injury. *(The original relates, that they will be wounded either by an arrow, or pointed instrument in the head: and further says, that, Harold King of England, and Henry King of France, were both under this figure, the former of whom was shot through the head with an arrow, and the latter slain by a spear, at a tournament, but these weapons now being disused, another signification must be taken.)* They will be fond of battle, war, blood-shed, and destruction. And be successful in colors of a sanguine, and blood-red hue. If born at noon-day, while the Sun is on the cusp of the meridian, and in the month of December, they will scorn the control of every one, even of heaven's puissant monarch, and be a curse to all mankind. If born at the *rising* of the Sun, and *setting* of the Moon, their fate will be a little altered for the better, but not essentially good. (Scarcely *one* in a *million,* is born entirely under this fatal symbol, it being so mischievous, that even in Astrology, every celebrated Professor of that sublime art, knows it to be a certain fact, that the *Dragon's Tail,* which this symbol represents, is *worse* than the most *evil* Planet.— Therefore the diviner, need not fear being under such a sign, as it so *rarely* happens.)

Tuesday is their uniform fortunate day. Let them also choose the very point of a new Moon, or Eclipse, as *that* alone can favor their dark designs. They are under the Angel of Destruction, *Barzabel.*

CAPUT DRACONIS

* *
*
*
*

From the above-mentioned horrible and destructive sign, we turn with a pleasing emotion to the rich and fortunate symbol, *Caput Draconis,* of the earthy triplicitie, ruled chiefly by Jove and Venus, in their exaltations.

They are firm, just, benevolent, and full of humane actions, always promoting the public good, and eminent in philanthropic undertakings. They have moles or marks on the face, and are subject to head-aches, and diseases proceeding from a redundancy of moisture. They are very fortunate in bringing to perfection other men's labors, making also eminent Poets, Musicians, Astronomers, Artisans, Mathematicians, Senators, and Law-givers. Invincible in battle, though loving peace and quietness. *(Solon, and Lycurgus, those famous, Law-givers, were under this symbol, as also the immortal Alfred, the divine Raphael, and the far famed Bards and Minstrels of olden times.)*

If born at sun-rising, noon-day, or sun-setting, they will bear rule and authority as Princes, in their household, and be the judge of other men's actions. Nevertheless, they shall not be entirely free from the attacks of an assassin. If in very inferior stations, they will utterly eclipse their contemporaries.

If a female, she will be as a Cleopatra, without her lustful coquetry, being followed and beloved by every one; but in matrimony let her beware, or she will meet with a sting. If they have a son to survive, he shall be the advancer of his house, first amongst his brethren, and reflect immortal honor upon his ancestors.

If a man, who has this symbol, he will marry rich and wealthy, felicitous and happy, but will, notwithstanding, see the object of his dearest affections snatched in an instant, from his grasp, by the icy hand of death; and with tears of heartfelt remorse, follow her cold remains to the dreary and remorseless sepulchre. After this, a bright and joyful sun-shine shall arise upon his fate, and rank and fortune bend submissive to his grasp.

The persons under this sign shall travel much, but not often, as the whole events of their lives will happen in climaxes and extremes, both of good and evil. The Bar of Justice will be *once* graced with their presence, but they will vanquish every opponent, and come off as conquerors. —*(In veritate victoria.)*

They have no particular fortunate day, but will generally succeed better while the Moon increases in the Constellation, *Gemini.*

They are under the Angels, *Raphael* and *Uriel.*

BIBLIOGRAPHY

Agrippa, Henry Cornelius — 'On Geomancy' in the *Fourth Book of Occult Philosophy*. London, 1655, reprinted Askin Publishers, London, 1977.

Agrippa, Cornelius (pseudo) — *The Ladies Oracle*. Evelyn, London, 1962.

Amar, K. Avv Hali ben (pseud) — *Vollenkommende Geomantia*. Leipsic, 1735.

Bascom, William Russell — *Ifa Divination*. Bloomington, London, 1969.

Cicero, Marcus Tullius — *De Divinatione*.

Cole, J.A. Abayomi — *Astrological Geomancy in Africa*. London, 1898.

Cotton, Christopher — *The Geomancy of Master Christopher Cotton* (1591) in *A Publication of Surveying*. 1616.

Crowley, Aleister — *Magick in Theory and Practice* (Chap. XVIII) Lecram, Paris, 1929.

The Equinox, Vol I. No. 2. Simpkin, Marshall, London, 1909.

Deacon, Richard — *The Book of Fate*. Muller, London, 1976.

Dumézil, Georges — *Archaic Roman Religion*. 2 vols.

Evans-Pritchard, Edward Evan	University of Chicago Press, Chicago, 1970. *Witchcraft, Oracles and Magic Among the Azande.* Clarendon, Oxford, 1937.
Fahd, Toufic	*La Divination Arabe.* Brill, Leiden, 1966.
Fludd, Robert	*Tractatus de Geomantia in quatuor libros divisus (see Paschius, Fasciculus Geomanticus).* 1687. *Utriusque Cosmi.* Oppenhemii, Frankfurt, 1617.
Forsyth, J. S.	*Demonologia.* London 1827.
Gaule, John	*Mag-astro-mances.* London, 1652.
———	*Geomantia.* Jordan, Meintz, 1532.
Goetze, Albrecht	*Old Babylonian Omen Texts.* O.U.P. London, 1947.
Hartmann, Franz	*The Principles of Astrological Geomancy.* Rider, London, 1913.
Heydon, John, MD.	*Theomagia, or the Temples of Wisdom.* 3 Vols. London, 1662-4.
Ibn Khaldun (Abd al-Rahman Ibn Muhammad)	*The Magaddimah.* (ed. Franz Rosenthal) 3 Vols. R.K.P., London, 1958.
Josten, C. H.	'Robert Fludd's Theory of Geomancy and His Experiences at Avignon in the Winter of 1601 to 1602, in *JWCI*, Vol. XXVII. London, 1964.
King, Francis & Skinner, Stephen	*Techniques of High Magic.* C.W. Daniel Co., London, and Warner Destiny, New York, 1976.
Kirchenhoffer, Herman	*The Book of Fate*, London, 1822.
Lutz, Henry Ludwig Frederick	*Old Babylonian Divination Text.* 1929.
Paschius, Georgius (see Fludd, Robert)	*Fasciculus Geomanticus in quo varia variorum opera geomantica continentur.* Verone, 1687.
Plutarch	*De Oraculorum Defectu.*
Raphael (i.e. Robert Cross Smith)	*The Familiar Astrologer.* London, 1831. *The Straggling Astrologer, or The Astrologer of the Nineteenth Century or Compendium of Astrology, Geomancy and Occult Philosophy*, (edited for the Society of the Mercurii). London, 1825. *The Philosophical Merlin.* London, 1822. *Pythoness of the East*, Lon-

	don, 1894. *The Royal Book of Fate,* London, 1828.
Regardie, Dr. Francis, Israel	*The Golden Dawn.* Vol. 4. Llewellyn, St. Paul, 1970.
	A Practical Guide of Geomantic Divination. Aquarian, London, 1972.
Thorndike, Lynn	*A History of Magic and Experimental Sciences.* Vols. I-VIII. Macmillan, New York, 1923-58.
Turner, Victor Witter	*Ndembu Divination: its Symbolism and Techniques.* Manchester University, Manchester, 1961.
———	*Volkommene Geomantia oder so genante Punctier-Kunst.* Freystadt, Jena, 1702.

A number of manuscripts in the British Library and Bodleian Library were also consulted.